Secondary School

MATHEMATICS for the

LEARNING DISABLED

Contributors

Colleen S. Blankenship

Anne M. Fitzmaurice Hayes

Henry A. Goodstein

Mahesh C. Sharma

Robert A. Shaw

Raymond E. Webster

Secondary School

MATHEMATICS for the

LEARNING DISABLED

Editor
John F. Cawley, Ph.D.
University of New Orleans
Lakefront

AN ASPEN PUBLICATION®
Aspen Systems Corporation
Rockville, Maryland
Royal Tunbridge Wells
1985

Library of Congress Cataloging in Publication Data

Main entry under title:

Secondary school mathematics for the learning disabled.

"An Aspen publication."
Includes bibliographies and index.
1. Mathematics—Study and teaching (Secondary) 2. Learning
disabilities. I. Cawley, John F.
QA11.S37   1985   510'.7'12   84-16946
ISBN: 0-89443-597-3

Publisher: John R. Marozsan
Associate Publisher: Jack W. Knowles, Jr.
Editorial Director: Margaret Quinlin
Executive Managing Editor: Margot G. Raphael
Managing Editor: M. Eileen Higgins
Editorial Services: Jane Coyle
Printing and Manufacturing: Debbie Collins

Library of Congress Catalog Card Number: 84-16946
ISBN: 0-89443-597-3

Printed in the United States of America

1   2   3   4   5

Table of Contents

Preface ix

Chapter 1— Learning Disabilities and the Secondary School 1
John F. Cawley

    Determining Status 2
    Mathematics Programs 3
    What Are the Characteristics of the Learning
        Disabled? 5
    Clinical Perspectives 13
    Algorithmic Variations among Adolescents 20
    What Descriptive Data Indicate 23
    From Characteristics to Individual Needs to Program
        Design 24
    Summary 26

Chapter 2— Measurement and Assessment: Group and Individual
        Techniques 29
Henry A. Goodstein

    Approaches to Secondary Special Education 29
    Developmental versus Remedial Needs 30
    Purposes of Assessment 31
    Measurement Scales 32
    Achievement Tests in Assessment 33
    Diagnostic Tests in Assessment 40
    Informal Assessment 44
    Proficiency Tests 48
    Vocational Education 57
    Summary 57

Chapter 3— Individualizing Mathematics Instruction for Students
        with Learning Problems 61
Colleen S. Blankenship

    What is Individualized Instruction? 63
    When Is It Necessary To Individualize Instruction? ... 64

Which Aspects of Instruction Can Be Modified? 66
What Steps Are Involved in Individualizing
    Instruction? 75
What Are the Benefits of Individualizing Instruction
    for Students and Teachers? 79
Summary 80

Chapter 4— Whole Numbers: Concepts and Skills 83
Anne M. Fitzmaurice Hayes

Questions: What and How Much To Teach? 83
Whole Numbers and Computation: Content Outline ... 86
Teaching Suggestions 88
Calculators 109
Microcomputers 113
Assessment in the Arithmetic of Whole Numbers 113

Chapter 5— Fractions, Decimals, Percentages 115
Anne M. Fitzmaurice Hayes

From 1, 2, 3, to the Square Root of 3 115
Rational Numbers: What To Teach? When?
    How Much? 119
Fractions 119
Decimals 142
Percentages 147
Summary 149

Chapter 6— Geometry Concepts and Skills 151
Robert A. Shaw

Geometry—Options and Structure 151
Expected Performance of Learners 153
Some General Guidelines 154
Adapting Geometry To Meet the Needs of
    Learning-Disabled Students 155
An Introductory Lesson 155
Points, Lines, and Planes 161
Measurement: The Connecting Link 162
Introduction to Proof 166
Introduction to Angles 167
Triangles 171

Beyond Development of Triangles 176
Summary 177

Chapter 7— Measurement Concepts and Skills 179
Robert A. Shaw

The Measurement Function 179
Prerequisites and Conditions 180
Length 181
Angle Measure 188
Area 191
Volume 197
Measurement in the Sciences 198
Mass (Weight) 198
Summary 200

**Chapter 8— Mathematics and Vocational Preparation for the
Learning Disabled 201**
John F. Cawley

Employment Settings 202
Vocational Preparation 203
Basic Skills and Applications 205
Instructional and Curriculum Planning 221
Instructional Procedures 222
Summary 232

Chapter 9— Applications of Mathematics in Other Subject Areas 235
Mahesh C. Sharma

The Value of Mathematics Applications 237
Mathematical Content for the High School Student 241
Mathematical Applications 244
Important Mathematical Skills for a High
School Student 255
Summary 270

**Chapter 10—Adapting the College Preparatory Program for
the Learning Disabled 271**
Robert A. Shaw

Curriculum Concerns 272
College Preparatory Program 272

Curriculum Essentials 274
Types of Lessons 275
Methods and Alternatives 277
A Plan of Action 278
Algebra I: The Course Sequence 279
Geometry 284
Algebra II 285
Pre-Calculus 289
Summary 289

**Chapter 11—Organizing the Secondary Mathematics Program
        for Learning-Disabled Students 291**
Raymond E. Webster

Orienting the Mathematics Program 292
Contents of the Mathematics Curriculum 296
Meeting the Educational Needs of the LD Student 300
Coordinating Mathematics with Other Subject
    Areas 310
Assessing Student Performance 316
Introducing New Programs 317
Summary 319

Index 321

Preface

The interface among mathematics, the secondary school, and the learning disabled stimulates concern regarding a variety of issues. These issues relate to curriculum and instruction, to patterns of school organization and special education delivery systems, to the need for cooperative efforts between special educators and regular educators, and to the challenge of serving the learning disabled and their families.

Individuals who are referred to as learning disabled exhibit diverse combinations of strengths and weaknesses. A student might be fully capable of satisfactory performance in the most rigorous of secondary mathematics classes. Yet, this same individual might be such a poor reader that his or her level of functioning in mathematics will be impaired unless instructional modifications are made to compensate for the reading problem. Other individuals may demonstrate discrepancies in attainment and other performance characteristics such that educational achievement in even the most basic arithmetical functions is adversely affected.

The secondary school is the terminal point in the educational process for many learning-disabled students. They know this. Their parents know this. The schools know this. Extreme pressure is brought to bear on all. All need to collaborate. The learner must keep trying. The family must relieve some of the pressure. The schools must respond with their best effort to provide an appropriate education.

Secondary School Mathematics for the Learning Disabled takes somewhat of a middle-of-the-road approach. Some of the mathematics included in this book extends far beyond the computational topics that have been emphasized in many programs for the learning disabled. Yet, the mathematics may be somewhat less difficult than what many deem appropriate for the secondary school.

Chapters 6 and 7 are illustrative. Clearly there is more geometry and more measurement in these chapters than is emphasized in any special

ix

education resource. At the same time, by design, they cover less than what is typically included in mathematics programs, particularly in the area of geometry.

Chapter 8 discusses the mathematics of vocational education and Chapter 9 focuses on the application of mathematics to other subject areas. Should the individual not be able to perform many of the indicated skills, he or she will be less than a full participant in these courses. Full participation may be achieved through selected modifications, as shown in Chapter 10, where suggestions for modification of the college preparatory program are discussed.

Learning-disabled youth frequently require assistance with the basic skills and operations in arithmetic and fractions even though they have reached the secondary school. Chapters 4 and 5 focus on these two important areas.

In developing the program at the secondary school level, it is important to remain cognizant of the fact that we lack a full and comprehensive set of descriptors of the learning disabled at this level (Chapter 1). Chapters 2 and 3 provide more functional and basic approaches to assessment, individualization of instruction, and development and implementation of an effective means of delivering services to the learning disabled at the secondary level. Chapter 11 focuses on the latter.

Mathematics in all its diversity can be integrated into the total program of the learning disabled at the secondary level. We have a vehicle for this. This vehicle is the Individualized Education Program. It should be used throughout the secondary level to assure the learning disabled that the mathematics they need will be appropriately delivered.

Secondary School Mathematics for the Learning Disabled is the product of a diverse but coordinated group of specialists who have conducted research and developed programs for the learning disabled. As such, there is a wide range of in-depth coverage. Such an approach is basic to meeting the needs of the learning disabled at the secondary level.

John F. Cawley

Chapter 1

Learning Disabilities and the Secondary School

John F. Cawley

Learning disability can be defined as a concept (Cawley, 1984). As a concept it is an organizer or a heading under which traits or qualities can be grouped according to rules or attributes. This enables us to respect the variation with which different perspectives present learning disability and to understand the multitude of approaches used in research, training, and programming.

As one begins to examine the concept of learning disability and mathematics at the secondary school level, it is important to consider the secondary school itself as well as the various aspects of the learning disability per se. Schools at the secondary level are as varied and different as any set of children who are referred to as learning disabled. Yet, once we set forth the rules and attributes, it is possible to develop an acceptable conceptualization of the secondary school.

For purposes of this text, the term *learning disabled* will refer to any youngster who manifests a significant discrepancy between present level of functioning and an established level of expectancy in mathematics or in developmental areas (e.g., reading) that impair performance in mathematics.

The term *secondary school* encompasses any grade equivalent from sixth to seventh grade through twelfth grade. In the U.S. learning-disabled children are entitled to a free and appropriate public education until they graduate from secondary school or until they reach the age of twenty-two.

Developing descriptors that characterize secondary school children with learning disabilities is difficult because we truly lack the needed longitudinal research to serve as a base for ascribing attributes to these children across the years or ages. In effect, we cannot definitively answer the question "What are the attributes of learning-disabled children at the various levels of secondary school?" However, while this limits us, it does not preclude our ability to set forth standards. Attributes are but one facet of a concept approach. Rules are the other. Accordingly, we can establish rules or guidelines that enable us to delimit the set of individuals who will be included within our sample of learning disability.

The Thirty-Fifth Yearbook of the National Council of Teachers of Mathematics is entitled *The Slow Learner in Mathematics*. In three chapters, one on characteristics (Schultz, 1972), one on prescriptive teaching (Glennon & Wilson, 1972), and one on research (Pikaart & Wilson, 1972), there is not a single comprehensive reference to support the descriptors ascribed to the term "slow-learning children." In fact, one study cited in the chapter on research (Pikaart & Wilson, 1972) is concerned with children who have an IQ of 100 or more but who are at least one year below grade level in arithmetic. These children are described as slow learning rather than slow-learners. An approach such as this focuses attention on the condition or status rather than on the individual. Perhaps a similar perspective toward learning disability would be helpful.

DETERMINING STATUS

Youngsters of the type referred to by Pikaart and Wilson should not be classified or serviced under the rubric of learning disabled. The concept of learning disability needs to be viewed within the dimension of difficulties that adversely affect educational performance and that clearly demonstrate educational performance is below expectation.

Learning disability takes on a special meaning in mathematics at the secondary level, a meaning quite different from learning disability with respect to reading. To establish a basis for this special meaning, the utmost consideration must be given to the criteria and procedures for conducting the pupil appraisal used in determining the learning disability. If, for example, the tests used emphasize computation of whole numbers and the individual is able to generate a grade equivalent score in the upper grade levels (e.g., 5 or 6 at the 7th grade level; 8 or 9 at the 10th grade level), a significant discrepancy might not exist. However, this could be due to the fact that the student had so much work in computation, with no experience in other areas, that he or she was able to wade through the "computes" to acceptable levels of performance. A learning disability could exist and performance could be discrepant from what is the curriculum-based expectancy for that grade level. One might expect reasonable progress from the individual only to find that he or she encounters severe problems in attempting to handle new materials. In fact, it might take as many years to attain proficiency with fractions or percents, say, as it did for the operations on numbers. Thus, we may begin to see the impact of a determination of learning disability when learning is defined in terms of the number of repetitions needed to attain mastery or the amount of time needed for original learning.

Some children may be included within the realm of the learning disabled as the result of curriculum standards. We must keep in mind that a learning disability does not exist simply because a child is having difficulty with mathematics. It may be that 9th grade algebra is simply too hard for the individual and that it is inappropriate to take this subject at this time. Another year or more of instruction and maturation may make the topic relevant and appropriate for study. Or it may not, and all concerned will have to deal with the fact that there is a leveling off of capability to handle more difficult topics. This is a sensitive matter, but one to which secondary schools realistically must attend. It suggests the need for considerable individual and family guidance.

MATHEMATICS PROGRAMS

Mathematics programs at the upper-grade levels provide unique opportunities to move on from attention to rote computation and explore topics that may have more, or at least equivalent, value in life. Sedlak and Fitzmaurice (1981) indicate that concepts of time, measurement, and geometry play roles in actions performed daily in post-secondary school environments. They point out that many of these mathematical concepts in fact play a greater role than computational skills. It will be necessary to consider all facets of mathematics. An inability to compute cannot be perceived as a disability while an inability to perform in geometry is simply seen as failure.

Secondary schools must have a plan in mathematics that will allow each child to attain his or her maximum potential. The learning-disabled child is protected in a sense in that needs in mathematics can be written into the Individualized Education Program (IEP) and the school is obligated to provide a program to meet these needs. Mathematics can be written into the IEP until proficiency is obtained.

Patterns of school organization at the upper-grade levels vary as do the types of schools learning-disability children attend. Crucial to the development of the learning-disabled child are the middle grades, those approximating 6 though 8. These are crucial because the child may be included or excluded from certain schools or certain school programs on the basis of level of proficiency in mathematics. Of particular importance at these levels is the need to ensure that the child has experiences with a broad range of mathematics and that the concepts associated with these areas are developed to the fullest possible extent. Measurement could be among the more important topics, because the ability to measure and to measure accurately is an important skill in vocational education.

The longer the individual is enrolled in school, the greater the amount of time for the discrepancy between performance and expectation to increase, the greater the amount of time for cumulative deficits to occur, and the greater the amount of time for problems of attitude and frustration to emerge and to become habituated. With higher grade levels the range of ability levels and achievement levels widens. The teacher of older children has a wider range of problems to deal with and a wider range of difficulties to overcome.

There is extraordinary stress upon the school, the individual, and the family in the upper grades. A lesser amount of time exists to attain the desired levels of proficiency and there is the concern as to whether standards, both within the school and those established by state competency programs, will be met for graduation and for life beyond school.

The organization of the upper grades and the emphasis on departmental structures is both to the advantage and disadvantage of the individual. The primary advantages are that (1) the student is more likely to encounter subject-matter specialists who are uniquely qualified in their fields and thus able to provide specialized types of assistance, (2) the student is maturing and likely to be able to display more mature cognitive functioning, and (3) the student's needs may be better met by the flexible schedules and time periods that are features of such organization.

The primary disadvantages are that (1) the subject-matter specialist might not be interested in meeting the unique needs of the child, (2) the special education teacher might not be able to provide the appropriate amount of extensive assistance in mathematics, and (3) going to six or seven different teachers during each day can create problems for children who have difficulty in making rapid adjustments to new demands and to new content.

In any area of mathematics, an important goal is to assist the child to habituate proficiency and to become rapid, efficient, and automatic in responding to stimuli. The stages in this process are described by Shaw (1981). The child's first encounter with a topic is at the *problem level*. At this level the child does not know how to process the algorithm or to demonstrate the concept, largely because all of this is new. Through proper instruction, the problem level is modified to the level of *example*. Here the child must ponder, organize strategies, and consciously follow a plan to arrive at a solution. There is no problem because the child knows what to do. The third stage is to modify the example to that of an *exercise*. Stimuli at the exercise level require only limited analysis. The individual glances at the item and immediately provides a response, calls out the correct formula, and substitutes the numbers to obtain a solution or matches the item with a known tactic and responds without delay or effort. Proper planning for the learning-disabled child will take the child to the exercise level before going on to a new topic. The learner cannot be continuously functioning at the problem level.

Teachers of the learning disabled were surveyed with regard to their concerns in mathematics for upper-grade-level students (McLeod & Armstrong, 1982). Their concerns are listed in order of priority from highest to lowest as follows: division, fraction operations, decimals, percent, fraction terminology, multiplication of whole numbers, place value, measurement skills, use of fingers to count, and language of mathematics. These concerns indicate a need for attention to several aspects of mathematics and not just one or two topics. The teachers seem to be seeking help in those areas of general mathematics that are associated with the upper grades. They do not focus on topics that might be found in college preparatory sequences. The emphasis is on basic skills in areas related to functional applications or to basic skill requirements that may be demanded by state testing programs.

WHAT ARE THE CHARACTERISTICS OF THE LEARNING DISABLED?

Alley, Deshler, and Warner (1979) conducted a study to identify learning-disabled adolescents at the secondary level. In a search of the literature for disability descriptors associated with learning disability a total of 67 descriptors was identified. Each of these component disabilities was rated according to its prevalence among learning disabled (LD) and non-LD populations. The four component disabilities found to best differentiate LD and non-LD populations at the secondary level were

1. Word decoding or inability to sound out words
2. Sight word deficiencies
3. An inability to detect spelling errors
4. Disability in mathematics such as being unable to set up a problem for its solution.

These four component disabilities were used to construct a scale with which teachers rated 494 9th-grade students as to whether they were learning disabled or nonlearning disabled. A total of 35, or 7.7 percent, were identified as learning disabled. Each of the 35 was individually tested and 9 were confirmed as learning disabled.

Sharma (1979) developed a comprehensive interpretation of the learning-disabled adolescent with respect to math learning problems. He cites the following as characteristics of the adolescent who has difficulty in mathematics.

- Directional confusion and spatial disorientation
  Many youngsters produce work that is immature. They still reverse letters and draw geometric forms in the reverse direction.
- Spatial orientation and difficulties with mathematical symbols
  Many children must constantly rethink the mathematical symbols. They may misread signs. For example, in a math problem is it 2 or 5, 6 or 9, 1/2 or 2/1, 12 or 21.
- Breaks in continuity of thought
- Intrusions from the outside or extraneous material may interrupt thought
- Overlooking or not noticing
  Children turn pages and omit problems or pages. They do part of a problem, but do not complete it.
- Poor organization
  Items are not organized into the correct columns. Materials are scattered all about.
- Perseveration
  Children work on one process such as addition and then continue addition even though the work calls for subtraction.
- Language difficulties
  The language of mathematics is akin to a foreign language to many students with learning disabilities. It is not nearly as explicit as we often conclude. "Divide" does not mean divide in the problem, John divided his apples among his 6 friends so that each friend has 2 apples. How many apples did John start with?

Pieper (1979) conducted a study of cognitive abilities among students specifically learning disabled in arithmetic. Within all his comparisons, two visual-spatial and one reasoning task significantly differentiated the research sample. Pieper notes that students who are impaired in arithmetic but doing average work in reading suffer in that they have difficulty comparing and differentiating numbers, identifying and manipulating shapes in space, and establishing equivalency statements as a result of their cognitive deficits.

White (1980) posits that the effectiveness of any match between curriculum and cognitive ability for effective instruction is dependent upon our knowing the student's stage of cognitive development. She studied 27 learning-disabled and 27 nonlearning-disabled adolescents on a battery of five measures. She found significant differences in verbal flexibility. Both groups achieved conservation of volume and demonstrated comparable skill in hypothetico-deductive reasoning on spatial and numerical tasks. Some differences were noted in specific language usage. White indicates that the limitations in precise language use may impair communication and thinking.

McEntire (1981) examined the relationships among listening, speaking, reading, and mastery of writing, vocabulary and grammar and mathematics performance in computation, concepts, and problem solving. Subjects of this study were 112 8th-grade students. Comparisons were made among remedial, basic, and honors English classes or among mathematics groups divided into quartiles. Results indicated that reading proficiency correlated most highly with mathematics concepts and computation and less significantly with problem solving. The author concluded that the relationship between mathematics and language may be due more to syntactical or structural matters than to semantics or content.

Bennet (1981) investigated syntactical and mediational effects on problem solving among learning-disabled and nonlearning-disabled individuals. Nonlearning-disabled individuals performed significantly better than the learning disabled across syntactical and computational levels. It was concluded that commercially available materials do not control syntactical complexity and, therefore, may not be appropriate for children with language problems. If the conclusion is valid, one of the problems facing secondary school personnel is overcoming the many years of inappropriate experiences to which the language disabled may have been exposed. Another problem is the adaptation of materials.

In a study of two types of learning disabilities among college students, Williams (1980) tested a group of 25 students with the WAIS, WRAT, and Tennessee Self-Concept Scale. Three combinations of basic skills disabilities were discovered: high reading-low mathematics, high mathematics-low reading, and low reading-low mathematics. None of the measures was significantly related to mathematics achievement. Given the fact that information processing scores were not critical factors in mathematics and that self-concept scores were average, the author concluded that other factors might be contributing to mathematics deficiencies at this level.

Cawley et al. (1979) studied selected developmental characteristics of 340 learning-disabled youngsters in the 11 through 17 age range. Their mean age was 12 years and 6 months mean IQ was 98.09, and mean mental age was 11.06 on the *Peabody Picture Vocabulary Test* and 10.97 on the *Raven Progressive Matrices*. Each individual was administered Level III of the *Mathematics Concept Inventory* (MCI), a test covering mathematics content approximating the 3.0 to 4.5 grade equivalent levels. Table 1-1 contains two types of data. One type shows the overall performance on the MCI.

The second type illustrates the variation in performance across small samples of individuals whose group membership was determined by discriminant function analysis. The MCI contains a total of 81 items to measure 60 mathematics concepts or skills. Mean number correct was 51.16. The mean number correct for the smaller samples ranged from 43.2 to 64.0. Learning-disabled individuals tended to respond in all areas tested and to show some degree of improvement with age.

The data in Table 1-2 (Warner, Alley, Schumaker, Deshler, & Clark, 1980) also show increments in achievement across the school years, although overall performance changes only slightly. Given the fact that the samples are cross-sectional and not longitudinal, one must be a bit cautious with respect to any conclusions. However, over the six-year span of the achievement data, grade equivalent performance increases approximately one and one-half years in reading, one year and seven months in mathematics, and about one year in written language.

A number of factors are worthy of consideration. One would be to examine the program of each child to determine its effectiveness and validity. The program could be one with an instructional emphasis or one

---

Table 1-1 Summary Characteristics of Learning Disabled
Adolescents by Population and by Age Samples

	Mean Scores by Topics:	Geometry $\bar{x}$: 10.86
		Measurement $\bar{x}$: 13.56
	N = 340	Fractions $\bar{x}$: 6.33
		Numbers $\bar{x}$: 20.41
		Total $\bar{x}$: 51.16/81

| | *Small Sample Characteristics* | | |
N	*Age*	*MCI*	*PPVT IQ*
15	12.3	43.2	101.1
19	12.4	50.6	93.7
35	13.1	62.0	105.1
11	14.3	62.6	107.3
12	14.8	64.0	87.6
15	15.1	59.7	90.3
15	16.2	63.1	96.3

Table 1-2 Mean Cluster Scores and Grade Equivalents for Learning
Disabled on *Woodcock-Johnson Psychoeducational
Battery*

Grade Level	N	Rdg Cluster GEq Score		Math Cluster GEq Score		Written Lang GEq Cluster Score	
7	35	485.03	3–3	504.79	5–2	491.69	3–7
8	35	495.75	4–2	507.81	5–5	498.13	4–2
9	24	492.00	3–9	516.19	6–3	498.53	4–3
10	35	500.10	4–7	520.95	6–9	503.44	4–7
11	34	501.05	4–8	517.98	6–5	502.88	4–7
12	35	493.65	4–1	516.89	6–4	504.43	4–8

with a curriculum emphasis. The former receives strong support from
Glennon and Cruickshank (1981), who are quite critical of the curriculum
emphasis. They state, "We begin with the very obvious, but sometimes
ignored truism, that it is not possible to publish a mathematics program
that is specifically targeted for the dyscalculic. It is professionally irre-
sponsible to purport that [such] a program can be designed and written."
(p. 80) If one accepts this position, programmatic efforts in the form of
commercial materials and microcomputer delivery systems will play only
a minimal role or be nonexistent in programs for the learning disabled. Of
course, different persons may be referring to children with different characteristics and these persons may be using different conceptual and data
sources in the development of their views. As an example, Levy (n.d.)
lists 37 terms that are used to describe disorders of mathematical functioning. Levy intimates that the problems of nomenclature may be more
serious than the difficulties of the learner.

The individuals described by Warner et al. (1980) seemed to have made
a fair amount of progress in mathematics in the elementary years. By grade
7 they were achieving at the 6th grade level, but there does not seem to
have been much progress between 7th and 12th grade. Is this because the
programs between grade 7 and grade 12 were difficult and demanded more
than the student was able to give? Or does it have something to do with
measurement? Were the types of items the youngsters encountered in the
early years more direct and easier than the types of items found at the
upper levels? There is definitely a need for longitudinal research that will
track both subject and program characteristics if we are to figure out the
answers to questions such as these.

Norlander (1983) has prepared a summary of selected data from *Multi-
Modal Mathematics* (Cawley, Fitzmaurice-Hayes, Shaw, & Norlander,
1980). Tables 1-3 and 1-4 show the percentage of incorrect responses to

Table 1-3 Percent Incorrect on Number Concepts Test*

| | | Percent Incorrect | | N | |
		Grades 4–6	Grades 7–12	4–6	7–12
Concept	*Item Description*				
1. Cardinal Property Numeration	Identify the set of objects representing the number 12	20.3	9.8	59	51
2. Reading Number Names: Numeration	Say the number 7062	50.8	39.2	59	51
3. Numeration: Cardinal Property of 0	Matching the numeral 0 with the empty set	0.0	2.0	59	51
4. Numeration: Ordering Numbers	Ordering numbers	8.5	11.8	59	51
5. Ordinal Property	Choose a number that is in the fourth position in a series of numbers	20.3	21.5	59	51
6. Reading Ordinal Number Names	Matching numbers with ordinal names Ex: 3—third	35.6	21.6	59	51
7. Roman Numerals	Choose the Roman numeral that tells how many dots are in the set : : :	69.5	39.2	59	51
8. Place Value	Point to the number that is in the hundreds place 2406	44.0	27.4	59	51
9. Place Value	Meaning of 0 in 13,401 : No Tens	61.1	37.3	59	51
10. Place Value	460 How many tens?	61.0	68.7	59	48
11. Place Value:	376 = 300 + 70 + 6	69.5	49.0	59	51
12. Rounding Off	Point to the number that shows 736 rounded off to the nearest 10 736	72.9	70.6	59	51

*Data presented represent 18 of 33 concepts tested.

Table 1-3 continued

| | | Percent Incorrect | | N | |
| | | Grades 4–6 | Grades 7–12 | 4–6 | 7–12 |
Concept	Item Description				
13. Even/Odd	Given four numbers— choose the even number	81.3	78.4	59	51
14. Reading Numbers	Three hundred twenty-one. Select the number that is the same as the words	52.5	21.6	59	51
15. Addition: Commutative Property	$79 + 80 = : 80$ $\quad\quad +79$	39.7	25.5	58	51
16. Estimation: Subtraction	Choose the closest 342 -124	58.7	51.0	58	51
17. Multiplication: Repeated action	$8 \times 6 =$ from four choices select the expression that means the same $6+6+6+6+6+6+6+6$	50.0	51.0	56	50
18. Division: Signs of Operation	Point to all the division signs	44.7	32.0	56	50

selected number and fraction concepts among learning-disabled children in grades 4 to 6 and in grades 7 to 12. With the exception of a few number concepts (i.e., items 1, 3, 4, and 5) and fewer fraction concepts (i.e., items 1, 2, and 3) performance fails to indicate substantial mastery.

In spite of the formal interest in tests and other standardized measures as indicators of progress, school marks often constitute an item of great concern to the child, the family, and the community. Table 1-5 displays the marks received in mathematics for 366 learning-disabled youth in 17 vocational-technical schools in which four years of mathematics is a requirement (Cawley, Kahn, & Tedesco, in progress).

The data at the top of the table show the percentage of school marks for each grade level. At the 9th grade level, 13 percent of the grades were "F"s and 8 percent were "A"s. The lower part of the table shows the distribution of each mark by grade level. Of all the As received, 56 percent were earned at the 9th grade level, 25 percent were earned at the 10th

Table 1-4 Percent Incorrect on Fractions Concept Test

		Percent Incorrect		N	
Concept	*Item Description*	*Grades 4–6*	*Grades 7–12*	*4–6*	*7–12*
1. Basic Concepts	Identify a fraction 5 55 $\frac{5}{10}$ 505	16.7	7.3	36	55
2. Basic Concepts	Match ¾ with a pictured representation	25.0	10.9	36	55
3. Comparing Fractions	Seriating fractions (pictorial representation)	21.9	32.7	36	55
4. Equivalent Fractions	Choosing equivalent fractions (pictorial representations)	88.9	65.4	36	55
5. Basic Concepts	Choose a picture that does not represent a fraction	55.5	36.4	36	55
6. Basic Concepts	Choose a pictured representation 1/6	58.3	34.5	36	55
7. Basic Concepts	Match 3½ to a pictured representation	75.0	41.8	36	55
8. Comparing Fractions	Choosing a larger fraction ⅜ : ⅝	30.6	31.0	36	55
9. Comparing Fractions	Choosing a larger fraction 2/6 : 4/6	88.9	78.2	36	55
10. Comparing Fractions	Find a picture of a larger value ⅗	91.7	81.8	36	55
11. Comparing Fractions	Find the largest position (fraction)	77.7	61.9	36	55
12. Comparing Fractions	Ordering fractions from largest to smallest	63.9	47.3	36	55
13. Basic Concepts	Fractions to mixed numerals 8/5 = 1⅗	69.2	61.8	36	55

Table 1-4 continued

		Percent Incorrect			N
Concept	Item Description	Grades 4–6	Grades 7–12	4–6	7–12
14. Subtraction	Use of pictured subtraction problem	38.9	44.4	36	55
15. Subtraction	Find picture of ⅓ taken away ⅔	75.0	50.9	36	55
16. Comparing Decimals	Ordering of decimal fractions	82.8	66.1	35	53

grade level, 12 percent were earned at the 11th grade level, and 6 percent were at the 12th grade level.

CLINICAL PERSPECTIVES

In addition to the variability within and among groups of learning-disabled youth at any given age and across age ranges, there exists considerable variation in the development characteristics of each individual.

Cohn (1971) is an excellent historical source for case study comparisons across ages. Cohn presented 31 case studies separated into groups labeled *much improved, improved, no overall change,* and *worse.* The following are summaries of three cases, one each from the *much improved,* the *improved,* and the *worse* categories as established by Cohn. The original case studies are presented in greater depth.

Case 1: Much Improved*

The first patient of the greatly improved category was seven years old at the time of the initial examination. In speaking the boy failed to enunciate the first syllables of the word utterances. His father had had a similar childhood speech difficulty but became a successful biophysicist. The mother insisted that though the father was a gifted mathematician, he was

---

*The following three case studies are taken from "Arithmetic and Learning Disabilities" by R. Cohn (Chapter 12) in *Progress in Learning Disabilities, Vol. II,* M. Myklebust, ed., with permission of Grune & Stratton. Copyright © 1971.

Table 1-5 School Marks in Mathematics of Learning-Disabled Adolescents

		Grade Level			
		9	10	11	12
	F	13	11	12	20
School	D	23	50	46	39
Marks	C	35	25	28	25
	B	21	9	11	13
	A	8	3	3	2
	N	111	114	82	59

Distribution of School Marks by Percent at Each Grade Level

		Grade Level			
		9	10	11	12
	F	30	26	20	24
School	D	18	39	26	16
Marks	C	36	27	21	14
	B	46	21	17	15
	A	56	25	12	6

Distribution of Each Mark by Percent at Each Grade Level

unable to do anything mechnical. She said, "the boy is just as discoordinate as his father."

He was discoordinate in all types of motor tests such as succession movement, heel-and-toe walking, finger-to-nose-to-finger and heel-knee testing. He was unable to tie his shoelaces or to carry out other complex manual actions. He was right-left oriented for his person, but could not transpose right and left in a picture.
In graphic functions, the boy was unable to place letters of his name or geometrical figures in proper orientation with one another; this is shown in Figure 1-1. He was unable to write numbers or to make letters of the alphabet other than those comprising his first name. In forming geometric figures, he would often say, "We make a square and then make a line"; in spite of the correct statements he was never able to accomplish the figure. He was unable to read any combination of letters other than his name.

On reexamination on September 11, 1959, at the age of 9 years and 4 months his speech had improved considerably. His general information

Figure 1-1 Much Improved

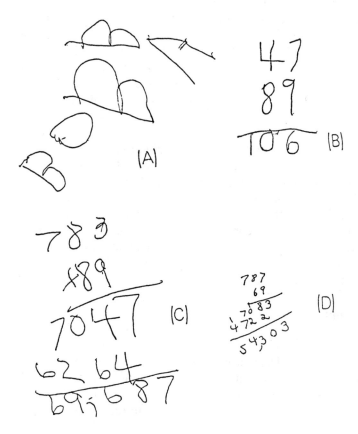

Source: Reprinted from: "Arithmetic and Learning Disabilities" (Chapter 12) by R. Cohn. In M. Myklebust (Ed.), *Progress in Learning Disabilities, Vol. II,* with permission of Grune & Stratton, © 1971.

fund was almost adequate: Christopher Columbus discovered American and the Pilgrims came with him, Christmas was the birthday of Jesus and he was born in Japan. His attempt to add 47 + 89 is shown as part B in Figure 1-1.

At the time of examination on May 18, 1962, the patient was attending regular school. He now played baseball sufficiently well for associates to call him out to play. He was interested in baseball players, past and present; he knew "all" their pitching and batting records. He knew that "Goose" Goslin was a good first baseman for the Washington baseball team, and he knew his home run record. It was interesting to note that he came to the examination room with a fielder's mitt, as well as his textbooks. He wrote "Our Father who arts in heaven hallobea they name." He multiplied 783 × 89 correctly, as noted in part C of Figure 1-1; the numbers were large and discoordinate. He handled geometric problems reasonably correctly. His fund of general information was adequate: he knew about the Civil War, holidays, and so on correctly.

At the time of the final personal examination on March 24, 1967, the patient was 16 years old and 10 months of age. His writing was adequate and the multiplication of 887 × 69 was correct and the numbers were well formed (see part D of Figure 1-1). In describing the action picture he now named all the elements comprising the picture, but not the action. Geometric problems were incorrectly solved. He read rapidly but tended to omit many small words. When he was asked about the Revolutionary War, he said, "I'm glad you asked about that, I love history." He did know many historical facts, but was unable to synthesize this knowledge.

Case 2: Improved

The next patient was 8 years and 3 months of age at the time of the initial examination. Discoordination was evident whenever he engaged in any rapid movements. He drew a picture which he said was me [himself]. He printed "man" and "boy" correctly. As noted in part A of Figure 1-2, some numbers were reversed. He was able to read such words as "and" and "to."

At the age of ten and a half, in September 1959, he had grown quite heavy. He could only read the words "it," "a," and "them." The numbers 4 and 9 were large and partly superimposed, as shown in part B of Figure 1-2.

In December 1961 he was facetious; in speech he often omitted the "r" sounds, and "first" was sounded as "fast." For the Lord's Prayer he wrote "How arts in heaven, howould be thy name." When asked to multiply 769 × 89 he wrote 700 × 69 (part C of Figure 1-2); the 9 × 7 operation was incorrect, and the additions were incorrectly performed because of a displacement of the numbers. He said that Columbus was not the first discoverer of America, that Lief Ericson and the Vikings had come

Figure 1-2 Improved

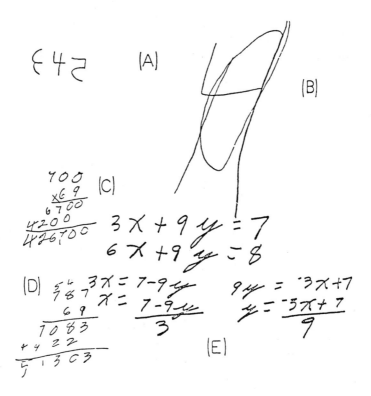

Source: Reprinted from: ''Arithmetic and Learning Disabilities'' (Chapter 12) by R. Cohn. In M. Myklebust (Ed.), *Progress in Learning Disabilities, Vol. II,* with permission of Grune & Stratton, © 1971.

first. It was clear that a different intellectual capacity was in effect.

In February 1964, at nearly 15, he was tall, thin, gawky, and unusually quiet. He was now in the eighth grade of regular school; he indicated that he would like to go to college. He wrote the Lord's Prayer as ''Are farther whow heaven hallood.'' As observed in part D of Figure 1-2, he multiplied 787 × 69 with only one error. He was able to read quite well but his enunciation had poorly developed consonant sounds.

At the age of 17 years and 11 months he was a well-built 6 ft.; he was a junior in high school. He wrote: ''Our father thour are in heaven hallow by thy name." As seen in part E of Figure 1-2, he was able to solve a pair of linear simultaneous equations in a proper way. He read the test paragraph correctly, but often accented the words incorrectly.

In 1970 attempts were made to reexamine him. It was learned that he was a student at the University of Maryland. The informant indicated that he was passing in his work.

Case 3: Worse

This boy of 9 years and 2 months was first examined in June 1957. His coordination was adequate; his speech was mechanically good. He was unable to read from printed material, even after several drills with the same sentences. He wrote his name in script with his right hand. He wrote the dictated numbers 7, 9, 6, and 3 (part A of Figure 1-3). He could not write any two-digit numbers. The EEG was abnormal.

In September 1959 when he was 11 years and 5 months of age it was stated that he played with paper dolls, liked to wear dresses, and to cook and to act. Writing was done in a rough, large style. For "dogs are brown," he wrote "doges er dan." For the dictated 48 + 16 he obtained 17 (part B of Figure 1-3). The picture of a person was unusually detailed, but compositionally adequate. Reading was inaccurate; for "because we might wake them" he read "before the night walking by the."

At 13 years and 10 months of age, he had become a tall gawky fellow with massive feet and large hands. For the Lord's Prayer he wrote, "Ore Father Hw oor in Hvine." He added 82 + 16 correctly, but added the number on the left first (part C of Figure 1-3). When asked if he had a dollar and spent 25 cents how much would he have left, he answered 53 cents. He read the phrase "because it might wake them a match was denied him" as "It might work with then a much was him."

In February 1964 at 15 years and 11 months of age, he was overactive and clumsy in all of his actions. He wrote several phrases to dictation correctly. Multiplication of 87 × 9 = 85 is shown in part D of Figure 1-3; the arithmetic was done by serial counting from his constructed marks; when he counted 55, he put down the 5 and carried the other 5. He read the test paragraph with many mistakes, but the overall comprehension was quite good. He seemed to have accumulated a considerable amount of information, but could not use it appropriately.

At the age of 19 years he came to the examination room singing "Let me hold your hand." He was working for the government.

Figure 1-3 Worse

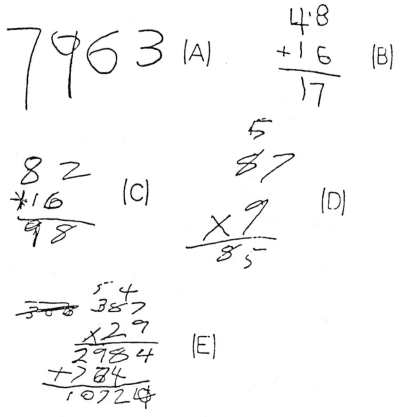

Source: Reprinted from: "Arithmetic and Learning Disabilities" (Chapter 12) by R. Cohn. In M. Myklebust (Ed.), *Progress in Learning Disabilities, Vol. II,* with permission of Grune & Stratton, © 1971.

He wrote "Our father ohwre in heven give us thes day our daylie bread etc." He multiplied 387 × 29; the multiplication by 2 and the subsequent additions were correct. Initially he wrote 300 for the 387 (part E of Figure 1-3). He read in a scanning way but he appeared to comprehend the material. His acquired fund of information was adequate, and he was unable to utilize the information for proper communication.

The individuals described by Cohn were quite severely disabled. An examination of the performance of individuals somewhat less disabled provides an additional clinical perspective from which to view the learning-disabled adolescent.

ALGORITHMIC VARIATIONS AMONG ADOLESCENTS

Pelosi (1977), while working as a member of a group at the University of Connecticut, acquired a most interesting set of individual responses to computational items in numbers and fractions. These were collected solely from a population at the secondary level. The fact that so many individuals manifested such distorted algorithms clearly suggests that meaningful intervention at earlier levels was meager, at best.

The difficulties with secondary school youngsters extend far beyond what is shown by individual performance. When intervention is introduced with these students, great opposition is encountered in getting them to use manipulatives and to produce responses with blocks, sticks, and toothpicks. They often argue that these are childish activities even though they cannot do them. They remember using manipulatives as young children and are reluctant to get involved because they were not particularly successful then. Nonetheless, manipulatives offer an alternative because the distorted algorithm that is produced in the paper-pencil activity cannot usually be performed by the learning disabled when they use manipulatives.

Throughout the following cases, the one most disconcerting factor is the stability of individual performance. The students use the same approach over and over again. The illustrations below are presented for two purposes. The first is to enable us to analyze and compare the performance of a group of children with learning disabilities. The second is to provide an opportunity to ponder the actions that may or may not have taken place with these learners in previous years.

INDIVIDUAL RESPONSES

Item		What the learners did
1. $\begin{array}{r} 12 \\ + 5 \\ \hline 8 \end{array}$	2. $\begin{array}{r} 10 \\ + 7 \\ \hline 8 \end{array}$	This set of problems displayed the following rule: add together all the digits to obtain the answer. Place value was ignored.
3. $\begin{array}{r} 80 \\ + 04 \\ \hline 12 \end{array}$		In number 1, $5 + 2 + 1 = 8$ In number 2, $7 + 0 + 1 = 8$ In number 3, $4 + 0 + 0 + 8 = 12$ Error made by student: grade 11 age 16

Item		*What the learners did*

$$\begin{array}{r} 93 \\ -7 \\ \hline 94 \end{array} \qquad \begin{array}{r} 30 \\ -14 \\ \hline 24 \end{array}$$

This set of problems displayed the following rule: *always* subtract the larger digit from the smaller digit, no matter where it is. Errors made by students:

$$\begin{array}{r} 423 \\ -12 \\ \hline 415 \end{array} \qquad \begin{array}{r} 543 \\ -195 \\ \hline 452 \end{array}$$

grade 10 age 17
grade 11 age 17
grade 11 age 16
grade 9 age 15
grade 11 age 18
grade 10 age 16

$$\begin{array}{r} 621 \\ -335 \\ \hline 314 \end{array}$$

The student borrowed 1 from the 9 in the hundreds place and made the 0 in the tens place 10. Then he borrowed 1 from the tens place and the 10 became 9 and the 3 in the ones place became 13. Now, $13 - 4 = 10$ (computational error—lack of basic skills). He brought the 0 in the answer and added the 1 from $13 - 4 = 10$ to the 9 in the tens column and it became 10 again. Thus, $10 - 1 = 9$ and 8 (in the hundreds place) $- 4 = 4$.

$$\begin{array}{r} 903 \\ -414 \\ \hline 490 \end{array}$$

To obtain this answer the student borrowed from the tens column. He renamed 3 ones to 13 and 8 tens became 7. Now $13 - 4 = 10$, (computational error—lack of basic skills). He wrote 0 in the answer and added the 1, from $13 - 4 = 10$, to the 7 in the tens column and it became 8 again. $8 - 4 = 4$ and $9 - 2 = 7$. Error made by student: grade 10 age 16.

$$\begin{array}{r} 983 \\ -244 \\ \hline 740 \end{array}$$

The student borrowed 1 from the tens place and the 1 in the tens became 9 (computational error) and the 8 in the ones place became 18. $18 - 9 = 9$ and $9 - 0 = 0$; $6 - 4 = 1$ (computational error). Error made by student: grade 9 age 16.

$$\begin{array}{r} 618 \\ -409 \\ \hline 109 \end{array}$$

This set of examples displayed the following rule: Borrow 1 from the hundreds place and put it in the ones column. The students *did not* borrow from the tens column. Errors made by students:

$$\begin{array}{r} 423 \\ -18 \\ \hline 315 \end{array} \qquad \begin{array}{r} 983 \\ -244 \\ \hline 649 \end{array}$$

grade 10 age 16
grade 10 age 17
grade 12 age 18

$$\begin{array}{r} 300 \\ -105 \\ \hline 105 \end{array}$$

$$\begin{array}{r} ^{1}6\overset{3}{1}8 \\ \times\ 4 \\ \hline 2522 \end{array}$$

$4 \times 8 = 32$. Wrote the 2 carried the 3, now, "4×1 does not mean anything since it does not change the 4" so multiply 4×3 (the carried 3). $4 \times 3 = 12$, write the 2, carry the 1. Next, $4 \times 6 = 24$, then $24 + 1 = 25$. Error made by student: grade 9 age 16

$$\begin{array}{r} 40\overset{2}{4} \\ \times\ 7 \\ \hline 2948 \end{array}$$

$7 \times 4 = 28$. Wrote down the 8 carried the 2. Now, 7×0 is meaningless, so use 7×2. Now, $7 \times 2 = 14$ wrote down the 4 carried the 1. $7 \times 4 = 28$ and $28 + 1 = 29$. Error made by students: grade 10 age 15 and grade 11 age 16

$$5\overline{)618}^{\ 13}$$

In this problem, the student split up the problem so that 5 was at least larger than the dividends.

$$5\overline{)618} \ =\ 5\overline{)6}^{\ 1} \qquad 5\overline{)12}^{\ 3}$$

Each example was divided and the quotients were the closest answer, and no remainders were recorded. Error made by student: grade 9 age 15

$$36\overline{)726} \qquad 36\overline{)72600}^{\ 2010}$$
$$\begin{array}{r} 72 \\ \hline 06 \\ 00 \\ \hline 60 \\ 36 \\ \hline 24 \\ 0 \\ \hline 24 \end{array}$$

The student did not add a decimal point. When asked to explain, she replied just keep adding zeros since zeros at the end of a number do not change the number. Error made by student: grade 10 age 15

$$7\overline{)217}$$

The problem indicated a correct answer; however, the divisor was performed backwards.

$$7\overline{)217} \ =\ 7\overline{)7} \quad \text{then} \qquad 7\overline{)21}$$

With a 2-digit divisor, the second digit in the divisor was divided into the last digit in the dividend $0\overline{)0}^{\ 1}$ then the 1st digit of the divisor was divided into the first 2 digits of the divi-

$$50\overline{)250}^{\ 5\,1}$$

dend: $5\overline{)25}^{\ 5}$

$\frac{2}{3} + \frac{3}{5} = \frac{5}{8}$

$$\begin{array}{r} \frac{2}{3} \\ + \frac{3}{5} \\ \hline \frac{5}{8} \end{array}$$

The learners added the numerators and denominators in *both* forms of the addition problem. Errors made by students:
   grade 9 age 13; grade 10 age 16
   grade 9 age 15; grade 10 age 15
   grade 12 age 17;   grade 11 age 16
   grade 10 age 16

$\frac{3}{4} + \frac{5}{4} = \frac{15}{8}$

The learner multiplied the numerators and added the denominators. Error made by student: grade 12 age 18

$\frac{3}{5} - \frac{2}{5} = \frac{1}{5}$

$\frac{3}{5} - \frac{3}{10} = \frac{0}{5}$

In this problem set, the learners were able to solve the problem correctly if the denominators were equal; however, if the denominators were unequal, they subtracted the numerators and the denominators (smaller from larger). Errors made by students:
   grade 10 age 16
   grade 9 age 14
   grade 10 age 15
   grade 9 age 14
   grade 10 age 16
   grade 10 age 15

WHAT DESCRIPTIVE DATA INDICATE

Descriptive data on the learning-disabled adolescent provide a basis for conclusions such as the following:

- To some degree, there is evidence that some individuals achieve in some areas of mathematics.
- The amount achieved across the secondary years is minimal, a factor which suggests that if we do not help the youngster early we may not be much help at all.
- Wide ranges of conceptual, perceptual, and language deficiencies characterize the learning-disabled adolescent.
- Achievement is difficult to predict. Some severely handicapped individuals get worse, some improve considerably.
- Adolescents not only demonstrate discrepancies in achievement. In some instances, performance is distorted and disordered.

- Remedial programs and approaches do not seem to have ameliorated the problem of many children, although we must recognize that those who remain in learning-disability programs are likely to be those with whom the greater difficulty is encountered.

FROM CHARACTERISTICS TO INDIVIDUAL NEEDS TO PROGRAM DESIGN

A primary reason for developing a better understanding of the characteristics of the learning disabled at the secondary level is to establish a more comprehensive and stable program base. Program development is predicated upon addressing individual needs. The situation is somewhat circular in the sense that we must understand the characteristics to determine the needs. These affect program design, which in turn affects characteristics. Let us examine some of the factors that influence our practices. Among these are:

- Degree of severity   Mild, moderate, severe
- Concept or skill   Gets 3 from $2\overline{)6}$ but does not understand what 3 represents.
  Understands 23 in $12\overline{)276}$, but unable to do computation.

- Discrepancy   Below level of expectancy, proceeding at slower
  or   rate.
  disorder   Distortions and aberrations in performance; illogical and unusual algorithms.

- Curriculum   Programs consist of limited content; items presented even though not ready; sequence inappropriate; many topics skipped.
  or
  instruction   Incorrect responses habituated; no stability in instructional approach.

- Direct   Teaches directly to item.
  or   Develops processes thought to be impairing performance.
  indirect   Inordinate number of repetitions required in
  learning   original learning even though adaptions to level of functioning have been made.
  or
  achievement   Learner is behind, but able to progress at level of functioning at rate similar to others at same level.

- Pattern of learning   General or specific
  disability
- Combinations of   Poor reader/good math
  learning   Poor math/good reader
  disability   Poor math/poor reader
- Program commitment Developmental, remedial, or compensatory

Program decisions at the secondary level will be influenced by the factors listed above as well as others in the specific school district and region.

Program commitment is high among the priorities. A choice must be made for one or a combination of developmental, remedial, or compensatory orientations. In a developmental approach all topics of mathematics are presented to the learner even though specific attention might be devoted to more limited topics. The child in need of assistance with computation problems will get this assistance, but will not sacrifice experiences in geometry, measurement, and other topics to attain the assistance. In a remedial approach energies will be concentrated on one or two specific topics (e.g., addition, subtraction) with little attention to other topics. A compensatory approach will attempt to develop coping and survival skills so that the individual will be able to function at as high a level as possible. Such an approach would train the child to take notes, use tape recorders, become skillful with the use of hand calculators, and to monitor behavior during the performance of specific tasks. Behavior monitoring is expanded upon in the fine text by Alley and Deshler (1979).

The compensatory approach at the secondary level has merits far exceeding other alternatives. Remedial work in computation has little effect. Far better to develop concepts and understanding and to perform the calculations with the use of a mechanical device. Perhaps the biggest drawback to such an approach is the increased use of competency testing in local school districts. Again, it is far better to give the youngster a test of problem solving in which thinking, information processing, logic, and applications to real-life experiences dominate and to permit the learner to use a calculator to perform the operations. The data generated in this chapter are certainly supportive of such an approach. Admittedly, the data are limited. But in no instance in the studies cited was it shown that substantial progress was made by learning-disabled youngsters during the secondary school years. Further, although there were some data on concepts and skills, there were almost none on problem solving.

SUMMARY

Program development for the learning disabled at the secondary school level has been limited. We have yet to determine the comprehensive nature of their proficiency in mathematics or to determine which types of program approaches might be most appropriate for which type of youngster. The test data tend to show only limited progression across the upper grades, although school marks showed a reasonable capability to meet teacher expectations.

Given that the needs in mathematics are so great, more math, not less seems to be needed in the program. One possible alternative is to undertake a compensatory approach at the secondary level and to instruct the learning disabled to use mechanical devices for computation. Instructional time could be directed toward concepts and applications.

REFERENCES

Alley, G.R., Deshler, D.D., & Warner, M.M. (1979). Identification of Learning Disabled Adolescents: A Bayesian Approach. *Learning Disability Quarterly, 2*(2) 76–83.

Alley, G.R., & Deshler, D.D. (1979). *Teaching the learning disabled adolescent: Strategies and methods*. Denver: Love.

Bennet, K. (1981). *The effects of syntax and verbal mediation on learning disabled students' verbal mathematical problem scores*. Unpublished doctoral dissertation, Northern Arizona University, Flagstaff, AR.

Cawley, J.F., Fitzmaurice, A.M., Shaw, R.A., Kahn, H., & Bates, H. (1979). LD youth and mathematics: A review of characteristics. *Learning Disability Quarterly, 2*, 29–44.

Cawley, J.F., Kahn, H.K., & Tedesco, A. The learning disabled in vocational education. Unpublished research project in progress. University of New Orleans.

Cawley, J.F. (1984). Learning disabilities: Issues and alternatives (Chapter 1). In J.F. Cawley (Ed.), *Teaching of developmental mathematics for the learning disabled*. Rockville, MD: Aspen Systems.

Cohn, R. (1971). Arithmetic and learning disabilities (Chapter 12). In M. Myklebust (Ed.), *Progress in learning disabilities, Vol. II*. New York: Grune & Stratton.

Glennon, V., & Cruickshank, W. (1981). Teaching mathematics to children and youth with perceptual and cognitive processing deficits (Chapter 3). In *The mathematical educators of exceptional children and youth* (pp. 50–94). Reston, VA: National Council of Teachers of Mathematics.

Glennon, V., & Wilson, J. (1972). Diagnostic prescriptive teaching (Chapter 9). In *The slow learner in mathematics* (pp. 282–318). Reston, VA: National Council of Teachers of Mathematics.

Levy, W. (n.d.) *Dyscalculia: More confusion than clarity*. Unpublished paper. University of Connecticut, Storrs.

McEntire, M.E. (1981). *Relationships between the language proficiency of adolescents and their mathematical performance*. Unpublished doctoral dissertation. University of Texas, Austin.

McLeod, T., & Armstrong, S. (1982). Learning disabilities in mathematics: Skill deficits and remedial approaches at the intermediate and secondary level. *Learning Disability Quarterly, 5*(8), 305–311.

Norlander, K. (1983). *A comprehensive mathematics curriculum for upper grade students with handicaps to learning: Design, development and instructional implications.* Unpublished research report. University of Connecticut, Storrs.

Pelosi, P. (1971). *A report on computational variations among secondary school students.* Unpublished research project. University of Connecticut, Storrs.

Pieper, E. *Analysis of cognitive abilities of students learning disabled specifically in arithmetic computation.* Unpublished doctoral dissertation. University of Kansas, Lawrence, KS.

Pikaart, L., & Wilson, J.W. (1972). The research literature (Chapter 3). In *The slow learner in mathematics* (pp. 26–51). Reston, VA: National Council of Teachers of Mathematics.

Schulz, R.W. (1972). Characteristics and needs of the slow learner (Chapter 1). In *The slow learner in mathematics* (pp. 1–25). Reston, VA: The National Council of Teachers of Mathematics.

Sedlak, R., & Fitzmaurice, A.M. (1981). Teaching arithmetic. In D.P. Hallahan & J.M. Kaufmann (Eds.), *Handbook of special education.* Englewood Cliffs, NJ: Prentice-Hall.

Sharma, M. (1979). *Math learning problems of the adolescent student.* Framingham, MA. Center for Teaching/Learning of Mathematics.

Shaw, R.A. (1981). Designing and using non-word problems as aid to thinking and comprehension. *Topics in Learning and Learning Disabilities.* l(3) 73–80.

Warner, M., Alley, G., Schumaker, J., Deshler, D., & Clark, F. (1980). *An epidemiological study of learning disabled adolescents in secondary schools: Achievement and ability, socioeconomic status and school experiences.* Research Report 13, Institute for Research in Learning Disabilities, University of Kansas, Lawrence.

White, J. (1980). *Cognitive processes indicative of readiness of hypothetico-deductive thought: A comparison of learning disabled and normal adolescents.* Unpublished doctoral dissertation, Bryn Mawr College. Bryn Mawr, PA.

Williams, H. (1980). *An investigation of two types of learning disabilities among college level students.* Unpublished doctoral dissertation, Carbondale, IL: Southern Illinois University.

Chapter 2

Measurement and Assessment: Group and Individual Techniques

Henry A. Goodstein

APPROACHES TO SECONDARY SPECIAL EDUCATION

There are three special education models or approaches at the secondary level for the adolescent with a learning disability: (1) remedial, (2) compensatory, and (3) vocational (Marsh & Price, 1980; Wiederholt & McNutt, 1979). Remedial education is typically the responsibility of special education personnel and is often offered in conjunction with other programmatic alternatives. Attempts are made to identify weaknesses or deficiencies that affect achievement and activities; techniques and practices are implemented to ameliorate those deficiencies. The focus of remedial models is upon changing the learner so that he or she can relate to the educational program as it is provided and administered for all students (Marsh & Price, 1980). Wiederholt and McNutt (1979) observe that remedial education encourages the identification of skills that students lack, focuses upon decreasing students' weaknesses rather than ignoring them, and offers an option to students unable to cope with regular education programs.

Compensatory approaches stress coping strategies, accommodation, and compensatory teaching to help students learn by circumventing their handicaps. The focus of compensatory models is to modify the instructional environment with direct, pragmatic strategies that allow the learner to cope with instructional demands (Marsh & Price, 1980). Advantages attributed to compensatory models include providing for the attainment of a high school diploma and entry into post-secondary educational opportunities, as well as the presumed opportunity to participate more completely in a "least restrictive environment" (Wiederholt & McNutt, 1979).

Vocational education includes both prevocational and vocational training of students designed to lead to their immediate or short-range employment as semiskilled or skilled workers. The basic purpose of vocational models is to provide job skills through a combination of classroom and on-the-job training. Advantages attributed to vocational models include the opportunity for students to learn marketable skills as an alternative to the traditional college preparation focus of the secondary school and the opportunity to learn a trade in a manner similar to an apprenticeship. (Wiederholt & McNutt, 1979).

DEVELOPMENTAL VERSUS REMEDIAL NEEDS

Goodstein and Kahn (1974) reported data supporting the proposition that a typical population of LD students is likely to have divergent patterns of achievement with respect to reading and mathematics. Many LD students with a primary pattern of disability in reading will not demonstrate any degree of disability in mathematics beyond the difficulties imposed by the requirement to respond to written directions. For these students any underachievement in mathematics is likely to be developmental in character, reflecting slowed progress as a result of the failure of prior instruction to compensate or accommodate to the reading disabilities of the student (Cawley, 1978). Specific gaps in the mathematics repertoire of such students would more likely be found for those concepts and skills more dependent upon comprehension of written directions (e.g., verbal problem solving). Compensatory strategies are appropriate for such students. The determination of the appropriateness of vocational or regular education (general or college preparatory curriculum) would be a function of students' interests, aptitudes, and general levels of achievements.

The main tasks of mathematics assessment for the compensatory student (with a primary reading disability) are (1) to identify the degree of developmental underachievement in mathematics, (2) to determine the extent to which this underachievement is a direct function of failure to comprehend written directions (thus creating a discrepancy between performance on standardized achievement tests and classroom performance where accommodation to the reading disability has been implemented), and (3) to identify any specific mathematics concepts and skills requiring remediation.

For the adolescent with a primary disability in mathematics (with or without an accompanying reading disability) the central focus of the assessment process shifts to remedial planning. The operative assumption is that there is a likelihood of the student demonstrating significant gaps in skill and concept development, reliance upon incorrect or inappropriate computational algorithms, and a history of failure in mathematics with corresponding negative attitudes toward mathematics. For such students whose disabilities have persisted into the secondary school, the likelihood of effectively participating in the college preparatory mathematics sequence (algebra, geometry, trigonometry) is indeed slim. The primary instructional planning emphasis is upon remediation of basic mathematics concepts and skills to provide the basis for more effective participation in vocational programs or general mathematics courses (e.g., consumer mathematics). In addition, instructional planning will be heavily influenced by the requirement (in most states) that the LD student pass a minimal-competency, basic skills proficiency test to be eligible for a standard high school diploma.

The dichotomy described above between the compensatory assessment focus for the LD student with a primary reading disability and the remedial assessment focus for the LD student with a primary mathematics disability is better pictured as a continuum. Many students will not fit neatly into the categories constructed to classify them and there will be infinite variations between the ends of this continuum. In spite of this limitation, this conceptualization of assessment strategies will provide a useful means of describing the emphasis of this chapter, the assessment of those LD students with a primary mathematics disability.

PURPOSES OF ASSESSMENT

Assessment has been described as the systematic process for determining the current status of the learner's knowledge and skill and identifying any additional information required for effective instructional planning (Goodstein, 1984). Assessment includes quantitative descriptions of the learner (typically measurements derived from tests), qualitative descriptions of the learner, as well as value judgments, as both quantitative and qualitative data are weighted and synthesized (Gronlund, 1981). While administration of tests remains the most common means of obtaining quantitative descriptions of learner performance, tests alone will never prove adequate for the assessment of secondary students with learning disabilities in mathematics.

Assessment is also the process of collecting data to make decisions about students (Ysseldyke & Algozzine, 1982). Salvia and Ysseldyke (1981) identified five kinds of decisions regarding students made by using assessment data: (1) evaluation of the individual, (2) program evaluation, (3) screening, (4) placement, and (5) intervention-planning decisions.

Public Law 94-142 mandated the systematic assessment of learners that might require special education programming in order to identify, diagnose, or label students according to handicapping condition and to aid in individual program planning (Myers & Hammill, 1982). However, there are both conceptual and practical difficulties in designing assessment strategies that might differentiate categories of underachievement in mathematics (e.g., Coles, 1978). The lack of specificity in the definition of learning disabilities and assessment practices has become compounded at the secondary level (Marsh & Price, 1980), with federal regulations adding to the confusion (Goodman & Price, 1978). There is a clear trend at the secondary level to diagnose and label students as learning disabled on the basis of poor academic skills.

It remains important to "diagnose" a specific learning disability in mathematics in order to secure resources to underwrite remedial programming. However, it is speculative as to the degree that psychological or neuropsychological process data obtained in a traditional diagnostic assessment contributes to the effectiveness of remedial planning for students with a specific mathematics disability (see, for example, Kosc, 1982). Very few tests have the reliability and validity to adequately assess process functioning with adolescents and there is little empirical support for remediation aimed at process disorders, especially with adolescents (Marsh & Price, 1980).

The emphasis in this chapter will be on assessment for the purpose of assisting in instructional planning. The most useful assessment data for instructional planning will focus on the mathematics to be learned, with consideration both of its structure and cognitive demands (Goodstein, 1984). In addition, the chapter will provide an overview of proficiency testing in mathematics in view of its increasing importance in instructional planning for students with learning disabilities.

MEASUREMENT SCALES

Norm-Referenced

Achievement test scores are interpreted with reference to either relative or absolute measurement scales. Tests that yield scores interpreted on a relative measurement scale are termed *norm-referenced*. Raw scores must be converted or transformed to derived scores (e.g., grade- or age-equivalents, standard scores, percentiles, stanines) to allow comparison of the student's performance with that of some clearly defined reference group, i.e., the norm.

For norm-referenced tests the total raw score typically has little meaning in any absolute sense. The score obtains meaning by comparison with scores obtained by other students. While the item pool from which test items will ultimately be selected has been presumably developed with respect to a content-valid set of specifications, the actual test items will be selected on the basis of certain statistical, psychometric properties. Simply, for most norm-referenced tests, items will be favored that are of mid-range difficulty and contribute to the discrimination of good and poor performers on the test as a whole. Tests constructed in this manner provide for maximum differentiation among students. Such differentiation contributes to the reliable interpretation of norm-referenced test scores.

Criterion-Referenced

Tests that yield scores interpreted on an absolute measurement scale are termed *domain-referenced* or more commonly *criterion-referenced*. Raw scores are typically converted to percentages. Meaning is explicitly or implicitly conferred to the score with respect to some domain of performance. That is, the score is viewed as an estimate performance that the student would have obtained if he or she were administered all similar items from the domain. Reliable and valid test scores are directly related to the clarity of domain specifications and representative selection of items from the domain (Goodstein, 1982).

Most criterion-referenced tests will describe the item domain with a behavioral or instructional objective. However, a chart or table linking test items with instructional objectives (while potentially useful in suggesting possible additional assessment tactics) does not suggest that the test be legitimately considered criterion-referenced. Criterion-referenced tests must provide a sufficient number of items to reliably assess each objective (domain). Test items will be selected as representative of the range of items in the domain (generally without regard to their difficulty or discrimination indices). Norm-referenced tests will tend to sample more objectives with fewer items. Criterion-referenced tests will tend to sample fewer objectives (on a single test form) with more items.

ACHIEVEMENT TESTS IN ASSESSMENT

The typical assessment plan for the secondary LD student begins with the administration of an achievement test to document the degree of disability in an academic area and direct attention to potential remedial needs (Sabatino, 1982). Depending upon the perceived degree of disability or, more likely, the orientation and training of the person responsible for the assessment, the achievement test selected may be designated a "diagnostic" achievement test. In the section that follows, the use of achievement tests (individual and group, norm-referenced and criterion-referenced) in the assessment process will be reviewed. "Diagnostic" achievement tests will be discussed in the succeeding section.

Individual Norm-Referenced Achievement Tests

Special education mathematics assessments traditionally include individual rather than group measures of mathematics achievement (McLoughlin & Lewis, 1981; Sabatino, 1982). Individual achievement tests are often designed to minimize the effect of poor reading ability on mathematics achievement. The test materials are typically more attractive than and less similar to classroom materials (worksheets and informal tests) with which the learner might associate previous failure. Of course, individual administration provides the opportunity for close observation of the learner and for motivation within the limitations of standardized administration procedures.

Three norm-referenced individual achievement tests are available for the assessment of secondary LD students. The most popular individual achievement measure is the mathematics subtest of the *Peabody Individual Achievement Test* (PIAT) (Dunn & Markwardt, 1970). The mathematics subtest consists of 84 multiple-choice items (four option) to assess mathematics skills taught from kindergarten through grade 12. The test stresses application of mathematics skills.

Two limitations are acknowledged by the authors. The content of the PIAT is limited to problems that can be solved mentally. Thus, problems that might require application of complex algorithms could not be included. Also, the items had to fit the multiple-choice format. Thus, the ability of the student to construct or supply the correct response cannot be evaluated.

The *Woodcock-Johnson Psychoeducational Battery* (Woodcock, 1978) includes two subtests designed to assess mathematics achievement. The two subtests form a mathematics achievement cluster (the term "mathematics" suggesting a broader range of content than the arithmetic skills evaluated). The Woodcock-Johnson is designed to be administered to persons from 3 to 80 years of age, although its main application will be with school-aged students. The Woodcock-Johnson has been praised as a model for excellence in the development of norm-referenced psychoeducational test development (Salvia & Ysseldyke, 1981). However, its usefulness as a total battery appears greater than its usefulness as an individual achievement test in mathematics.

The *Wide Range Achievement Test* (WRAT) (Jastak & Jastak, 1978) is divided into two levels. Level II is intended for persons 12 years 0 months to adulthood and includes 46 computational problems ranging from simple arithmetic calculations to problems requiring knowledge of algebra and geometry. The WRAT will severely penalize those students who do not respond well to the speeded conditions of administration. The range of content is largely restricted to arithmetic computation skills.

McLoughlin and Lewis (1981) observe that the arithmetic subtests of the WRAT and PIAT measure different skills. The WRAT arithmetic subtest requires a written response to computational problems, while the PIAT mathematics subtest requires a selection response to items that require not only computation, but reasoning and applications. They note the correspondingly low correlations between scores on the WRAT and PIAT.

Unfortunately, the three most commonly used individual achievement tests in mathematics were designed exclusively as norm-referenced instruments. While providing an estimate of a learner's performance with respect to the performance of a normative population, little diagnostic or prescriptive inference can be drawn from test results because of the extremely thin sampling of skills and concepts.

In recent years, some test publishers have attempted to capitalize on the interest in criterion-referenced measurement by describing the links between individual test items with instructional objectives on their norm-referenced instruments. However, since this often results in only a single item to assess an objective, reliable interpretation is problematic at best.

Ashlock (1982) suggests another weakness associated with the typical norm-referenced achievement test. Such instruments tend to focus more on the measurement of skills, giving less attention to concepts. Yet remediation of faulty concepts is the key to assisting adolescent students with mathematics disabilities to learn skills, remember basic facts of arithmetic, and know when to use the skills they do learn. Norm-referenced achievement tests offer little guidance as to the status of concept development in mathematics.

Individual Criterion-Referenced Achievement Tests

An increasing number of special education authorities have been urging replacement of norm-referenced achievement tests with criterion-referenced measurement systems in the initial stage of assessment for instructional planning. The proposition advanced is that administering a norm-referenced achievement test solely to document the degree of disability (in relation to normative expectations) lacks practical utility for planning remedial programs. This may be particularly true for the secondary LD student who at an earlier grade probably had been administratively "identified" as in need of special education services.

The increased interest in recent years in criterion-referenced assessment has given impetus to the development of a number of criterion-referenced measures in mathematics. Some of these tests are independent of an instructional program, while others are closely linked to an instructional system, such as the *Math Concept Inventory,* the assessment component of *Project MATH* (Cawley, Goodstein, Fitzmaurice, Lepore, Sedlak, & Althaus, 1975, 1976).

Typically, criterion-referenced measures closely linked to *developmental* instructional systems will not be as useful in the assessment of secondary LD students. Such tests have exceptionally high content validity for placement decisions and formative evaluation of instructional outcomes when students are engaged in a particular developmental instructional system. However, the exceptionally high content validity becomes a drawback in using the assessment instrument for more generalized remedial planning. An exception to this conclusion would be for any criterion-referenced measure linked to a program oriented toward remediation, such as *Multi-Model Mathematics,* a remedial program designed specifically for adolescent students with learning disabilities by Cawley and his associates (Cawley, Fitzmaurice-Hayes, Shaw, & Bloomer, 1980).

An individually administered criterion-referenced test that assesses sequences of instructional objectives through high school is *System Fore* (Bagai & Bagai, 1979). Skill sequences are correlated with instructional objectives and arranged developmentally through age 14. A feature of *System Fore* is the linkage of the instructional objectives with commercially available materials.

Diagnosis: An Instructional Aid in Mathematics, Level B (Troutman, 1980) is designed to assess specific mathematics skills from third through eighth grade. Each skill is assessed by a criterion-referenced test (described as a probe). A survey test is available to obtain a global assessment of the learner and to determine which specific probes should be administered. The assessment system is correlated with a wide range of mathematics curriculum materials.

Two additional individually administered criterion-referenced mathematics assessment systems are popular among special education professionals: *The Diagnostic Inventory of Basic Skills* (Brigance, 1977) and the *Criterion-Referenced Curriculum* (Stephens, 1982). Both of these instruments extend their coverage of skills assessed only to the sixth grade. However, for students with severe mathematics disabilities, administration of either test may provide sufficient initial information with respect to possible remedial objectives.

The mathematics subscale of Brigance's *Diagnostic Inventory of Basic Skills* includes 64 tests (sequences). Each sequence is referenced to the grade level at which the content of the sequence is first taught. A norm-referenced computation test in the basic arithmetic operations is included with the Inventory.

Stephens' *Criterion-Referenced Curriculum* (CRC) is the commercial revision of the assessment/instructional system outlined in *Teaching Children Basic Skills* (Stephens, Hartman, & Lucas, 1978). The CRC is referenced to the scope and sequence of skills in the primary grades. A total of 376 skill objectives in mathematics are referenced to the level at which handicapped children normally learn the skills in the elementary grades. Each assessment task is correlated with a set of instructional activities and materials. The CRC has been field tested over a ten-year period with mildly handicapped learners.

The Concept and Skills Assessment component of *Multi-Model Mathematics* (Cawley et al., 1980) is organized in six categories (Number Skills, Number Concepts, Fraction Skills, Fraction Concepts, Measurement, and Geometry). The concept items are multiple-choice in format, whereas the skill items require the student to make computations and supply correct answers. Items are linked to an informal assessment process (Clinical Mathematics Interview) to further clarify the source of the poor performance and prescribe remedial modules. The *Concept and Skills Assessment* has been extensively field tested. Reliability of the inventory is quite high for secondary LD students, with internal consistency estimates ranging from .75 to .97 (median, .86). A more complete description of the Clinical Mathematics Interview will be provided in the section on informal assessment later in this chapter.

A cutoff or advancement score (often referred to as a criterion score) is a feature associated with many criterion-referenced tests. This is a score suggested by the test author that represents the minimum level of mastery of the domain represented by the test items. Most of the cutoff scores suggested are arbitrary, representing the application of judgments as opposed to empirical validation. Suggested criterion scores are often unrealistically high (demanding 100 percent performance), thus failing to reflect the probability of random errors of measurement (instrument-based or student-based). Accordingly, special educators are advised to exercise judgment in the determination of skills or concepts requiring remediation as a result of the failure to achieve the suggested criterion score.

Group Norm-Referenced Achievement Tests

Group achievement tests are less widely used at the secondary level. Three alternative types of norm-referenced tests are common (Gronlund,

1981). One type of achievement test extends assessment of basic skills through the high school years. A second type emphasizes the course content and skills of the secondary mathematics curriculum. A third type (closely linked with aptitude testing) measures general educational development in intellectual skills and abilities that are not dependent upon specific courses.

The first type of achievement test might be appropriate for use with some LD students whose mathematics disabilities are not severe. Examples of this type of group achievement test include the *California Achievement Tests* (CTB/McGraw-Hill, 1977) (Level 19, grade levels 9.6–12.9), the *Metropolitan Achievement Tests* (Prescott, Balow, Hogan, & Farr, 1978) (Level Advanced 2, grade levels 10.0–12.9), and the *Stanford Achievement Tests* (Gardiner, Rudman, Karlsen, & Merewin, 1981) (Level TASK 2, grade levels 9.0–13.0). For severe cases of disability, administration of tests designed for secondary students may prove to be a frustrating exercise. Such tests will have limited content validity for such learners.

A preferred tactic is often the administration of a test that more closely parallels the functional level of mathematics achievement of the student. Administering a level of a test designated for an age range that does not include the age of the student to be assessed is referred to as "out-of-level" testing. Out-of-level testing with a norm-referenced test seriously compromises the ability of the special educator to use the normative data for interpretation (Berk, 1981). That is, since no students of this older age were included in the normative population, the norms become inadequate for comparing the performance of the older student.

If the group achievement test to be given to the older student has a reasonable basis for a criterion-referenced interpretation of performance, out-of-level testing does not present as significant a problem. However, it should be emphasized that, as was the case with individual norm-referenced achievement tests, mathematics objectives on group norm-referenced measures will be assessed quite thinly, often with only a single item.

Group Criterion-Referenced Achievement Tests

A number of excellent group-administered criterion-referenced achievement tests are currently available. The *Metropolitan Achievement Tests* now include a series of *Mathematics Instructional Tests*. The tests parallel the survey tests as to levels and mathematics strands included. A principal difference between the survey tests and instructional tests rests in the number of items (a minimum of three) to evaluate each objective. The

Mathematics Instructional Tests are also norm-referenced. However, the design of the test allows for legitimate criterion-referenced interpretations.

The *Diagnostic Mathematics Inventory* (DMI) (Gessel, 1975) is based on a purportedly comprehensive set of objectives of mathematics curricula from grade 1.5 through 8.5. It is divided into seven levels (of one year each). Each level includes only those objectives ordinarily covered in that grade level. Some objectives are measured at more than one level (with the same item). Each concept (e.g., place value) is evaluated with a minimum of two items (although the majority are evaluated with three or more items). Each item is keyed to a specific objective within the concept being evaluated. A *Guide to Ancillary Materials* and a *Learning Activities Guide* are available to the teacher for selecting or developing instructional materials correlated with DMI performance.

The *Multilevel Academic Skill Inventory* (MASI) (Howell, Zucker, & Morehead, 1982) includes a mathematics component to evaluate basic skills objectives that range in curriculum level from grades 1 through 8. The MASI is organized to assess at three levels. Survey tests provide a general sample of performance on key objectives. The results of the survey test suggest specific skill clusters to be assessed by placement tests (the second level of assessment). Finally, individual skills are evaluated by the specific level tests, where typically ten items are used to assess each skill. The authors of MASI claim that suggested mastery criteria were derived from a review of academic skills mastery by normally achieving students and field tests with normal achievers.

The *Individual Criterion-Referenced Tests* (Hambleton, 1981) consist of a series of criterion-referenced tests organized by strand (e.g., measurement, operations) within six levels intended for use in grades 1 through 6. The *"Math Basics +"* component evaluates 384 objectives. Eight objectives are assessed for each booklet, with each objective evaluated by two items. Parallel forms of each booklet are available for retesting purposes. Performance is reported on an objective attainment basis (100 percent as mastery), as well as in reference to national norms.

Achievement Tests in Action

The use of group achievement tests with secondary LD students could tend to either overestimate or underestimate mathematics performance with respect to their true level of achievement. Group achievement tests rely heavily upon multiple-choice test items (unfortunately, many individual achievement tests also rely upon such recognition-type items). Learners who benefit from the opportunity to guess but whose performance on supply-type items would be poorer will tend to have overestimated test scores. Learners who do not respond in a motivated fashion under group testing conditions or demonstrate reading disabilities will tend to test poorer than would be predicted from their actual level of mathematics achievement. Unfortunately, we have little data to judge which of these potentially biasing effects is more prevalent in the use of group achievement test with secondary LD students.

One final note with respect to assessment of achievement. Numerous criterion-referenced inventories are becoming available for assessment of mathematics achievement, many of which have been developed locally by school systems. In determining whether to use a particular criterion-referenced test or inventory or another, various features of the instruments ought to be evaluated and compared.

Test items should be judged as the best or most representative measurement tactic to assess the content suggested by the instructional objective. Sufficient items of similar content and format should be provided to reliably measure the objective. Items should be free of technical flaws. Objectives (and items) should be arranged in a reasonable developmental progression in order to facilitate efficient assessment. (Survey tests designed to aid in planning strategies for inventory administration may prove helpful.) Most important, the instructional objectives evaluated by the inventory should closely correlate with the instructional goals for the student. Hambleton and Eignor (1978) present a more complete listing of potential evaluative criteria.

DIAGNOSTIC TESTS IN ASSESSMENT

In mathematics, as in reading, many test publishers have attempted to distinguish diagnostic tests from achievement tests. The presumed distinction between mathematics achievement tests and diagnostic tests resides in the intent of the diagnostic test to define the causes of nonachievement (Goodstein, 1975). It should be pointed out that simply because a test author determines to call his or her instrument a diagnostic test this does not necessarily endow it with diagnostic properties (Cronbach, 1970).

Gronlund (1981) suggests that defining properties of diagnostic tests are more intensive measurement of specific skills, use of test items that are based on a detailed analysis of specific skills involved in successful performance and a study of common errors, and the inclusion of items with lower levels of item difficulty than would be appropriate for survey achievement tests. The presumption being made is that a diagnostic achievement test would be more typically administered to learners with low levels of normative achievement. Underhill, Uprichard, and Heddens

(1980) suggest that diagnostic tests are more systematic over a narrower range of content.

Gronlund (1981) cautions that each diagnostic test reflects the author's concept of the subject area and viewpoint towards diagnosis. Diagnostic tests do not necessarily indicate the cause of errors and differ widely in the ability to allow one to infer the cause of errors. While many experts in mathematics education have suggested that diagnosis not be limited to the abstract level and modeled after classroom situations, instrument development has been largely limited to symbolic skills. Unfortunately, clinicians and diagnosticians have not agreed upon standards for diagnostic instruments (Underhill et al., 1980).

Reisman (1982) summarizes the challenge of creating a comprehensive diagnostic mathematics test:

> It is impossible to construct a test that taps the total range of a mathematics curriculum and that provides information as to why a child misses one item and has answered the preceding item correctly. An analysis of published tests that purport to be diagnostic shows that between most items, several missing relations and concepts may exist. Furthermore, most tests do not provide enough information as to why a child has answered an item or a group of items incorrectly. (p. 44)

Norm-Referenced Diagnostic Tests

The *Key Math Diagnostic Arithmetic Test* (Connolly, Nachtman, & Pritchett, 1976) is the most widely used diagnostic test of mathematics in special education (McLoughlin & Lewis, 1981). *Key Math* is an individually administered norm-referenced test designed to assess mathematics performance of learners from kindergarten through grade 8. The test is composed of 14 subtests organized into three areas: Content, Operations, and Applications. Grade equivalent scores are available for interpretation of both the total score and for individual subtest scores. Items are arranged within subtests in ascending order of difficulty and are calibrated (and displayed) with respect to the grade equivalent scale.

Salvia and Ysseldyke (1981) observe that *Key Math* performance can be interpreted in four ways: total test performance, relative area strengths and weaknesses, relative performance on the 14 subtests, and a criterion-referenced interpretation based on item performance and the description of behaviors sampled by each item. With respect to area strengths and weaknesses, it would appear that the analysis would be of dubious merit since no factorial validity has been demonstrated for the areas as defined by *Key Math* (Goodstein, Kahn, & Cawley, 1976). With respect to a criterion-referenced interpretation of performance, this would appear to be limited by the fact that most objectives are measured by a single item. Substantial skill gaps exist between items. If a criterion-referenced evaluation of performance is desired, better assessment instruments are available.

The diagnostic value of *Key Math* is limited to comparisons of normative subtest performance. However, low subtest reliabilities for some subtests make such comparisons subject to considerable error (Salvia & Ysseldyke, 1981). Further, some subtests such as Mental Computation and Missing Elements may assess mathematics skills not found in the typical mathematics curriculum (McLoughlin & Lewis, 1981). The skill gaps between items and inability to assess an objective with more than one item limits the interpretation of *Key Math* with respect to remedial strategies. Since it fails to intensively measure specific skills and provides no data with respect to causality for failure, *Key Math* more closely resembles a multiple-subtest individually administered achievement test than a diagnostic test.

Given the limitations of *Key Math* as a diagnostic mathematics test, it is difficult to understand its enthusiastic endorsement by authors of assessment textbooks. For example, Wallace and Larsen (1978) describe *Key Math* "as a good example of a comprehensive arithmetic battery that provides an overall indication of a child's arithmetic skills, along with more detailed information for teaching specific skills" (p. 449). Salvia and Ysseldyke (1981) claim its real value is as a criterion-referenced device, with apparently little regard to lack of comprehensive skill coverage. Perhaps the endorsements reflect the current lack of alternative individual diagnostic tests.

Another widely used mathematics diagnostic test is a group-administered measurement, the *Stanford Diagnostic Mathematics Test* (SDMT) (Beatty, Madden, Gardiner, & Karleson, 1976). The SDMT is organized into four levels: the Red level (grades 1.5 to 4.5), the Green level (grades 3.5 to 6.5), the Brown level (grades 5.5 to 8.5) and the Blue level (grades 7.5 to High School). At each level skills and knowledge are organized into three subtests: Number System and Numeration, Computation, and Applications.

The SDMT is essentially a norm-referenced instrument, with norm-referenced scores available for each subtest and total score. However, it contains many more easy items than most norm-referenced achievement tests. This provides more opportunities for the student to answer items correctly, facilitating valuable insights into differential patterns of achievement. However, Alley and Deshler (1978) report that LD students administered the appropriate normalized level of the SDMT still found many of the basic items extremely difficult to solve. They urge out-of-level testing strategies and criterion-referenced interpretation of the SDMT.

The SDMT provides more items for each skill area. This latter feature facilitates more reliable criterion-referenced interpretations of performance. Items that measure a specific skill are grouped and assigned a criterion score (called Progress Indicator cutoff scores). Cutoff scores were suggested by the authors judgmentally on the basis of the importance of the skill as a prerequisite for other skills and normative item difficulties. Patterns of performance or specific areas of weaknesses can be identified.

The SDMT is an exceptionally well-constructed group-administered measurement. Parallel forms exist that facilitate retesting for reevaluation of learner performance. As a group-administered measurement instrument, the SDMT may not be as motivating for the child as some of the more attractive individual tests (e.g., *Key Math*). While it is more likely to yield instructionally relevant information on specific performance problems than *Key Math*, the SDMT does not contribute substantially in suggesting the cause of the poor performance.

Criterion-Referenced Diagnostic Tests

Wallace and Larsen (1978) suggest that the *Diagnostic Chart for Fundamental Processes in Arithmetic* (Buswell & John, 1925) cannot be considered a test because of its lack of standardization, final scores, or quotients or grade equivalents. However, since it does present a standardized set of items to the learner in a standardized manner, it will be included in our discussion of diagnostic tests.

With the Buswell-John the learner is given a worksheet with a graded series of arithmetic computational problems arranged in order of increasing difficulty for the four basic operations with whole numbers. The learner is asked to work each of the problems aloud so as to assist the examiner in determining the algorithm employed in solving each problem. The need to consider the algorithm (or process) used that resulted in errors in computation is a consistent theme in the remedial mathematics literature (Goodstein, 1975; Underhill et al., 1980). The examiner classifies errors according to one of the numerous categories of error provided on the Diagnostic Chart. A more complete discussion of error analysis is included in this chapter in the section on informal assessment.

The Buswell-John instrument is basically a test of algorithms with no diagnosis on the structure of mathematics. No provision is made for diagnosing problem-solving techniques or for diagnosing place value either independently or in relation to algorithms (Underhill et al., 1980). However, the test is relatively easy to analyze for sequence of processes and learner errors are readily isolated.

A new criterion-referenced inventory under revision for commercial dissemination is the Reisman *Sequential Assessment in Mathematics Inventory* (SAMI) (Reisman, 1984). Described in *A Guide to the Diagnostic Teaching of Arithmetic* (Reisman, 1982), the SAMI is intended for use with learners through grade 8. The SAMI assesses mathematics content in 18 mathematics topics (ideas). Specific objectives (goals) are stated for each topic. Test items are classified by behavior (e.g., show, write, interpret, compute) required of the learner. The psychological nature (e.g., arbitrary association, relationship, concept, generalization) and mode of representing the content for each item (enactive, iconic, symbolic) are also specified.

Reisman (1982) describes the SAMI as a diagnostic screening instrument. Unlike typical criterion-referenced inventories, the domains represented by the topics (at each level of the instrument) are broader, inclusive of a number of related, but different, goals assessed with fewer items for each goal. Whether the ability to identify diagnostically meaningful patterns with respect to the various descriptive schemes for labeling items will contribute to effective remedial planning remains untested. The SAMI will constitute the most comprehensive single diagnostic instrument available. However, its interpretation will require considerable clinical experience and knowledge of how children acquire mathematics knowledge and skill.

INFORMAL ASSESSMENT

Myers and Hammill (1982) contrast two assessment paradigms: the test-based approach and the informal approach. There has been an increasing dissatisfaction with the test-based approach (much of this criticism specifically directed at norm-referernced tests). Most critics have observed that the test-based approach simply fails to provide significant data for intervention-planning decisions. Poplin and Gray (1982) contend that the classroom teacher should have the primary responsibility for the assessment of student needs and most teachers now perform the informal assessments most relevant for instructional planning for handicapped students. This is representative of the increasing advocacy for the development and use of informal assessment techniques for acquiring data for intervention-planning decisions in special education programs for mildly handicapped adolescents (e.g., Mercer, 1979).

The informal approach relies heavily on the interpretation of children's performance in natural settings. It stresses criterion-referenced interpretations and is educationally task oriented (Myers & Hammill, 1982). At a minimum, it is often advocated as a necessary supplement (as opposed to a replacement) to more formal test-based approaches. Sedlak, Sedlak, and Steppe-Jones (1982) describe informal assessment as a dynamic process that verifies, probes, or discards the conclusions and recommendations of a formal assessment.

Informal assessment strategies are especially relevant for use with adolescent students with a learning disability in mathematics. Many of these students will present skill deficits as a result of incomplete concept formation. The importance of concept mastery as a prerequisite to skill development in mathematics is gaining prominence in the special education literature (e.g., Ashlock, 1981). Ashlock warns professionals working with students who have not learned basic mathematics skills not to ignore concepts in their assessment and instructional planning. He describes two classes of concepts (meanings of operations on numbers and meanings of numerals) as fundamental anchors to successful skill development.

These concepts are not to be confused with computational procedures (algorithms), as students are often asked to apply the correct procedure even though they do not understand the meaning of an operation. Cawley (1978) similarly notes that students may recognize the pattern and structure for completing the computation (meaning of operations on numbers), but may use the wrong procedure or algorithm or vice versa.

Examining the "cause" of poor test performance requires additional assessment data not available from sole reliance upon currently available "diagnostic" tests. As was described in the previous section, diagnostic tests are essentially content instruments. They provide little information as to either the student's most efficient or least efficient mode of performance or the appropriateness or efficiency of the algorithm employed (Cawley, 1978).

Often included under the rubric of informal assessment are criterion-referenced tests and inventories, behavioral observations, checklists and rating scales, interviews and questionnaires, work sample analyses (error analysis), and analyses of student responses to various instructional tasks (McLoughlin & Lewis, 1981; Sedlak et al., 1982). This section of the chapter will review the informal assessment tools of error analysis and interview strategies and discuss guidelines for the development of teacher-constructed tests and inventories.

Error Analysis

Error analysis is intended to determine the presence of systematic patterns underlying incorrect learner responses. Implicit in the use of error analysis is the expectation that most secondary LD student errors will not be random or simply the result of carelessness (Alley & Deshler, 1978). Rather, learner errors can provide diagnostic information to guide the remediation of specific concept or skill deficits (Goodstein, 1975). What might appear to be a total lack of comprehension may define itself as a single inappropriately applied concept or rule that quickly yields to precisely targeted remediation.

In the analysis of computational errors, three types of systematic errors are discriminated from careless, random errors (Cox, 1975; Moran, 1978; Reisman, 1982). These systematic error sources are inadequate facts, incorrect operations, and ineffective strategies or algorithms. A systematic error pattern is verified when students make at least three errors in five items requiring the same algorithm and the errors are of the same type (Cox, 1975). Of the three types of systematic errors, algorithmic errors are the most difficult to detect and confirm. Ashlock (1982) concentrates attention on the detection of defective algorithms and provides a wealth of examples to aid that process.

Error analysis can also be effectively used in the informal assessment of verbal problem-solving errors (Goodstein, 1981). If verbal problems have been developed in such a manner that the various factors or parameters that combine to describe a problem have been controlled, organizational matrices can be developed. Such matrices allow for task descriptions that are sufficiently complete to evaluate errors on individual problems and determine whether they are random or systematic.

Error analysis can be made solely from the examination of the student's work products. However, Alley and Deshler (1978) caution that the algorithmic errors of many LD students may be sufficiently aberrant that an error analysis system such as that proposed by Ashlock (1982) may not be sufficiently sensitive to detect systematic errors without additional clinical interviewing. Error analysis is often combined with a clinical interview to enhance its diagnostic value with LD students (Cawley, Fitzmaurice, Shaw, Kahn, & Bates, 1978; Lepore, 1979).

Romberg and Uprichard (1978) identified three approaches to the clinical interview: the structured interview, the Piagetian interview or clinique, and the teaching experiment. Regardless of how the interview is structured, the effectiveness of the assessment will depend upon the assessor's knowledge and ability to facilitate communication (Underhill et al., 1980). Clearly, *effective* use of the clinical interview will require significantly more training in mathematics education than is typically provided many assessment professionals (Wallace & Larsen, 1978).

Multi-Model Mathematics (Cawley et al., 1980) includes the *Clinical Mathematics Interview* (CMI) to provide a comprehensive diagnostic component to link the *Concept and Skill Assessment* component (screening) with appropriate remedial modules. The CMI (first described by Cawley, 1978) is a structured interview, with questioning proceeding systematically in an effort to define systematic modality or faulty algorithm sources for concept or skill deficits.

Students are first screened with the Concept and Skill Assessment. Suggested concept or skill deficits are confirmed (reliability check) by presenting five additional written items. If the student makes only one or two careless errors, the student is assigned an appropriate drill activity. If the student makes more than two errors and/or some doubts emerge as to level of understanding, the assessor initiates the diagnostic phase.

The initial step of the diagnostic phase involves checking for understanding of the problem. An example is selected in which the student made an error. The student is asked to explain how the answer was obtained or how the answer might be obtained (if no answer was given) and to provide the correct answer. If the student provides incorrect answer(s) and/or doubts remain as to level of understanding, the assessor is provided a series of procedures requiring sequential decision making. Most errors made by remedial and LD students are consistent even though they may appear illogical to the teacher. One of the characteristics of the LD adolescent with a specific mathematic disability is to present idiosyncratic as opposed to random error patterns (Marsh & Price, 1980). While this consistency may be difficult to identify by simply looking at completed problems, it may be easier to spot when the problem is done one step at a time (Lyon & Karplus, 1980).

Teacher-Made Tests

Many authors have extolled the virtues of teacher-made tests in the assessment of mathematics disabilities (e.g., Bartel, 1978). However, the large number of criterion-referenced tests and inventories that are being commercially distributed would appear to obviate the need for teacher-made mathematics skill inventories. Though the correspondence to the classroom curriculum may not be perfect, a far better strategy may be to modify or adapt a commercially distributed test or inventory. Objectives (and/or test items) could be added or deleted and additional parallel items could be developed to ensure greater reliability in the assessment process.

Teacher-made tests or inventories do often prove quite helpful in providing more diagnostic information as to the nature and probable cause of specific skill deficits (Reisman, 1982; Underhill et al., 1980). These "informal" measures could assess the learner using a variety of formats, materials, and response modes that could not be cost-effectively employed by commercial test publishers. Unfortunately, the inability of teachers to prepare appropriate test items that will reliably assess learner performance is a major obstacle to valid teacher-made tests (Wallace & Larsen, 1978). Developing such tests does require more knowledge of the structure of mathematics, learning theories, developmental theories, and the nature of mathematics disabilities than many teachers have.

Reisman (1982) offers the following guidelines for preparing such a test: (1) select content, (2) isolate one concept that is to be diagnosed in depth, (3) determine which level of learning the individual is at, (4) decide on what behaviors you want the learner to display in order to demonstrate acquisition of the concept, and (5) write a table of specifications that includes behavior and content components. Items would then be developed of sufficient technical quality to adequately sample the table of specifications. Any of the several introductory textbooks in educational measurement (e.g., Gronlund, 1981) contain guidelines to the development of test items of high technical quality.

The format of test items is receiving increasing attention as a possible source of errors in mathematics (e.g., Sedlak et al., 1982). In the construction of teacher-made tests and inventories, considerable care should be taken to assess performance using a variety of formats for test items (with sufficient items to reliably assess performance within each format). Ashlock (1981) reminds us that skills need to be applied in varied contexts, and, until students can demonstrate skills in these contexts, it is hardly appropriate to say they are skillful. Even minor variations in content and format can significantly affect performance of mildly handicapped adolescents on informal criterion-referenced tests (Goodstein, Howell, & Williamson, 1982). Determining which formats the student is more successful with can be quite useful as a *starting point* for remedial programming aimed at enhancing the student's capability to apply skills in multiple contexts.

PROFICIENCY TESTS

Proficiency testing is becoming an increasingly potent force influencing the instructional planning for students with learning disabilities, especially at the secondary level. Most states now require that students pass a basic skills proficiency test to be eligible for graduation with a "standard" high school diploma. While many states will allow special education students to graduate if they satisfactorily complete agreed-upon objectives in the student's IEP, the diploma earned may be differentiated from the standard diploma. A standard diploma is valued as a means of gaining admission to further opportunities for education or training or securing employment in an increasingly competitive marketplace. This results in considerable pressure to prepare the secondary student with a learning disability to pass the state proficiency test.

In view of the increasing emphasis on proficiency testing in instructional planning, it is important that the special education professional have an understanding of the process of developing a typical mathematics basic skills proficiency test. Such knowledge will provide a basis for planning appropriate instructional strategies for preparing secondary LD students to achieve passing scores on these tests. Special education professionals are urged to become familiar with the test program and test development process in their own state since there are differences.

Typically, mathematics objectives are assessed in a single section or subtest of a basic skills proficiency test, with a predetermined passing score (e.g., 70 percent) assigned for certifying "minimal competence." The student is required to pass each section (e.g., mathematics, reading) in order to be eligible to graduate. However, failure to pass one section does not typically result in the student being retested on sections for which a passing score was achieved. It is common practice to provide students with a number of opportunities to retake sections of the test for which they failed to achieve a passing score.

In some states, the high school proficiency test is the culmination of a developmental testing program initiated in the early elementary grades. A series of achievement tests administered annually or biannually provides for progress monitoring of the development of prerequisite concepts or skills. Feedback is provided with respect to overall performance and performance on specific objectives is assessed in order to direct remedial assistance. In other states, parallel forms of the high school proficiency test are administered prior to entrance into high school (e.g., the eighth grade) to assist in the "diagnosis" of concept or skill deficits.

High school proficiency tests are designed as criterion-referenced tests. However, unlike criterion-referenced mastery tests where a single objective (or domain) is assessed and mastery or minimal-competence decisions are made on an objective-by-objective basis, the high school proficiency test more closely resembles a survey test. That is, the test is composed of a *collection* of objectives (with several items to assess each objective) and, most important, the passing score to determine minimal competence is some proportion of the total raw score on the test. This suggests that the student need not be able to demonstrate mastery of all objectives in order to achieve a passing score.

For example, assume that the mathematics section of a high school proficiency test has 15 objectives assessed with four items each, resulting in a total of 60 items. The passing score is set at 75 percent (45 items). Assuming that a student could achieve perfect performance on 11 of the objectives (44 items), he or she would have to answer only one item from the remaining four objectives. This method of scoring high school proficiency tests has important implications for the remedial mathematics instruction of the secondary LD student. First, the teacher should be thoroughly familiar with the objectives assessed on the test and the *manner* in which those objectives will be assessed. Second, the teacher should determine the most efficient strategy for preparing each student. Perhaps, individual objectives that the student has had extreme difficulty mastering in the format used to assess those objectives should be minimized or omitted in the instructional program in favor of improving performance levels on other objectives.

Some would criticize this strategy-based instructional planning as "gamesmanship." However, it should be noted that proficiency tests are able to sample only a portion of the mathematics curriculum appropriate for LD students. Thus, teachers will not want to limit their instructional planning to only the state-identified basic skills. Given the importance of passing this test for LD students, there would be a temptation to do just that. What is being proposed is simply that teachers not spend a disproportionate amount of time engaged in a potentially frustrating teaching-learning exercise for a single objective on the proficiency test. Mastery of all objectives is not required.

Proficiency Test Objectives

The following is a list of objectives for the Tennessee high school basic skills proficiency test. These can serve as an overview of the "scope and sequence" of a typical proficiency test.

1) **Writing a numeral for a word name**—Given a word name for a number less than one billion, the student will determine the equivalent numeral.
2) **Rounding off numbers**—Given a whole number with fewer than seven digits, the student will determine the answer which represents the nearest multiple of ten, hundred, thousand, or ten thousand.
3) **Place value**—Given a whole number or a decimal number, the student will identify the digit that is in a given place.
4) **Adding whole numbers and decimal numbers**—Given a problem to add either two or more whole numbers or two or more

decimal numbers, the student will solve the problem with regrouping.

5) **Subtracting whole numbers or decimal numbers**—Given a problem to subtract either two whole numbers or two decimal numbers, the student will solve the problem with regrouping.

6) **Multiplying whole numbers**—Given a problem to multiply a three-digit number by a two-digit number, the student will solve the problem by regrouping.

7) **Multiplying decimal numbers**—Given a problem to multiply two decimal numbers, each having no more than three decimal places, the student will solve the problem.

8) **Dividing whole numbers**—Given a problem to divide a four-digit number by a one-digit number or a two-digit number, the student will solve the problem for which the answer may have a remainder.

9) **Dividing a decimal number by a whole number**—Given a problem to divide a decimal number by a whole number, the student will solve the problem.

10) **Adding fractions**—Given a problem to add three fractions with unlike denominators, including mixed numbers, the student will solve the problem and express the answer in simplest form.

11) **Subtracting fractions**—Given a problem to subtract two fractions with unlike denominators, one of which may be a mixed number, the student will solve the problem and express the answer in simplest form.

12) **Multiplying or dividing fractions**—Given a problem to multiply or to divide two fractions, including mixed numbers, the student will solve the problem and express the answer in simplest form.

13) **Fraction, decimal number, and percent equivalency**—Given a simple fraction, a decimal number, or a percent, the student will determine either of the other equivalent forms of the number.

14) **Percent of number**—Given a problem that involves finding the percent of a number, the student will solve the problem.

15) **Finding perimeter and area**—Given the lengths of the adjacent sides of a rectangular figure, the student will determine the perimeter or the area.

16) **Determining the arithmetic mean**—Given a problem involving five two-digit numbers, the student will determine the arithmetic mean.

17) **Operations for solving simple word problems**—Given a simple one-step word problem, the student will identify the operation required for the solution of the problem.
18) **Interpreting graphs**—Given illustrations of bar, circle, picture, or broken-line graphs, the student will interpret their meanings.
19) **Equivalent measures**—Given either customary or metric units of measure of (1) length, (2) weight (customary) or mass (metric), (3) volume, or (4) time, the student will determine an equivalent measure within the same system.
20) **Linear measurement**—Given a drawing of a ruler and an object, the student will determine the length of the object to the nearest one-fourth of an inch or to the nearest centimeter.
21) **Measuring temperature**—Given an illustration of a thermometer with either the Celsius or Fahrenheit scale, the student will determine the pictured temperature.

Developing Proficiency Test Items

The process of developing test items to assess an objective typically includes an intermediate step of defining the measurement domain. The most prevalent means of deriving this definition involves utilizing versions of detailed test specifications proposed by Popham (1978, 1981). The specifications identify the boundaries of the domain (i.e., what items may be included in the potential item pool) and the format for the presentation of the items. In addition, the characteristics of the alternative responses (distractors) are described for the multiple-choice questions and guidelines for the selection or arrangement of items may also be included.

There is considerable debate over the appropriateness of providing these test specifications to teachers and/or general public. Some argue for confidentiality fearing that their availability will encourage "teaching for the test." However, teachers ought to have complete knowledge of the measurement domain so that they might ensure that their instructional domain is consistent. Proficiency tests *already* limit and prioritize instructional objectives. If the domain established for the objectives is so narrow that the specifications provide for only a small pool of items, the objective is probably inappropriate. In most cases, what the domain specifications provide is useful information for teachers to incorporate in instructional planning.

At a minimum, most states will provide teachers with sample items for each objective. Careful examination of these sample items will often enable the teacher to infer the test specifications that define the potential item pool. The following sample detailed test specifications for the Tennessee high school proficiency test offer an opportunity to observe the process of moving from the general statement of an objective to the development of a pool of test items and selection of items from that pool for assessing the objective.

Title of
Objective: **Fraction, Decimal Number, and Percent Equivalency**

Statement
of
Objective: Given a simple fraction, a decimal number, or a percent, the student will determine either of the other equivalent forms of the number.

Definition of Domain
1. Denominators of simple fractions shall be limited to single-digit numbers, to multiples of ten not to exceed 100, and to the number 25.
2. Decimal numbers to be converted to percents shall consist of two or three digits.
3. Decimal numbers to be converted to simple fractions shall consist of two digits.
4. Percents to be converted to simple fractions may be any whole number less than 100.
5. Percents to be converted to decimal numbers may be any number greater than zero and less than 100 that is expressed as a whole number or to the tenths place.

Guidelines for Item Writer
1. Denominators of simple fractions shall be limited to single-digit numbers, to multiples of ten not to exceed 100, and to the number 25.
2. All fractions will be written in simplest form.
3. One-sixth of the test items will be written for each category described in guidelines 4–10 below.
4. For fraction-to-decimal items, consideration should be given to the choice of distractors obtained by:
   a. dividing the denominator by the numerator.
   b. misplacing the decimal point.
   c. reversing numerator and denominator and then dividing correctly.
   d. writing "zero, decimal point, denominator" in that order as a distractor for simple fractions with a numerator of one.

5. For decimal-to-fraction items:
   a. all decimal numbers shall consist of two digits.
   b. consideration should be given to the choice of distractors obtained by:
      1) writing a fraction with a numerator of one and a denominator consisting of the two digits given in the decimal number.
      2) writing a fraction consisting of the first digit over the second digit given in the decimal number.
      3) rounding the decimal number to the nearest tenth and then converting correctly to simplest form.
6. For fraction-to-percent items, consideration should be given to the choice of distractors obtained by:
   a. writing the numerator followed by the denominator.
   b. dividing the denominator by the numerator.
   c. multiplying the numerator by the denominator.
7. For percent-to-fraction items:
   a. percents may be any whole numbers less than 100.
   b. consideration should be given to the choice of distractors obtained by:
      1) writing a fraction with a numerator of one over a denominator consisting of the two digits given in the percent number.
      2) writing a fraction consisting of the first digit divided by the second digit given in the percent number.
      3) writing a fraction with a numerator consisting of the two digits of the percent number and a denominator of 1,000.
8. For decimal-to-percent items:
   a. decimal numbers shall consist of two or three digits.
   b. all response alternatives should have the decimal point in different places and the percent sign attached.
9. For percent-to-decimal items:
   a. percents may be any number greater than zero and less than 100 and expressed as a whole number or to the tenths place.
   b. all distractors should have misplaced decimal points; one distractor, in particular, should have the same numerical value as the given percent but without the percent symbol (%).
10. For fraction-to-decimal and for fraction-to-percent items:
    a. all response alternatives will be expressed in hundredths.

    b. correct answers that do not terminate in the hundredths place shall be rounded appropriately to the hundredths place.

    c. distractors may not be used which have a value $\pm$ 0.03 of the correct answer.

    d. the stem of the item should use the expression "is closest to" as in the following example:

    2/3 written as a decimal fraction is closest to:

        a) 0.23
        b) 0.60
        c) 0.67
        d) 0.75

Guidelines for Selecting Items

Only one item should be selected from a given category (e.g., fraction-to-decimal).

Guidelines for Arranging/Printing Items

    None

Sample Test Items

1. 37/50 written as a decimal fraction is closest to:
    a) 0.07
  *b) 0.74
    c) 0.80
    d) 1.35

2. 0.075 written as a percent is:
    a) 0.075%
    b) 0.75%
  *c) 7.5%
    d) 75%

3. 0.45 written as a fraction is:
    a) $\frac{1}{45}$ *c) $\frac{9}{20}$
    b) $\frac{2}{5}$ d) $\frac{4}{5}$

4. 12% written as a fraction is:
    a) $\frac{1}{12}$ c) $\frac{3}{20}$
  *b) $\frac{3}{25}$ d) $\frac{1}{2}$

---

*Correct answer

5. 14.5% written as a decimal is:
   a)   0.0145
  *b)   0.145
   c)   1.45
   d) 14.5

6. ¾ written as a percent is:
   a) 12%
   b) 13%
   c) 34%
  *d) 75%

Hopefully, the availability of such detailed test specifications will offer the secondary LD teacher specific guidance for developing appropriate instructional sequences and practice exercises to maximize performance.

Of course, use of detailed test specifications is no guarantee that all items written will have equivalent levels of difficulty. As teachers develop sample items for practice exercises, efforts should be made to expose the students to a wide variety of tasks (consistent with the specifications). Teachers should also keep in mind that practice on sample items is not a substitute for planned instructional activities to ensure full understanding of the concepts and skills underlying item performance.

Commercially Distributed Proficiency Tests

With the rapid adoption of proficiency tests to certify eligibility for high school graduation, commercial test publishers have attempted to capitalize on the need for tests that school systems might wish to administer to assess learner achievement of basic skills objectives. In mathematics there seems to be a greater (but by no means complete) level of agreement on a core set of basic skills. However, the usefulness of any commercial test to assist in directing remediation of basic skill deficits will depend on the content validity of the test with respect to each state's basic skills objectives.

The *Iowa Tests of Achievement and Proficiency* (Scannell, 1978) is partially an assessment of basic skills. The *Stanford Achievement Tests Task I* (Gardiner et al., 1981) is a basic skills proficiency test. Scott-Foresman's test division has recently introduced a *Minimum Essentials Test* (Wick & Smith, 1980) based on those objectives considered basic to minimum competence in mathematics. Basic skills proficiency tests might be considered an appropriate assessment tool for initiating the evaluation of the secondary school age child with a mathematics disability.

VOCATIONAL EDUCATION

The assessment of mathematics skills in job-related tasks may be markedly different from the assessment of basic skills in school and on high school basic skills proficiency tests. A distinction must be made between assessments of contrived applications and assessments of real applications (Cawley, 1982). Contrived applications are those that take place simultaneously with the acquisition of concepts and skills. Real applications are the direct application of skills and concepts in job-related and social situations.

Poplin and Gray (1982) point out that the advantage of natural (real) assessments as opposed to synthetic (contrived) ones is the opportunity to observe the application of skills in natural contexts, an ultimate determination of competence. Unfortunately, there exists almost no data on the importance of various mathematics skills for vocational success within or across various occupations and little experience in the design of assessment tools appropriate for determining progress in application of mathematics skills on job-related tasks. This is an area of future inquiry that demands research and development.

SUMMARY

The assessment of secondary school LD students with primary mathematics disabilities represents a challenge to the special education teacher. While a variety of tests are available, most require considerable skill in administration and interpretation when used with secondary school students. Recent advances in the development of criterion-referenced achievement tests and state-sponsored proficiency tests represent the most promising alternative to the use of norm-referenced achievement tests which have associated psychometric difficulties. The application of clinical judgments in observing the mathematics performance of secondary LD students remains the most important diagnostic tool for the special education professional.

REFERENCES TO TESTS CITED IN CHAPTER

Bagai, E., and Bagai, E. (Eds.). (1979). *System Fore*. North Hollywood, CA: Forewords.

Beatty, L.S., Madden, R., Gardiner, E.F., & Karleson, B. (1976). *Stanford Diagnostic Mathematics Test*. New York: Harcourt Brace Jovanovich.

Brigance, A. (1977). *Brigance Diagnostic Inventory of Basic Skills*. North Billerica, MA: Curriculum Associates.

Buswell, G.T., & John, L. (1925). *Diagnostic Chart for Fundamental Processes in Arithmetic.* Indianapolis: Bobbs-Merrill.

Cawley, J.F., Fitzmaurice-Hayes, A.M., Shaw, R., & Bloomer, K. (1980). *Multi-Model Mathematics.* Storrs, CT: The University of Connecticut. *(Concept and Skills Assessment)*

Cawley, J.F., Goodstein, H.A., Fitzmaurice, A.M., Lepore, A.V., Sedlak, R., & Althaus, V. (1975, 1976). *Project MATH: Levels I, II, III & IV.* Tulsa, OK: Educational Development Corp. *(Math Concept Inventory)*

Connolly, A.J., Nachtman, W., & Pritchett, E.M. (1976). *Key Math Diagnostic Arithmetic Test.* Circle Pines, MN: American Guidance Service.

CTB/McGraw-Hill. (1977). *The California Achievement Tests.* Monterey, CA: CTB/McGraw-Hill.

Dunn, L.M., & Markwardt, F.C. (1970). *Peabody Individual Achievement Test.* Circle Pines, MN: American Guidance Service.

Gardiner, E.F., Rudman, H.C., Karlsen, B., & Merewin, J.C. (1981). *Stanford Achievement Tests.* New York: Psychological Corp.

Gessell, J.K. (1975). *Diagnostic Mathematics Inventory.* Monterey, CA: CTB/McGraw-Hill.

Hambleton, R.K. (1981). *Individual Criterion-Referenced Tests.* Tulsa, OK: Educational Development Corp.

Howell, K.W., Zucker, S.H., & Morehead, M.K. (1982). *MASI: Multilevel Academic Skill Inventory.* Columbus, OH: Charles E. Merrill.

Jastak, J.F., & Jastak, S. (1978). *Wide Range Achievement Tests.* Wilmington, DE: Jastak Associates.

Prescott, G.A., Balow, I.H., Hogan, T.P., & Farr, R.C. (1978). *Metropolitan Achievement Tests: Survey Battery and Instructional.* New York: Psychological Corp.

Reisman, F.K. (1984). *Sequential Assessment in Mathematics Instruction.* Columbus, OH: Charles E. Merrill.

Scannell, D.P. (1978) *Iowa Tests of Achievement and Proficiency.* Lombard, IL: Riverside.

Stephens, T.M. (1982). *Criterion-Referenced Curriculum.* Columbus, OH: Charles E. Merrill.

Troutman, A.P. (1980). *Diagnosis: An Instructional Aid in Mathematics, Level B.* Chicago: Science Research Associates.

Wick, J.W., & Smith, J.K, (1980). *Comprehensive Assessment Program: Achievement Series.* Glenview, IL: Scott, Foresman. *(Minimal Essentials Tests)*

Woodcock, R. (1978). *Woodcock-Johnson Psychoeducational Battery.* Boston: Teaching Resources.

REFERENCES

Alley, G., & Deshler, D. (1978). *Teaching the learning disabled adolescent: Strategies and methods.* Denver: Love.

Ashlock, R.B. (1981). Mathematics instruction for behaviorally disordered adolescents. In G. Brown, R.L. McDowell, & J. Smith (Eds.), *Educating adolescents with behavior disorders.* Columbus, OH: Charles E. Merrill.

Ashlock, R.B. (1982). *Error patterns in computations: A semi-programmed approach.* Columbus, OH: Charles E. Merrill.

Bartel, N.R. (1978). Problems in mathematics achievement. In D.D. Hammill and N.R.

Bartel, *Teaching children with learning and behavior problems*. Boston: Allyn & Bacon.

Berk, R.A. (1981, May). *Identification of children with learning disabilities: A critical review of methodological issues*. Paper presented at The Johns Hopkins University Colloquium on Gifted/Learning Disabled Children, Baltimore, MD.

Cawley, J.F. (1978). An instructional design in mathematics. In L. Goodman and J.L. Wiederholt (Eds.), *Teaching the learning-disabled adolescent*. Boston: Houghton Mifflin.

Cawley, J.F. (1982). *The relationship of mathematics to vocational education and job specific requirements: A proposal*. Storrs, CT: Psychoeducational Associates. (Mimeographed).

Cawley, J.F., Fitzmaurice, A.M., Shaw, R.A., Kahn, H., & Bates, H. (1978). Mathematics and learning disabled youth: The upper grades. *Learning Disability Quarterly, 1*(4), 37–52.

Coles, G.S. (1978). The learning disability test battery: Empirical and social issues. *Harvard Educational Review, 48*(3), 313–340.

Cox, L.S. (1975). Diagnosing and remediating standard errors in addition and subtraction computations. *The Arithmetic Teacher, 22*, 151–157.

Cronbach, L.J. (1970). *Essentials of psychological testing*. New York: Harper & Row.

Goodman, L., & Price, M. (1978). BEH final regulations for learning disabilities: Implications for the secondary school. *Learning Disability Quarterly, 1*(4), 73–79.

Goodstein, H.A. (1975). Assessment and programming in mathematics for the handicapped. *Focus on Exceptional Children, 7*(7), 1–11.

Goodstein, H.A. (1981). Are the errors we see the true errors?: Error analysis in verbal problem solving. *Topics in Learning and Learning Disabilities, 1*(3), 31–46.

Goodstein, H.A. (1982). The reliability of criterion-referenced tests and special education: Assumed versus demonstrated. *Journal of Special Education, 16*, 37–48.

Goodstein, H.A. (1984). Assessment: Examination and utilization from Pre-K through high school. In J.F. Cawley (Ed.), *Developmental teaching of mathematics for the learning disabled*. Rockville, MD: Aspen Systems.

Goodstein, H.A., Howell, H., & Williamson, K. (1982). The reliability of criterion-referenced tests for special education and regular education students: The impact of item format and content sampling. Unpublished manuscript.

Goodstein, H.A., & Kahn, H. (1974). Patterns of achievement among children with learning disabilities. *Exceptional Children, 41*, 47–49.

Goodstein, H.A., Kahn, H., & Cawley, J.F. (1976). The achievement of educable mentally retarded children on the *Key Math Diagnostic Arithmetic Test*. *Journal of Special Education, 10*, 61–70.

Gronlund, N.L. (1981). *Measurement and evaluation in teaching*. New York: Macmillan.

Hambleton, R.K., & Eignor, D.R. (1978). Guidelines for evaluating criterion-referenced tests and test manuals. *Journal of Educational Measurement, 15*, 321–327.

Kosc, L. (1982). Neuropsychological implications of the diagnosis and treatment of mathematical learning disabilities. In J.T. Neisworth (Ed.), *Assessment in special education*. Rockville, MD: Aspen Systems.

Lepore, A.V. (1979). A comparison of computational errors between educable mentally handicapped and learning disability children. *Focus on Learning Problems in Mathematics, 1*, 12–33.

Lyon, L., & Karplus, E. (1980). *Math in and out of the mainstream*. Novato, CA: Academic Therapy Publications.

Marsh, G.E., & Price, B.J. (1980). *Methods for teaching the mildly handicapped adolescent.* St. Louis: C.V. Mosby.

McLoughlin, J.A., & Lewis, R.B. (1981). *Assessing special students.* Columbus, OH: Charles E. Merrill.

Mercer, C.D. (1979). *Children and adolescents with learning disabilities.* Columbus, OH: Charles E. Merrill.

Moran, M. (1978). *Assessment of the exceptional learner in the regular classroom.* Denver: Love.

Myers, P.I., & Hammill, D.D. (1982). *Learning disabilities: Basic concepts, assessment practices and instructional strategies.* Austin, TX: Pro-Ed.

Popham, W.J. (1978). *Criterion-referenced measurement.* Englewood Cliffs, NJ: Prentice-Hall.

Popham, W.J. (1981). *Modern educational measurement.* Englewood Cliffs, NJ: Prentice-Hall.

Poplin, M., & Gray, R. (1982). A conceptual framework for assessment of curriculum and student progress. In J.T. Neisworth (Ed.), *Assessment in special education.* Rockville, MD: Aspen Systems.

Reisman, F.K. (1982). *A guide to the diagnostic teaching of arithmetic.* Columbus, OH: Charles E. Merrill.

Romberg, T.A., & Uprichard, A.E. (1978). The nature of clinical investigation. In *Clinical investigations of mathematics education.* Washington, DC: Research Council for Diagnostic and Prescriptive Mathematics.

Sabatino, D.A. (1982). Preparing individual educational programs (IEPs). In D.A. Sabatino & L. Mann (Eds.), *A handbook of diagnostic and prescriptive teaching.* Rockville, MD: Aspen Systems.

Salvia, J., & Ysseldyke, J.E. (1981). *Assessment in special education and remedial education.* Boston: Houghton Mifflin.

Sedlak, R.A., Sedlak, D.M., & Steppe-Jones, E. (1982). Informal assessment. In D.A. Sabatino & L. Mann (Eds.), *A handbook of diagnostic and prescriptive teaching.* Rockville, MD: Aspen Systems.

Stephens, T.M., Hartman, A.C., & Lucas, V.H. (1978). *Teaching children basic skills: A curriculum handbook.* Columbus, OH: Charles E. Merrill.

Underhill, R.G., Uprichard, A.E., & Heddens, J.W. (1980). *Diagnosing mathematics disabilities.* Columbus, OH: Charles E. Merrill.

Wallace, G., & Larsen, S.C. (1978). *Educational assessment of learning problems: Testing for teaching.* Boston: Houghton Mifflin.

Wiederholt, J.L., & McNutt, G. (1979). Assessment and instructional planning: A conceptual framework. In D. Cullinan & M.H. Epstein (Eds.), *Special education for adolescents: Issues and perspectives.* Columbus, OH: Charles E. Merrill.

Ysseldyke, J.E., & Algozzine, B. (1982). *Critical issues in special and remedial education.* Boston: Houghton Mifflin.

Chapter 3

Individualizing Mathematics Instruction for Students with Learning Problems

Colleen S. Blankenship

Imagine if you will 25 freshmen in a general mathematics course. The students have just entered the room. After calling the class to order, the teacher asks them to turn in their homework. Amid a flurry of activity, assignments are passed to the front of the room. For the third time this week, Harold has not completed his homework. Upon questioning, he offers yet another lame excuse. Directing the students to open their texts, the teacher begins to review procedures for computing simple interest. When the teacher turns to write on the blackboard, Jim and Sam begin to chat. Their discussion continues, as it does almost every day, whenever the teacher's attention is not riveted on them. Pausing for the fifth time to reprimand Jim and Sam, the teacher finds it difficult to regain her train of thought. Then there's Marla, listening so intently and struggling to keep up with the other students. Much of the discussion goes over her head, as she lacks so many basic concepts and skills. There never seems to be enough time to work with her. Bob is a real trouble maker, constantly disrupting the class. He lacks knowledge of the basics and does not appear to be interested in learning. Jeremy is another student with a problem; he simply cannot read the text. He catches on to demonstrations though, and seems eager to learn.

An almost universal recommendation to the teacher in our example would be to "individualize instruction." While proponents stress the logic of tailoring instruction to meet the needs of individual students, critics point out that individualizing instruction is more time consuming for teachers, more costly, and perhaps no more effective than traditional instruction (Schoen, 1976). In summarizing the research on individualizing instruction in mathematics, Fey concluded that educators "contemplating a move to individualization can probably find research evidence to support a decision for or against such innovation" (1980, p. 412).

While teachers tend to support the concept of individualization, few apply the principle in their own classrooms (Bosco, 1971; Stern & Keislar, 1975). Despite the fact that teachers feel that individualization is necessary for subjects such as mathematics, they prefer to work with the entire class most of the time (Denny, 1978; Weiss, 1978). Many who favor individualizing instruction suggest that the lack of curriculum materials or the dread of excessive record-keeping prevents them from implementing this practice in their classrooms (NACOME, 1975). The fact that many teachers agree with the concept yet find it difficult to implement suggests that individualization is viewed as a lofty but unworkable goal.

Although educators continue to debate the merits as well as the practicality of individualizing instruction for *all* students, its appropriateness is unquestioned in teaching students classified as learning disabled. Currently, a controversy exists concerning the nature of secondary level programs for the learning disabled. Some educators maintain that instruction should stress the attainment of basic skills; others advocate placement in the regular curriculum; still others recommend that instruction should focus on career development combined with attention to functional academic skills (Touzel, 1978). The problem with trying to determine what should be the nature of the mathematics curriculum for secondary level LD students is that experts disagree as to the nature of learning disabilities (Tucker, Stevens, & Ysseldyke, 1983).

Serious doubts concerning our ability to identify students with learning disabilities have been raised by Ysseldyke, Algozzine, and their colleagues. In one study the relationship between data presented at placement meetings and decisions made by placement teams was evaluated (Ysseldyke, Algozzine, Richey, & Graden, 1982). No significant relationship was found "between presentation of statements supportive of ability/achievement discrepancies, verbal/performance discrepancies, or federal definition criteria and the placement team decision" (p. 40). In some cases, identical data were used to support different outcome decisions, which resulted in some students being classified as LD and others not. In another study, the decision-making practices of teachers, school psychologists, and administrators were investigated (Ysseldyke, Algozzine, & Thurlow, 1980). Although decision makers were presented with test scores indicative of *normal* performance, in about half the cases they declared students eligible to receive special education services, labeling most of the students learning disabled. In yet another study, the scores of low achievers and students classified as LD were compared on 49 different psychometric measures including the WISC-R, achievement tests, perceptual motor tests, a self-concept test, and a behavioral rating scale (Ysseldyke, Algozzine, Shinn, & McGue, 1982). No significant differences in performance were found between students classified as LD or as low achievers. Results such as these suggest that it is relatively easy to be classified as learning disabled and that there are no discernible differences in performance between students classified as LD or as low achievers.

Intervention practices as well as identification methods have been questioned. Research does not indicate that students classified as LD learn differently from normal students. In fact, programs aimed at remediating underlying deficits, such as poor perceptual motor skills or psycholinguistic abilities, have consistently failed to affect these purported deficits or to improve academic skills (Arter & Jenkins, 1979).

Given this state of affairs, one cannot specify what the nature of the mathematics program should be for students classified as LD, nor can one martial much support for remediating supposed underlying deficits rather than focusing directly on improving students' mathematical skills. While the needs of many students labeled as LD can best be met in college preparatory courses, others may profit from courses in functional mathematics (Cawley, 1978). Considering the diversity in performance among students labeled as LD, it is far more prudent to consider each student as an individual. As Cawley noted, "instructional planning for the individual, is of course, where it all begins and ends" (1978, p. 205).

While it is difficult to specify *what* mathematics should be taught to students classified as learning disabled, it is possible to make recommendations concerning *how* one might vary mathematics instruction to accommodate students with a variety of learning problems. Actually, it makes no difference whether a student is classified as learning disabled, or educable mentally retarded, or is perceived as a slow learner or a low achiever, because these terms provide no instructionally relevant information. In teaching students with learning problems, whether they be classified as handicapped or not, the overriding question is "How can I adapt instruction to better meet their needs while continuing to meet those of the other students in my classroom?" The focus of this chapter is on assisting secondary level mathematics teachers in answering that question.

WHAT IS INDIVIDUALIZED INSTRUCTION?

Individualized instruction in mathematics means something different to almost everyone. Some educators equate individualized instruction with self-paced instruction (Schoen, 1976). Others define individualized instruction in mathematics more broadly, as encompassing a continuum of arrangements including "continuous progress plans, team teaching, flexible scheduling, differentiated assignments, grouping, programmed instruction, computer-assisted instruction, independent study, use of contracts, performance-based curricula, and mathematics laboratories" (Miller, 1976, p. 636). While different instructional delivery systems, such as team teaching and mathematics laboratories, may allow teachers to individualize instruction, the essence of individualization involves matching instruction to fit the needs and abilities of individual students.

In this chapter, individualized instruction is defined as the practice of matching instruction to the needs and abilities of students by (1) modifying the content, (2) adjusting the instructional sequence or pace, (3) altering the demands of a task, (4) changing the instructional delivery system, or (5) selectively applying different teaching techniques on the basis of their effect on individual pupil's progress. Implied in this definition is the idea of direct and frequent measurement of pupil performance, for without continuous data on pupil progress one cannot adjust instruction to meet the ever-changing needs and abilities of individual students.

Before proceeding, a number of points need to be clarified. First, individualized instruction means far more than providing students with special materials. The ability to individualize is not acquired by making wise purchases of educational materials; rather it is the result of what one *does* while providing instruction. Second, to individualize instruction one need not vary all five of the previously mentioned components, i.e., content, sequence or pace, task demands, delivery system, and techniques. Modification of one or a few of these components would allow teachers to better match instruction to the needs and abilities of individual students. In some cases it might be sufficient to vary only one component. For example, one might alter the demands of a task by allowing a student with reading problems to preview his or her assignment with a peer. In other cases, it may be necessary to vary several components at once; for a student who has not mastered necessary prerequisite skills and is slow to acquire new concepts, one might modify the content by providing supplementary materials that focus on prerequisite skills as well as alter the pace of instruction. Third, individualized instruction neither requires nor precludes one-to-one instruction. As we shall see, a number of different instructional arrangements are possible. Lastly, one need not individualize instruction for all students in a class. Of course, as a teacher becomes adept at individualizing instruction and experiences some success in using the method, there is a tendency to individualize instruction for increasingly larger number of students.

WHEN IS IT NECESSARY TO INDIVIDUALIZE INSTRUCTION?

In order to understand when it is necessary to individualize instruction, let's examine typical instructional procedures in teaching mathematics at the secondary level. Studies of current instructional practices (Stake, Easley, & collaborators, 1978; Weiss, 1978) indicate that instruction is typically based on a single text and is commonly directed to the class as a whole. Following a lecture/discussion period students are given individual assignments to complete. Use of this method makes a number of assumptions concerning the appropriateness of the text, the students' ability to understand mathematical concepts and to perform computational tasks, to engage in and profit from large group discussions, and to work independently. Briefly, the assumptions made in using a single text and providing only large group instruction may be summarized as follows. First, reliance on a single text assumes that (1) its content is appropriate for all students' needs, (2) concepts and skills are presented in a logical and sequential manner without large gaps between one skill and another, (3) sufficient examples are provided to ensure mastery by all students, and (4) adequate review lessons are included to facilitate maintenance of newly learned material. Second, with respect to the academic abilities of students, it is assumed that each can read the text and that each has mastered necessary prerequisite concepts and skills. Finally, regarding students' behavioral skills, it is assumed that they will (1) attend to demonstrations, (2) participate in class discussions, (3) follow directions, (4) work independently, and (5) complete assignments and submit them on time.

Let's examine the validity of these assumptions for some typical students in a general mathematics course. What is the probability that all students can read and understand the text? Secondary level teachers frequently point to students' poor reading skills as one difficulty that must be circumvented in providing mathematics instruction (Denny, 1978). Because mathematics texts are often written a grade or two above the level in which they are used (Suydam & Osborne, 1977), many students with reading problems have struggled for years just to decipher what is written in their texts.

Next, how likely is it that all students have mastered necessary prerequisite concepts and skills? Many teachers find that they must reteach concepts and skills they believe students should have mastered in earlier grades. Because the text also assumes that students have mastered a great deal of content and are ready to learn more advanced material, little time is devoted to reviewing prerequisite concepts and skills. Further, texts present information under a fixed-frequency system whereby each problem or task occurs with a specific frequency (Cawley, 1978). While a fixed-frequency system implies that all students learn at the same rate, teachers know that some students require more examples, more finely sequenced instruction, greater opportunities for practice, and more frequent reviews in order to acquire, generalize, and maintain mathematical concepts and skills.

Consider a student who lacks certain prerequisite mathematical skills, has difficulty reading, and does not attend to demonstrations, participate in class discussions, work well independently, or complete assignments on time. The lecture/discussion approach requires students to be able to perform all these behaviors. How well will this weaker student do in the typical classroom? Not very well!

When students have mastered prerequisite mathematical skills, are capable readers, can acquire new skills at the rate the text suggests, can attend to demonstrations, participate in large group discussions, and work independently, the lecture/discussion method is both appropriate and efficient. While most normally achieving students demonstrate these abilities, some or none may be evidenced by students with learning problems. To the extent that any or all of these abilities are not demonstrated by a given student, a mismatch will exist between what that student needs to learn, or is capable of learning, and the nature of his or her instructional program. Because many mathematical skills are hierarchical in nature, a faulty understanding of basic concepts or computational procedures serves to hinder the ability to solve more complex mathematical problems. Students who lack such an understanding can only fall further and further behind unless their programs are modified in a constructive manner.

WHICH ASPECTS OF INSTRUCTION CAN BE MODIFIED?

It was previously suggested that instruction could be individualized by modifying any one or a combination of five components: content, instructional sequence or pace, tasks, instructional delivery system, or teaching techniques. Procedures discussed in this section are similar to those presented by Charles and Malian (1980), who suggested that teachers can individualize instruction by varying the elements of content, objectives, activities, time, and/or supervision. While slightly different terminology will be used here and greater emphasis placed on varying teaching techniques, the suggestions represent a variation of Charles and Malian's strategy and an attempt to apply it to the teaching of secondary school mathematics. Attention is focused on describing options for varying different aspects of instruction to better match the needs and abilities of individual students.

Modifying the Content

Modifying the content has to do with altering the type or amount of information presented to a student. Basically, there are three options for modifying the content. One can either supplement or adapt the information presented in the standard text or substitute other materials in its place. The type of modification required depends on the needs of the individual student. If, for example, a student lacks mastery of prerequisite skills, it is necessary to supplement the text by securing additional materials. If the standard text provides an insufficient amount of practice, additional exercises from other materials must also be obtained. To provide either, it is not necessary to purchase new materials. Typically, resource teachers have materials that regular classroom teachers may use to provide extra practice or to teach prerequisite skills not included in the standard text. In most districts there is a repository of materials, or perhaps a teacher center or a regional instructional materials center from which additional instructional materials may be borrowed. Facing declining supply budgets, many inventive teachers stalk book sales for outdated texts, which may be a little worse for wear but nevertheless provide students with needed practice on skills. Some teachers develop their own materials and share them with other teachers. While it is easier to purchase new materials, there's a lot to be said for combing through supply cabinets in search of materials or setting up a network to exchange materials with other teachers.

Modifying the content through supplementing it with additional material can be thought of as providing "more of the same" information as that presented in the text. Sometimes, providing "more" is not enough; instead, it is necessary to alter the way in which information is presented. One type of adaptation involves rewriting explanations and directions. For long, detailed explanations, the teacher may delete unnecessary words, substitute shorter words, and underline important terms. To clarify directions one may list steps and provide examples. Another modification designed to reduce the level of difficulty for students with reading difficulties is to present information in tables. When rewriting explanations and directions, it is wise to follow a standard format. For example, the reworded explanation might appear first followed by a list of steps and a few examples. Important terms may be underlined and keyed to short definitions that appear at the bottom of the page.

Another method of adapting the text involves reducing the number of problems presented on a page. Some students are easily overwhelmed by the sheer number of problems presented. Instead of assigning students 50 division of decimal problems, why not assign 10 problems? Provided that a student solves at least 8 problems correctly, does he or she really need to spend the whole period tediously computing 40 more problems? Why not use the time instead to focus on applied examples, which may be of more interest to students? Reducing the number of problems presents a number of advantages. First, it makes it worth a student's while to do well. Second, the student receives feedback on his or her work earlier than if he or she had had to finish all 50 problems. In case of errors, it is much more acceptable to correct 10 problems than to be told one has solved 50 problems incorrectly and must now redo them. Third, problems that are not assigned can be used another day to determine whether students have maintained their skills.

In planning adaptation of materials, keep the following points in mind. First, make use of resources for modifying instructional materials. Two federally funded projects have focused on adapting materials for secondary level students with learning problems. The Parallel Alternate Curriculum (PAC) developed at the Child Service Demonstration Center at Arizona State University teaches nine "high school courses in a nonreading format, using such methods as taped books, videotaped materials, movies, slides, lectures, and various forms of discussion" (Hartwell, Wiseman, & Van Reusen, 1979). The *Parallel Alternate Curriculum Guide for Consumer Mathematics* (Cusick, Wiseman, Hartwell, & Van Reusen, 1980) illustrates procedures for modifying a special consumer math text and provides general guidelines applicable to revising any type of textual material. Studies of PAC materials support their effectiveness and indicate a high level of satisfaction among teachers, students, and parents. PAC materials are available for dissemination from the Arizona Education Information System, as indicated in the reference section.

The University of Kansas Institute in Learning Disabilities developed procedures for visually marking key points and audiotaping textbook chapters to circumvent reading difficulties experienced by secondary level students (Schumaker, Deshler, Alley, & Warner, 1983). Learning-disabled students who used these materials in combination with a specific study strategy were able to make significant progress.

While paraprofessionals were employed to modify materials developed by the University of Kansas (Schumaker et al., 1983), Wiseman reported enlisting the aid of high school composition classes and volunteer adults to rewrite text passages (1980). By capitalizing on existing resources, including published guidelines and curriculum materials as well as human resources, teachers can adapt materials to better meet the needs of individual students.

Second, one need not have all materials requiring some adaptation ready by the beginning of the year. The object is to stay one step ahead of assignments and to keep copies of exercises that have been rewritten. One of the easiest ways to organize rewritten directions is to put them in plastic protectors, keep them in a notebook, and provide a list in the front of the notebook indicating which exercises are included. This list can be provided to future students or to other teachers should they wish to use the materials. Multiple copies of exercises for student use can be kept in folders arranged by topic.

The last modification of content to be discussed involves substitution of another text in place of the standard text. More and more frequently, publishers are developing parallel alternate texts, which, as their name implies, closely follow a particular text but attempt to reduce the reading level, provide more examples, and arrange exercises to be completed using a step-by-step approach. In cases where a student has significant difficulty reading the text, and a parallel text is available, this alternative is worth exploring.

In summary, it is possible to modify the content by supplementing or adapting the current text or by substituting another text or set of materials. Sometimes changing the content is the only modification a student may require. In other cases, one might also have to vary other aspects of instruction such as sequence or pace, task demands, delivery system, or teaching techniques. These components are discussed in the following sections.

Adjusting the Instructional Pace or Sequence

One of the most common methods of individualizing instruction involves altering the frequency with which new concepts and skills are presented. Adjusting the pace represents only a minor change and results in presenting the same information at a slower rate. While varying the pace is one method of individualizing instruction for students who have difficulty acquiring new skills, it should not be the only modification considered. Still, such a slight alteration may be all that is needed by some students.

Perhaps the most important consideration in determining how to set an appropriate pace for students is to examine the number of students who consistently master the topics presented in the allotted time versus those who seldom or never achieve mastery. By setting minimum criteria for mastery and sharing this information with students, teachers communicate their expectations. Through frequent testing, teachers can determine which students have and have not achieved mastery. By presenting supplementary exercises for students who have not achieved mastery and providing enrichment activities for students who have, some flexibility is built into teaching by the unit method.

It is sometimes necessary to alter the instructional sequence as well as the pace. Modifying the sequence is warranted when students lack prerequisite skills or have difficulty generalizing from one skill to another. Modifying the instructional sequence involves breaking tasks down into smaller steps. One way to gauge the amount of adjustment that is necessary is to (1) consider the prerequisite behaviors a student must have to do the task, (2) identify and sequence the task into a series of steps, and (3) observe the student at work to determine where in the sequence he or she experiences difficulty.

The following example illustrates the procedure one might use to alter the sequence for a student who lacks necessary prerequisite skills. The text might direct students to find the area of a given triangle, parallelogram, and trapezoid, but some students may have difficulty identifying these shapes. The task could be broken down by providing instruction first on identifying and naming each shape, then on discriminating among them. Next, the formula for each shape could be presented separately, accompanied by suitable practice activities. For students who have difficulty generalizing from one skill to another, the same procedure could be used. The text might illustrate how to round decimals to the nearest tenth, but fail to provide a detailed explanation of how to round to the nearest hundredth and thousandth. After making sure that a student can identify the hundredth's place, the teacher might reiterate rules for rounding and point out the similarity between rounding to the nearest tenth and hundredth. Following the successful completion of exercises on rounding to the nearest hundredth, the teaching process could be repeated for problems requiring rounding to the nearest thousandth. Finally, the student could be presented with several problems requiring rounding to either the nearest tenth, hundredth, or thousandth.

Modifying the sequence of instruction results in providing students with needed practice on prerequisite skills, which will allow them to better understand new concepts or help them see the relationship between similar tasks. While altering the instructional sequence or pace is sometimes necessary, these modifications alone may not be sufficient for students with significant reading and computational difficulties. In such instances, another aspect of instruction must be modified, namely, altering the demands of a task.

Altering the Demands of a Task

Certainly, some of the modifications we have already discussed, such as rewriting directions, decreasing the number of problems presented on a page, and presenting instruction in smaller steps, can be thought of as ways of reducing the demands of a task. All of the previous suggestions, however, involve modification of materials. Another method of altering the demands of a task involves providing supplementary instructional aids or extra assistance.

The most commonly used aid in mathematics class is the calculator. While NACOME (1975) recommended that all students past the eighth grade who are not proficient in the basic facts should have access to calculators, parents, teachers, and administrators are sometimes apprehensive about allowing students to use them. It appears that the use of calculators does not adversely affect achievement; in all but a few studies, achievement scores have been as high or higher when calculators were used for mathematics instruction than when they were not used for instruction (Taylor, 1981). Given the fact that calculators can take some of the tedium out of mathematics, allow teachers and students more time to focus on understanding concepts, and provide students who have not mastered computational skills with a chance to be exposed to relevant mathematical topics, their use should be encouraged. That is not to say, of course, that attention need not be paid to improving students' computational skills; however, for students who have not committed the basic facts to memory by the time they reach high school, emphasis might better be placed on learning when to add, subtract, multiply, and divide with the aid of a calculator than on continued attempts at rote learning of facts.

To compensate for lack of mastery of basic facts students should be allowed to use a calculator during instruction as well as during testing. Practice on such functional mathematical tasks at totalling purchases, computing interest rates, or figuring wages will probably be of more direct benefit to students with serious computational difficulties than will endless practice for mastery of basic facts that have eluded them during eight years of past instruction.

While calculators reduce the demands of a task for students with low computational skills, other modifications are necessary for students with reading problems. Although one could rewrite directions and explanations as previously suggested, another approach is to provide students with extra assistance in reading. Depending upon a teacher's preference, he or she might arrange for the student with reading problems to (1) ask the teacher or another student for assistance, (2) preview assignments with a peer, the resource teacher, or the student's parents, or (3) listen to an audio recording while following along in the text.

For students whose primary difficulty is reading, altering the demands of the task by providing them with reading assistance may be all that is necessary to ensure their progress. Multiple modifications, including changing the content, altering the instructional sequence or pace, and reducing the demands of a task may be necessary for students with more severe learning difficulties.

Changing the Instructional Delivery System

The previously noted modifications are all compatible with the lecture/discussion format. Teachers need, however, to consider a wide range of instructional delivery systems, as sometimes the system itself requires modification. It has been suggested that some students may not profit from the approach of lecture/discussion followed by the completion of assignments due to their inability to attend to demonstrations, participate in discussions, or work independently. Based upon reviews of research on the relationship between teacher behavior and student achievement, Grouws (1981) and Stevens and Rosenshine (1981) concluded that achievement is related to the amount of time students spend academically engaged on instructional tasks. During a lecture/discussion, students may not be actively involved. In cases where students are not profiting from the lecture/discussion approach or when it is necessary to provide them with additional instruction to remediate deficient skills, one might consider a choice from the following instructional delivery systems. Granted, all of the options presented may not be available to all teachers; however, they do represent systems that are worthy of consideration.

Computer-Assisted Instruction

Microcomputers are becoming increasingly common in our schools, particularly at the secondary level. In addition to providing drill and practice, computers can function in a tutorial manner by providing direct instruction and posing questions for the student to answer. Similarly, computers can be used to demonstrate mathematical concepts, thereby providing teachers with another way of modifying the content. Several computer magazines as well as issues of *The Mathematics Teacher* have included reviews of mathematics software as well as ideas for integrating microcomputers into the curriculum. Networks have also been established to encourage teachers who develop programs to exchange them with other teachers. Microcomputers can motivate students to practice mathematical skills, increase their computer literacy, and encourage them to learn programming skills.

Peer Tutoring

Students who are working far below grade level may profit from having a peer tutor them. Tutoring may take place as part of the normal class period or as a supplement to classroom instruction. If tutoring is conducted during class time, a certain portion of the period should be reserved for that activity. Students who typically finish their work early and who appear eager to provide assistance are the most likely prospects. Often students who are considering teaching as a career would rather tutor a student who needs help than spend an hour in study hall. If the tutoring arrangement is mutually agreeable to all concerned, and the teacher offers guidance to the tutor, tutoring can provide the means for remediating students' deficient skills while keeping them actively involved.

Programmed Instruction

Programmed materials represent another option available to teachers. While individualization means more than providing programmed materials, their judicious use can contribute to a teacher's ability to effectively individualize instruction. Programmed materials are often useful for students who lack mastery of prerequisite skills. Materials that focus on single topics such as decimals, fractions, and percents are particularly appropriate to use with students who may need to review these topics before proceeding to more advanced material.

While care must be taken to select carefully sequenced materials written at a suitable reading level, programmed materials can be used to both the student's and teacher's advantage, as they allow the student to proceed at his or her own rate and free the teacher from spending a great deal of time providing one-to-one instruction. While the teacher is occupied giving a large group lesson or supervising students working on assignments, students who require supplementary instruction can be spending their time profitably working with programmed materials.

Small Group Instruction

When three or more students experience difficulty on the same skill, it is efficient to group them for instructional purposes, at least on a temporary basis. While the remaining members of the class are working on individual assignments, the teacher can arrange to work with a small group of students to practice skills or provide them with further assistance in completing the assignment given to the other members of the class.

One-To-One Instruction

While it may be difficult to provide several students with one-to-one instruction for any extended period of time during class, it is usually possible to devote a few minutes each day to students who require additional assistance. While other students are completing assignments, the teacher can meet briefly with individual students to explain assignments, check completed work, or clarify procedures for solving problems. Students who require a great deal of assistance might profit more from computer-assisted instruction, programmed instruction, or peer tutoring, all of which make fewer demands on a teacher's time.

Several alternatives to the lecture/discussion format have been presented. Teachers may use these options in conjunction with lecture/discussion or as alternatives to that approach. For students who profit from the lecture/discussion format but who lack necessary prerequisite skills, one might opt for providing them with supplementary instruction using a different delivery system. For example, a teacher might have a student review percents using a programmed text prior to teaching a unit on computing interest to the whole class. For students with significant deficits, the primary instructional delivery system may not be lecture/discussion but some combination of approaches such as computer-assisted instruction, small group instruction, or peer tutoring, depending on the student's needs and ability to profit from these various approaches as well as on their availability in a given school.

Varying Teaching Techniques

Often teachers assume that major changes are needed to individualize instruction. One of the most neglected but easiest ways to individualize involves varying one's teaching techniques. There really aren't any special techniques or magic formulas to improve performance. Basically, all that is needed are general instructional strategies such as (1) verbal instruction, (2) demonstration, (3) modeling, (4) drill and practice, (5) prompts and cues, (6) feedback, (7) reinforcement, and (8) contingencies for errors. These very simple strategies have been shown to be effective in improving the performance of students with learning problems in a number of academic subjects (Haring, Lovitt, Eaton, & Hansen, 1978). Although the techniques are straightforward, the trick comes in knowing when to use a particular type of strategy. For example, when a student lacks prerequisite skills, reinforcement or feedback will probably be of little use; some type of instructional technique is warranted. Depending upon the skill to be learned, instruction might include a verbal explanation, followed by a teacher demonstration after which the student models the teacher's behavior. Next, a practice activity would be scheduled. Finally, feedback could be provided in the form of marking correctly and incorrectly computed problems.

Instruction could also take another form. For example, following a demonstration the teacher might leave a completed sample problem on the student's desk. Following a practice exercise, the student might self-correct his or her work. Students who have not reached criterion levels may be directed to complete a remedial exercise with a tutor.

Just as instructional techniques need to be used to improve the performance of students who "can't" perform certain skills, motivational techniques are required to improve the performance of students who "can, but won't, or at least don't" compute mathematical problems very accurately. Motivational techniques include reinforcing students for correct answers or improved performance by using naturally occurring classroom events such as teacher praise, free time, or extra privileges. It can even be reinforcing to some students to determine which of several math assignments to do first!

By making the simple distinction between "lack of knowledge" and "lack of motivation" and by adjusting one's instructional strategy accordingly, it is relatively easy to select appropriate techniques. By applying them consistently and evaluating their effects on each pupil's performance, teachers can identify effective techniques for individual students.

WHAT STEPS ARE INVOLVED IN INDIVIDUALIZING INSTRUCTION?

Previous sections have focused on explaining "what" is meant by individualizing instruction, "when" it is necessary to individualize, and "how" instruction can be modified to better match the needs and abilities of students. While knowing what, when, and how to individualize are important, of equal importance is the ability to implement individualized programs in an efficient manner. In this section, emphasis is placed on describing procedures for organizing and managing individualized programs.

Basically, there are four steps involved in individualizing instruction:

1. Assessing pupil performance
2. Deciding which instructional components to vary
3. Identifying available resources and organizing materials
4. Managing the daily operation of the system.

The first priority in developing individualized programs involves assessing pupil performance. Once a teacher has determined the needs and abilities of individual pupils, attention is focused on deciding how instruction can be modified. Next, concern shifts to locating available resources and organizing materials. Once the plan becomes operational, attention centers on the day-to-day management of the system. Each of the four steps involved in individualizing instruction is discussed in the following sections.

Assessing Pupil Performance

Assessment data provide the basis for individualizing instruction, for without adequate information teachers cannot plan programs to meet the needs of individual pupils. The primary focus of assessment is to identify students' levels of mathematical functioning. Unfortunately, it is often confused with testing. Some teachers as well as students may think it unfair to be assessed prior to instruction on a particular topic. The purpose of assessment is *not* to grade a student's performance, but simply to determine what a student knows and does not know.

When assessment does not precede instruction, teachers run the risk of boring some students and confusing others. Once the purpose of assessment is explained to students, they are usually eager to demonstrate their knowledge so as to avoid going over previously learned material. They may also feel more comfortable disclosing what they do not know when it is understood that instruction to improve their skills will be forthcoming.

While standardized test scores give a general indication of performance, they do not provide sufficient information to individualize instruction (Eaton & Lovitt, 1972; Freeman, Kuhs, Knappen, & Porter, 1982; Jenkins & Pany, 1978). Because the shortcomings of standardized tests were discussed in Chapter 2, they need only be summarized here. Standardized tests are given only on one occasion, thus preventing teachers from determining students' typical performance. Although these tests contain several skills, few examples of a given problem type appear, leaving teachers to guess whether or not a student really knows how to perform a particular skill. Also, items on standardized tests may not match those emphasized in the curriculum, thereby providing teachers with little information that is instructionally useful. For these reasons, teachers often find they must go beyond the results of standardized tests to determine students' academic skill levels.

Curriculum-based assessment (CBA) represents an alternative to standardized tests. While specific guidelines for constructing CBAs have been provided elsewhere (Blankenship & Lilly, 1981), the basic steps in developing one will be presented. Essentially, a CBA is a teacher-made criterion-referenced test. After analyzing the concepts and skills presented in the classroom text, a teacher selects and sequences the skills to be assessed; develops a series of assessment objectives that include criterion levels; and determines how to administer, score, and record pupil performance. Assessment materials are then developed. Performance is assessed on two or more occasions, thereby permitting teachers to determine students' typical performance. Following the administration of the CBA the teacher records each student's performance on a class summary sheet and notes which students did and did not achieve criterion levels. Information gleaned from a CBA can be used to form instructional groups or to identify specific skills that particular students need to learn.

All or part of the CBA could be given to the entire class at the beginning of the school year. A teacher could choose to administer part of a CBA at the beginning of the year and then administer other parts just prior to the introduction of each new unit. For example, a teacher in a general mathematics class who has developed a CBA might assess students' skills on whole number operations at the beginning of the year. Prior to the introduction of a unit of decimals and the metric system, the teacher would assess performance in just that area. By readministering parts of a CBA following instruction, teachers derive data on pupil progress.

Teachers who may not wish to develop their own assessment devices can approximate the CBA method by using a publisher's placement test or unit or chapter pretests. Information gained by analyzing students' performance on these tests, provided the items on the tests match the objectives of each unit or chapter, can be used to determine students' strengths and weaknesses.

In addition to determining mathematical skill levels, assessment must necessarily focus on identifying students who (1) evidence difficulty reading and understanding the text and (2) demonstrate behavior problems that interfere with their ability to learn under normal classroom conditions. Through direct observation of pupil performance during the first few weeks of school, teachers can determine which if any of their students are experiencing reading difficulties or are displaying inappropriate behaviors. Information gleaned from cumulative folders or from conferences with the resource teacher may also alert teachers to provide some students with extra assistance in reading or to arrange more motivating consequences to encourage appropriate behaviors. While observation and recording systems are available to quantify students' reading abilities as well as their classroom behaviors (Blankenship & Lilly, 1981), informal observations can alert one to the fact that some students may have reading problems or display behaviors that interfere with their learning in large group situations.

Deciding Which Instructional Components To Vary

Following assessment attention turns toward matching instruction to students' needs and abilities. As previously noted, teachers can modify instruction by (1) changing the content, (2) altering the instructional sequence or pace, (3) modifying the task demands, (4) changing the instructional delivery system, or (5) varying teaching techniques. Given that these modifications have been discussed in detail, no further elaboration appears necessary.

Identifying Available Resources and Organizing Materials

Once a teacher has determined needed instructional modifications for individual students, it is time to identify possible resources. Three questions need to be answered: "What materials do I need to individualize instruction for my students?" "How can I lay my hands on them?" and "Who can help me?" With respect to the latter question, "who" might very well be the resource teacher who can set up a behavior management program to encourage a student to pay attention during demonstrations or to complete assignments. Or, the "who" might be another pupil in the class who is capable of providing tutoring assistance.

Organizing materials need not be a time-consuming chore. One of the simplest systems for organizing materials is to arrange a file cabinet with dividers for each unit covered in the text. Individual folders can be used to separate exercises, tests, and supplementary materials. Other useful items, such as manipulatives and calculators, can be stored in the file when not in use. A master list of materials with their respective quantities noted should be used to keep track of available materials. By checking off consumable materials as they are used, a running inventory is provided which can be consulted prior to restocking the file.

Managing the Daily Operation of the System

Attention needs to be paid to structuring the classroom to ensure its efficient operation. Certain management details must be attended to regardless of the particular options selected to individualize instruction. These basic details include (1) scheduling who will do what and when, (2) explaining the features of the students' individualized programs to them, (3) making sure appropriate materials are available when needed, (4) developing a system for monitoring students while they are working independently, (5) determining general procedures for correcting students' work and providing feedback, and (6) establishing classroom behavior management strategies to encourage appropriate behavior and to reinforce performance on academic tasks.

Other management details may arise depending on the particular options used to individualize instruction. For example, if tutors are to be used to deliver instruction, they must be given procedures to follow in providing instruction, giving feedback, and recording their tutee's progress. Similarly, if students are allowed to use equipment such as a calculator, tape recorder, or microcomputer, procedures for their use need to be explained.

Another important aspect of managing the system involves developing procedures to evaluate and record pupil progress. Some teachers prefer to evaluate progress using pre- and post-tests. If this method is used, it's a good idea to keep track of the following information: (1) skill or topic, (2) pre-test score, (3) instructional modifications made, (4) scores on daily work, (5) post-test score, and (6) instructional decisions made based on pupil progress. By keeping information of this type on an individual record sheet, teachers compile useful information on which to base instructional programs.

While this system provides the minimum amount of information needed to make instructional decisions, more elaborate decision-making and recording systems are available. One such method involves charting pupil performance data (Blankenship & Lilly, 1981; Haring et al., 1978). Using the charting approach, direct and frequent measures of performance are collected prior to, during, and following instruction. Daily, each student's scores are plotted on a chart. As they are made, instructional modifications are noted on the chart. By comparing performance before, during, and after instruction teachers can evaluate pupil progress and gauge the effectiveness of their instructional modifications. Because performance is evaluated daily, or at least frequently, up-to-the-minute information on pupil progress is available. When progress is not being made, instruction can be changed immediately and the effect of a new teaching technique can be evaluated in the same manner. One other advantage of this system is that students often find charting to be fun as well as reinforcing because charts provide them with visible evidence of their improved performance.

WHAT ARE THE BENEFITS OF INDIVIDUALIZING INSTRUCTION FOR STUDENTS AND TEACHERS?

The advantages of individualizing instruction are usually discussed from the student's point of view. The beneficial aspects of this practice from the pupil's perspective are that he or she is presented with tasks of an appropriate level of difficulty; extra assistance or aids are available to compensate for deficient skills; and instruction is geared to the student's rate of learning. Further, academic tasks are presented using techniques and instructional arrangements that are particularly suited to the student's needs and abilities. Finally, frequent feedback is provided and positive consequences are arranged to reinforce improvements in academic performance. When instruction is individualized, students begin to experience success. With repeated successful experiences, students who may have previously had low self-concepts come to view themselves as capable learners and are eager to show what they can do!

While benefits clearly accrue to students when instruction is individualized, this practice also is advantageous for teachers. Students have less reason to act out when they are given materials that are at an appropriate level and when they are actively involved in learning. By individualizing instruction and by reinforcing improvements in performance, teachers establish a classroom environment that is conducive to learning. Individualization also encourages teachers to seek out and use all available resources. In this way, teachers acquire new materials that can make teaching easier and often gain assistance from the resource teacher, other teachers, parents, and students.

Individualizing instruction also tends to focus a teacher's attention on positive changes that can be made to facilitate learning. By modifying instruction along the dimensions discussed in this chapter, teachers can bring about dramatic changes in pupil performance and students' attitudes. This alone is sufficient reason for many teachers to try to individualize instruction.

SUMMARY

Individualization of instruction offers benefits to teachers and students alike. By approaching individualization as a goal, and by attempting to implement this practice gradually, teachers often become intrigued and seek to individualize instruction for increasingly greater numbers of students. Certainly, individualization requires more time and effort, but the benefits appear to far outweigh the costs.

REFERENCES

Arter, J.A., & Jenkins, J.R. (1979). Differential diagnosis-prescriptive teaching: A critical appraisal. *Review of Educational Research, 49,* 517-555.

Blankenship, C., & Lilly, M.S. (1981). *Mainstreaming students with learning and behavior problems: Techniques for the classroom teacher.* New York: Holt, Rinehart & Winston.

Bosco, J. (1971). Individualization: Teachers' views. *Elementary School Journal, 72,* 125-131.

Cawley, J.F. (1978). An instructional design in mathematics. In L. Mann, L. Goodman, & L.J. Wiederholt (Eds.), *Teaching the learning-disabled adolescent.* Boston: Houghton Mifflin.

Charles, C.M., & Malian, I.M. (1980). *The special student: Practical help for the classroom teacher.* St. Louis: C.V. Mosby.

Cusick, N., Wiseman, D.E., Hartwell, L.K., & Van Reusen, A.K. (1980). *The parallel alternate curriculum guide for consumer mathematics.* Arizona Education Information System, Office of Field Services, College of Education, Arizona State University, Temple, AZ 85281.

Denny, T. (1978). Some still do: River Acres, Texas. In R.E. Stake, J.A. Easley, Jr., & collaborators, *Case studies in science education.* College of Education, University of Illinois at Champaign-Urbana. Also published by the U.S. Government Printing Office, Washington, DC, under Stock No. 038-000-0377-1, 038-000-003763, and 038-000-00383-6.

Eaton, M., & Lovitt, T.C. (1972). Achievement tests vs. direct and daily measurement. In G. Semb (Ed.), *Behavior analysis and education—1972.* Lawrence, KS: University of Kansas Press.

Fey, J.T. (1980). Mathematics education research on curriculum and instruction. In R.J. Shumway (Ed.), *Research in mathematics education.* Reston, VA: National Council of Teachers of Mathematics.

Freeman, D.J., Kuhs, T.M., Knappen, L.B., & Porter, A.C. (1982). A closer look at standardized tests. *The Arithmetic Teacher, 29,* 50-54.

Grouws, D.A. (1981). The teacher variable in mathematics instruction. In M.M. Lindquist (Ed.), *Selected issues in mathmatics education.* Berkeley, CA: McCutchan.

Haring, N.G., Lovitt, T.C., Eaton, M.D., & Hansen, C.L. (1978). *The fourth R: Research in the classroom.* Columbus, OH: Charles E. Merrill.

Hartwell, L.K., Wiseman, D.E., & Van Reusen, A. (1979). Modifying course content for mildly handicapped students at the secondary level. *Teaching Exceptional Children, 12,* 28-32.

Jenkins, J.R., & Pany, D. (1978). Standardized achievement tests: How useful for special education? *Exceptional Children, 44,* 448-453.

Miller, R.R. (1976). Dialogue: Research on individualized instruction. The *Mathematics Teacher, 69,* 636-640.

National Advisory Committee on Mathematical Education. (1975). *Overview and analysis of school mathematics grades K-12.* Washington, DC: Conference Board of the Mathematical Sciences.

Schoen, H.L. (1976). Self-paced mathematics instruction: How effective has it been in secondary and postsecondary schools? *The Mathematics Teacher, 69,* 352–357.

Schumaker, J.B., Deshler, D.D., Alley, G.R., & Warner, M. (1983). Toward the development of an intervention model for learning disabled adolescents. *Exceptional Education Quarterly, 4,* 45–74.

Stake, R.E., Easley, J.A., Jr., & collaborators. (1978). *Case studies in science education.* College of Education, University of Illinois at Champaign-Urbana. Also published by the U.S. Government Printing Office, Washington, DC under Stock No. 038-000-0377-1, 038-000-003763, and 038-000-00383-6.

Stern, C., & Keislar, E.R. (1975). *Teacher attitudes and attitude change, Vol. 2: Summary and analysis of recent research.* Arlington, VA: ERIC Resources Information Center.

Stevens, R., & Rosenshine, B. (1981). Advances in research on teaching. *Exceptional Education Quarterly, 2,* 1–9.

Suydam, M.N., & Osborne, A. (1977). *The status of pre-college science, mathematics, and social science education: 1955–1975. Vol. II: Mathematics education.* Columbus, OH: The Ohio State University Center for Science and Mathematics Education.

Taylor, R. (1981). Computers and calculators in the mathematics classroom. In M.M. Lindquist (Ed.), *Selected issues in mathematics education.* Berkeley, CA: McCutchan.

Touzel, S.W. (1978). Secondary LD curricula—A proposed framework. *Learning Disability Quarterly, 1,* 53–61.

Tucker, J., Stevens, L.J., & Ysseldyke, J.E. (1983). Learning disabilities: The experts speak out. *Journal of Learning Disabilities, 16,* 6–14.

Weiss, I. (1978). *Report of the 1977 national survey of science, mathematics, and social studies education.* Research Triangle Park, NC: Research Triangle Institute.

Wiseman, D.E. (1980). Programs for secondary school students with learning problems. In L.A. Faas, *Children with learning problems: A handbook for teachers.* Dallas: Houghton Mifflin.

Ysseldyke, J.E., Algozzine, B., Richey, L., & Graden, J. (1982). Declaring students eligible for learning disability services: Why bother with the data? *Learning Disability Quarterly, 5,* 37–44.

Ysseldyke, J.E., Algozzine, B., Shinn, M., & McGue, M. (1982). Similarities and differences between low achievers and students classified learning disabled. *Journal of Special Education, 16,* 73–85.

Ysseldyke, J.E., Algozzine, B., & Thurlow, M. (1980). *Placement team decision-making: A naturalistic investigation* (Research Report No. 41). Minneapolis: University of Minnesota Institute for Research on Learning Disabilities.

Chapter 4

Whole Numbers: Concepts and Skills

Anne M. Fitzmaurice Hayes

The secondary school experience is both an exciting one and a frightening one for many, if not most, adolescents. A time of continuing cognitive development and a heightened awareness of self and others, ages thirteen through eighteen mark the passage from childhood to young adulthood. For the learning-disabled adolescent, these years are generally fraught with other problems as well: achievement deficits, high levels of stress, and a sense of repeated failure, to name but a few.

In this chapter we will examine one small part of the secondary school experience of most learning-disabled adolescents: instruction in whole numbers and the four operations of arithmetic. A necessary preface to this discussion considers the question of what concepts and skills in this area should be taught. Following that prelude we will outline the mathematics content, present some specific teaching suggestions culled from our own experience and that of others, offer some guidelines on the use and usefulness of hand-held calculators for the arithmetic of whole numbers, and briefly mention some criteria for assessment techniques appropriate and beneficial to the learning-disabled adolescent.

QUESTIONS: WHAT AND HOW MUCH TO TEACH?

The answers to the questions of what and how much arithmetic should be taught to learning-disabled secondary school students must reflect the uses to which those students will put the concepts and skills under consideration. The secondary school, for many students, has assumed the task of career preparation, either by way of vocational education programs or college preparatory sequences. In Touzel's proposal of a framework for the development of secondary school curricula for learning-disabled youngsters (1978), she noted that 84 percent of the respondents to a three-round Delphi probe agreed that secondary learning-disabilities curricula should include career and vocational development. An even larger number of the respondents, 92 percent, agreed that secondary school learning-disabilities curricula should include survival skills. Since mathematics skills are necessary in many situations in adult life, the inclusion of such skills among survival techniques follows logically. Hence, the question of what and how much arithmetic to teach seems to depend on the demands of survival in the twentieth and twenty-first centuries, and the requirements of secondary school programs in career preparation.

How does the educator determine what concepts and skills are necessary for survival in a world characterized by rapid change? Perhaps the most fundamental skill is that of being flexible, a skill outside the realm of mathematics instruction in and of itself, but one that can be developed through appropriate instruction in all areas. The determination of specific mathematics skills and concepts necessary for survival might reflect two sources: the requirement of successful daily living on a personal level and the demands made by entry-level positions in the job market.

With respect to arithmetic, the former set of requirements would include the abilities needed to handle cash, shop, pay bills, manage limited credit plans, maintain an automobile in reasonably good condition, read a newspaper with understanding, adhere to a schedule, take medication properly, plan a well-balanced diet, and the like. The demands made by entry-level positions in the job market of course reflect the nature of the employment under consideration. Employers also base their expectations on the amount of education experienced by the applicant. Swadener (1979) reported that of 22 hiring officials surveyed, 95 percent of the respondents considered addition and subtraction of whole numbers as necessary and/or desirable skills for high school graduates. Cowan and Clary (1978) noted that facility with addition and subtraction ranked second in a list of most desired mathematical skills. Sixty-five percent of the hiring officials polled by Swadener named skill in multiplication of whole numbers through six-digit by three-digit numbers as desirable or mandatory for a position in their place of business. Sixty percent of them expected high school graduates to have attained skill in computation with whole numbers through division of a five-digit number by a two-digit number, if job requirements were to be met successfully.

Neither Cowan and Clary's survey nor Swadener's study included many topics that might fall under the heading of "noncomputational use of whole numbers." Rounding whole numbers through hundred thousands, however, ranked twelfth in Swadener's list, representing selection by 27 percent of the respondents. In general, the evidence seems to indicate that skills in basic computation are necessary and desirable, but much practice with very large numbers would not seem to be a useful expenditure of time.

The requirements of secondary school programs in career preparation reflect the content of the courses selected or imposed. These courses range from carpentry to chemistry, from electronics to English. The mathematical requirements of the last named may not be too stringent, but those of the first three can be fairly demanding.

Huth (1979) included in his *Practical Problems in Mathematics for Carpenters* exercises in the use of exponents and in finding square roots. Huth also underscored the need for facility with ratio and proportion. Although these topics are considered under the umbrella of fractions, multiplication and division with whole numbers are necessary for solving proportions. In addition to the skill requirements, most secondary school mathematics teachers will attest to the difficulty most students have in working with ratio and proportion for solving problems.

Grob's *Basic Electronics* (1977) illustrates another necessary skill, the need to read and apply formulas involving computation with whole numbers. He gives as the formula for finding an unknown branch resistance the following:

$$R_x = \frac{R \times R_T}{R - R_T}$$

Where R_x represents the unknown branch resistance, R is the known resistance, and R_T is the desired resistance (p. 82). The following passage from Kreh's *Masonry Skills* (1976) highlights the need for skill in extracting numerical information from reading material.

> In modular design, the nominal dimension of a masonry unit (such as a brick or a block) is understood to mean the specified or manufactured dimension plus the thickness of the mortar joint to be used. That is, the size of the brick is designed so that when the size of the mortar joint is added to any of the brick dimensions (thickness, height, and length) the sum will equal a multiple of the 4-inch grid. For example, a modular brick whose nominal length is 8 inches will have a manufactured dimension of 7½ inches if it is designed to be laid with a ½-inch mortar joint, or 7 ⅝ inches if it is designed to be laid with a ⅜-inch joint. (p. 5)

Each of the examples cited above is taken from a textbook being used in classes taken by learning-disabled students in vocational educational programs. College preparation programs, of course, require the skills in whole numbers necessary for success in dealing with basic algebra and geometry, as well as the mathematics needed for courses in both the physical sciences and the social sciences, including the use of numbers for measurement, labeling, and identification. The learning-disabled student who cannot work with whole numbers is doubly disabled. Hence most teachers responsible for the mathematics programs of learning-disabled students at the secondary school level make arithmetic skills a priority, and rightfully so.

WHOLE NUMBERS AND COMPUTATION: CONTENT OUTLINE

Students with learning disabilities bring to a secondary school mathematics program a variety of degrees of preparation with respect to whole numbers. Some have mastered the basic number facts and the four operations. Others may have some computational skills, but accuracy and facility with the facts is very limited. Still others may have very faulty number concepts. These differences in background require the mathematics instructor to keep in mind a set of objectives, rather than a list of content defined by a starting point and a final destination.

The list of objectives presented in Exhibit 4-1 reflects a set of principles derived from the material in the introduction to this chapter:

1. Instruction in whole numbers and the operations of arithmetic should prepare the learning-disabled student to meet the mathematical demands day-to-day living makes on the average person.
2. Instruction in whole numbers and the operations of arithmetic should facilitate the learning-disabled adolescent's progress along the avenues of career preparation, either those already selected or those representing reasonable goals for the individual involved.
3. Instruction in whole numbers and the operations of arithmetic should foster the development of skills, concepts, and attitudes that will enable the student to flourish in a rapidly changing technological era.
4. Instruction in whole numbers and the operations of arithmetic should result in a good understanding of the skills and concepts needed for working with other rational numbers, and for success in other areas of the mathematics curriculum, especially geometry and measurement.

Exhibit 4-1 Secondary School Content Objectives—Whole Numbers and Operations

---

I.   Reading whole numbers
   A. Reads numerals of up to seven digits.
   B. Reads number words up to nine hundred ninety-nine.
   C. Reads the words and abbreviations for million and billion.
II. Writing whole numbers
   A. Writes numerals of up to seven digits.
   B. Writes number words up to nine hundred ninety-nine.
III. Using and recognizing the use of numerals for identification purposes
   A. Knows purpose, use of Social Security number.
   B. Knows purpose of other identification numbers: car registration, operator's license number, checking account number, and the like.
   C. Can use numbers and letters to locate places on a map, seats in a theater or stadium, and so on.
IV. Place value
   A. Can label and name the value of any digit in units place, tens place, hundreds place . . . . through millions place.
   B. Can rewrite a number given in standard form in a modified form of expanded notation. For example, $379 = 3 \times 100 + 7 \times 10 + 9 \times 1$.
   C. Can regroup or rename numbers in either direction, up to five digits. Examples: $379 = 3$ hundreds, 6 tens, and 19 ones; $379 = 2$ hundreds, 17 tens, and 9 ones; $379 = 2$ hundreds, 16 tens, and 19 ones; 2 hundreds and 13 ones can be written as 2 hundreds, 1 ten and 3 ones, and so on.
   D. Recognizes and can use zero as a digit in a numeral as signifying the absence of the power of ten involved. For example, $307 = 3$ hundreds, no tens, and 7 ones.
   E. Can round off numerals of up to seven digits to any place.
   F. Can order multidigit numbers.
V.   Addition of whole numbers
   A. Can represent the addition of whole numbers with some type of manipulative device: abacus, chips, or the like.
   B. When presented with any single-digit addition combination through $9 + 9$ in written form, can write and state aloud the answer.
   C. Can find sums of up to four addends of five digits each when presented with such examples in writing.
   D. Can translate sentences describing situations involving addition into addition expressions.
   E. Recognizes and uses the terms "addend" and "sum."
   F. Can estimate sums to a reasonable degree of accuracy.
VI. Subtraction of whole numbers
   A. Can represent the subtraction of whole numbers with some type of manipulative device.
   B. When presented with any basic subtraction combination through $18 - 9$ in written form, can write and state aloud the answer.
   C. Can find differences between any two numbers consisting of no more than five digits each.
   D. Can translate sentences describing situations involving subtraction into subtraction expressions.
   E. Can estimate differences to a reasonable degree of accuracy.

Exhibit 4-1   continued

VII. Multiplication of whole numbers
   A. Can represent a multiplication expression with one-digit factors with some type of manipulative device.
   B. When presented with any multiplication combination through 9 × 9 in written form, can write and state aloud the answer.
   C. Can find product between any two numbers consisting of no more than four digits each.
   D. Can translate sentences describing situations involving multiplication into multiplication expressions. In particular, knows that *of* indicates multiplication.
   E. Recognizes and uses the terms "factor" and "product."
   F. Can estimate products to a reasonable degree of accuracy.
VIII. Division with whole numbers
   A. Can represent the division of whole numbers with some type of manipulative device.
   B. When presented with any division combination through 81 ÷ 9 in written form, can write and state aloud the answer.
   C. Can find a quotient when the divisor has no more than three digits and the dividend no more than five digits.
   D. Can translate sentences describing situations involving division into division expressions.
   E. Can estimate quotients to a reasonable degree of accuracy.

TEACHING SUGGESTIONS

The activities described here fall into one of two categories: efficient methods for developing a skill or concept or experiences designed to provide rehearsal of a skill. Space does not permit coverage of each subtopic in the list of objectives, but many of the activities presented can be adapted to different content.

Reading and Writing Number Names; Numbers as Identification

1. Many word games can be adapted to provide experience with numerals and number words. Figure 4-1 illustrates a crossword puzzle for which the clues are numerals.

Figure 4-2 provides an example of a wordsearch task. The difficulty level of the wordsearch task can be controlled in several ways: (1) the words to be found can be listed next to the puzzle, or the student must find them on his or her own; (2) the words to be found can be written only horizontally, or only vertically, or in both directions, or horizontally, vertically, and diagonally; (3) the size of the puzzle, including the number of squares and the size of the letter, can be varied.

2. Many forms one has to complete in the course of daily affairs require information expressed through numbers. Obtain copies of such forms: job applications, W-4 forms, credit applications, insurance forms, and the

Figure 4-1 A Number Crossword Puzzle

¹S	E	V	E	N		²T	W	E	L	V	E
E						W					
V						O		³S		⁴O	
⁵E	I	G	H	⁶T				I		N	
N				H		⁷S	I	X	T	E	⁸N
⁹T	E	N		R				L		I	
E				E		¹⁰F	I	F	T	E	E	N
E			¹¹Z	E	R	O		I		V		E
¹²N	I	N	E			U		V		E		T
			R			R		E		N		E
			O									E
					¹³E	I	G	H	T	E	E	N

Across		Down	
1.	7	1.	17
2.	12	2.	2
5.	8	3.	6
7.	16	4.	1
9.	10	6.	3
10.	15	8.	19
11.	0	10.	4
12.	9	11.	0
13.	18		

Figure 4-2 A Word Search Puzzle

f	o	u	r	b	f	o	u	r	t	e	e	n
o	a	b	m	i	l	l	i	o	n	c	j	r
r	m	j	p	l	w	s	m	h	i	x	d	z
t	g	r	k	l	s	e	v	e	n	t	y	k
y	t	m	s	i	x	t	y	d	e	a	o	q
o	h	t	h	o	u	s	a	n	d	p	h	p
n	i	t	e	n	e	l	e	v	e	n	u	s
i	r	h	a	u	f	i	f	t	y	h	n	u
n	t	i	z	a	r	f	d	w	c	g	d	h
e	e	r	h	s	i	x	i	e	q	i	r	g
t	e	t	f	j	g	d	f	n	g	q	e	d
y	n	y	c	e	i	g	h	t	y	a	d	l
g	t	w	o	f	c	m	z	y	u	p	x	o

like. Help the students to fill out the forms, stressing the role numbers play in conveying information.

3. A major reason for the need to know how to write numbers with both words and numerals is found in the process of writing a check. Obtain copies of checks or facsimiles. On some checks write the amount of the check in numerals in the appropriate space. On others, write the amount of the check in words in the appropriate space. In each case the students are to complete the writing of the check.

4. On a transparency prepare a facsimile of a driver's operator license for your state. Help the students analyze the information presented by way of numbers.

Discuss with the students other "settings" for numbers used as identification: (1) In hotels and office buildings, the first digit or the first two digits of a room generally tell on what floor the room is located. (2) Certain digits of savings accounts numbers tell what kind of a savings account it is. (3) The first three digits of a telephone number (the area code) tell the general area in which the phone is located. (4) Each digit of a zip code refers to a specific geographic area within the area defined by the preceding digit to the left. Ask the students to provide other examples.

Place Value

There are very few contexts in which the adage "Haste makes waste" has greater application than in the area of mathematics instruction. As part of the mathematics curriculum, the topic of place value ranks high among those for which hasty instruction results in much waste, both of the student's time and energy and of the efforts of those mathematics teachers whose tutoring must build upon a firm foundation of place value concepts. An understanding of place value should be part of a student's set of knowledge very early in his or her work with numbers. Many learning-disabled adolescents lack such comprehension. In many cases, haste has been the culprit.

Our decimal system of notation determines not only how we read and write number names but also the algorithms with which we calculate sums and products, differences and quotients. Since this is so, even the student who must rely on mechanical devices for the latter will experience little success if a firm grasp of place value is not present.

Our number system is an example of a positional number system, in which the base is ten. Any digit in a given numeral represents a multiple of some power of ten, and the power of ten is determined by the position of the digit in the numeral. In the numeral 1,273, for example, the symbol 7 represents seven times ten to the first power, and all digits in the second position from the right in any numeral represent a multiple of ten to the first power. Students must understand this positional notation, and they must be familiar with the underlying principle that ten of anything can be expressed as one group of ten. Ten ones is the same as one ten, ten tens is the same as one group of hundred, and so on.

Although our numeration system is a system of symbols, much work with manipulatives is necessary to make the symbols meaningful. For the older student who may reject the use of popsicle sticks or chips as juvenile, pictures, or a sophisticated-looking abacus or odometer may provide some help. Activities like the following can be useful.

1. Obtain a manual (nonelectronic) hand calculator once used for keeping track of expenditures while shopping in a supermarket or similar store. Such a calculator is useful for demonstrating the working of our base ten number system. When one is added to nine ones, the calculator automatically regroups and notes one ten in the tens column. After demonstrating the use of the calculating machine, dictate numbers of one, two, or three places. Direct the student to show each number on the calculating machine.

2. Some students at the secondary school level might enjoy designing a calculator such as the one described above, or a simple odometer.

3. Provide the students with a worksheet on which several copies of the frame illustrated in Figure 4-3 are drawn:

Dictate different multi-digit numbers. The students are to write each digit in the appropriate space. Begin by naming numbers in standard form, for example, one thousand, three hundred eighty-six. For the last few numbers you dictate, warn the students that you will name the numbers in a "mixed up way." They must listen carefully and place the digits in the appropriate spaces. For example, dictate 1,478 as seven tens, one thousand, eight ones, and four hundreds.

4. The role of zero as a place holder in our decimal system is an important one. Activities such as those described above should include examples of numerals making use of zero as a place holder.

5. Estimation is a necessary skill that usually depends on the ability to round off numbers to a given place. To develop facility in rounding off, suggest that the students examine newspaper advertisements and advertising circulars and that they keep a record of prices they find. Examine the students' lists of prices, noting the frequency of such prices as $9.99, $19.95, and the like. Discuss the reasons for those advertised prices and the need to round off in order to get a reasonable estimate of what the cost is.

Addition

As an operation, addition has both a mathematical definition and a practical one. In mathematics, addition is an operation, denoted by the symbol +, that maps (assigns) any two real numbers to a unique third real number known as the sum of the first two. This third number is the cardinal property of the set formed by the union of two disjoint sets, each of which has one of the first two numbers as its cardinal property. From a practical

---

Figure 4-3 A Place Value Frame

mil-lions	hundred thou-sands	ten thou-sands	thou-sands	hundreds	tens	ones

perspective, addition is the algorithm or set of procedures that allows us to find the sum of any two numbers, for whatever the purpose may be. Students must know and understand both those interpretations of addition, although the words used to express the former may be less formal than those employed above.

That secondary school students do not always understand addition from either standpoint is made evident from the addition procedure illustrated in Figure 4-4. The rule being followed (add up all the digits in each example as if they were all single-digit addends) is one that is frequently found among examples of inappropriate algorithms used by students of all ages. The behavior shows that the students do not understand the numbers involved, and/or the meaning of the symbol ⁺, and/or the addition algorithm.

The learning-disabled secondary school student who has not memorized the single-digit addition combinations to a reasonable degree of facility of recall presents a quandary to the secondary school math instructor. Such a student usually has other weaknesses in his or her background. Is the time needed for drill and practice on the addition facts, or those of the other three operations, justifiably spent on that endeavor, when so much other content must be taught in so limited an amount of time?

The answer must depend on each individual case, but one caution should prevail, no matter which decision is made: The student who does not know the answers to basic combinations of single-digit numbers must learn to use some aid to accuracy, whether the combinations are being rehearsed on a regular basis or not. Such aid might take the form of pictures drawn to represent the combination under consideration, the use of an addition chart for addition and subtraction and a multiplication chart for multiplication and division, a hand-held calculator, or the like. Random guessing should be discouraged.

Figure 4-4 A Commonly Used, Inappropriate Addition Algorithm*

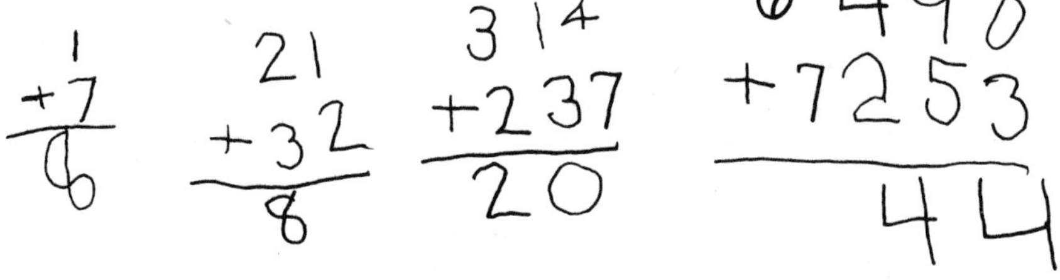

The instructor who wishes to provide structured rehearsal of the basic combinations will find suggestions in Fitzmaurice Hayes (1984) or in Suydam and Reys, *Developing Computational Skills,* the 1978 Yearbook of the National Council of Teachers of Mathematics.

The standard addition algorithm makes use of the principle "Ten ones equal one ten." A sequence of instruction is illustrated by the order of examples in Figure 4-5. Note the change from each example to the next.

The activities described below illustrate alternate ways of representing the standard algorithm.

1. A device, based on four squares arranged as illustrated in Figure 4-6 (a), can serve as a useful means of representing addends and sums. Any digit from 0 to 9 can be represented as shown in Figure 4-6 (b). To represent the addition of two-digit numbers, two grids may be used for each addend. Figure 4-6 (c) represents the addition of 37 and 42.

2. The use of coins, if the activity is structured properly, provides an experience-based approach to addition. Provide the student with pennies and dimes to be used in representing the numbers to be added. Combining all pennies for the sum of the ones and all dimes for the sum of the tens and exchanging ten pennies for one dime serves as a useful representation of examples such as 27 + 36.

3. Provide the students with models of number lines like those illustrated in Figure 4-7. For an example such as 327 + 236, the students can represent each column addition on the appropriate number line. The sum of 13 in the ones column can then be represented by an additional ten on the middle number line, with only three ones remaining on the top number line.

Much effort during kindergarten and first grade instruction is devoted to the development of left-to-right behaviors. Such reading and writing behavior does not come instinctively. Note the instance of a kindergarten child who had written his name on his paper thus: wehttaM. When questioned, Matthew simply explained in his own words that he had started there (and he pointed to the upper right-hand corner of the paper) and didn't have room to go to the right, so he went to the left. For Matthew, much instruction will be necessary before he learns that we read and write from left to right in our society. Chances are, however, that Matthew will learn the behavior and learn it well.

Some children learn it too well, and carry left-to-right behaviors over to arithmetic. For Steps 1–4, 6, 8, 10, and 12 of the sequence outlined in Figure 4-5, left-to-right addition gives the same answer as right-to-left addition. Children practice many examples of each of those steps. Hence it is not unusual that secondary school students are found to have devel-

Figure 4-5 A Sequence of Instruction for the Conventional Addition
Algorithm

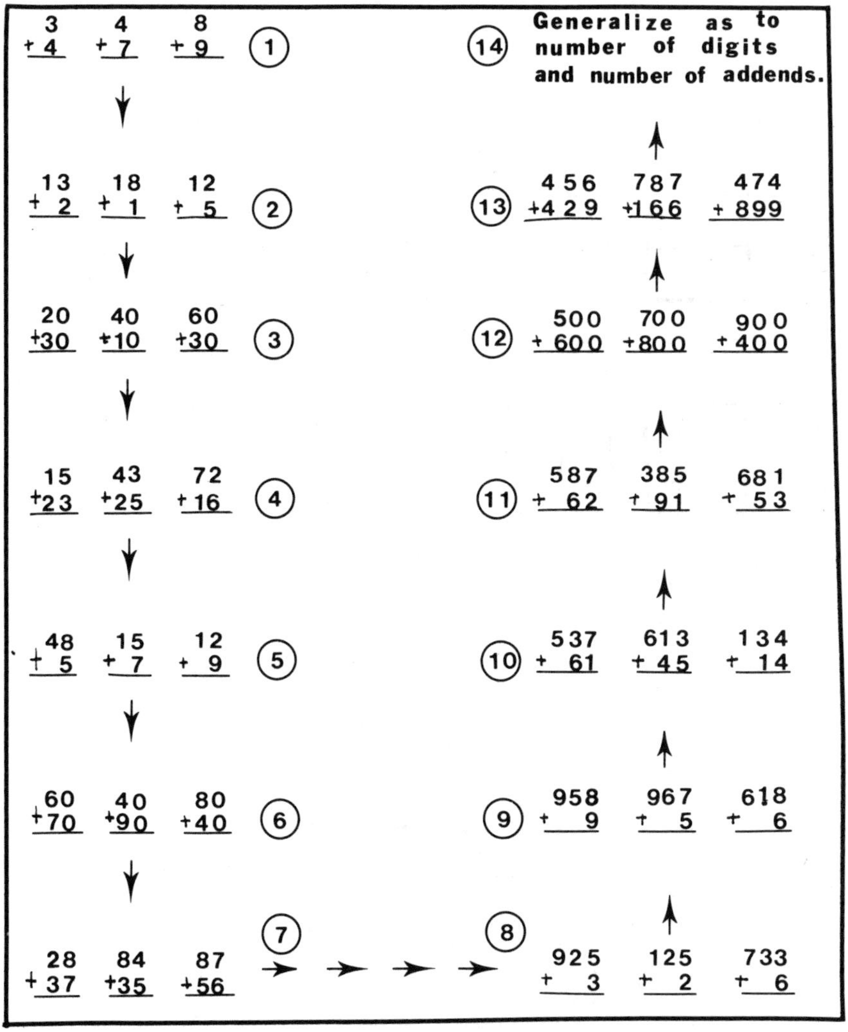

```
  3      4      8              ⎛  ⎞    Generalize   as  to
+ 4    + 7    + 9     ( 1 )    ⎝14⎠    number   of  digits
                                      and  number  of addends.
        │                                      ▲
        ▼                                      │

 13     18     12                      456    787    474
+ 2    + 1    + 5     ( 2 )    ⎛13⎞   +429   +166   + 899
                                      ⎝  ⎠
        │                                      ▲
        ▼                                      │

 20     40     60                      500    700     900
+30    +10    +30     ( 3 )    ⎛12⎞   + 600  +800   + 400
                                      ⎝  ⎠
        │                                      ▲
        ▼                                      │

 15     43     72                      587    385    681
+23    +25    + 16    ( 4 )    ⎛11⎞   + 62   + 91   + 53
                                      ⎝  ⎠
        │                                      ▲
        ▼                                      │

 48     15     12                      537    613    134
+ 5    + 7    + 9     ( 5 )    ⎛10⎞   + 61   + 45   + 14
                                      ⎝  ⎠
        │                                      ▲
        ▼                                      │

 60     40     80                      958    967    618
+70    +90    +40     ( 6 )    ( 9 )  + 9    + 5    + 6

        │                                      ▲
        ▼                                      │
                     ( 7 )    ( 8 )
 28     84     87      →  →  →  →       925    125    733
+ 37   +35    +56                     + 3    + 2    + 6
```

oped for themselves faulty left-to-right addition algorithms that they use
for all addition examples.

When working with a student who has been using a faulty left-to-right
algorithm fairly consistently, the teacher has a choice to make. One alternative is to teach the standard right-to-left algorithm. This involves cor-

Figure 4-6 An Aid to Addition

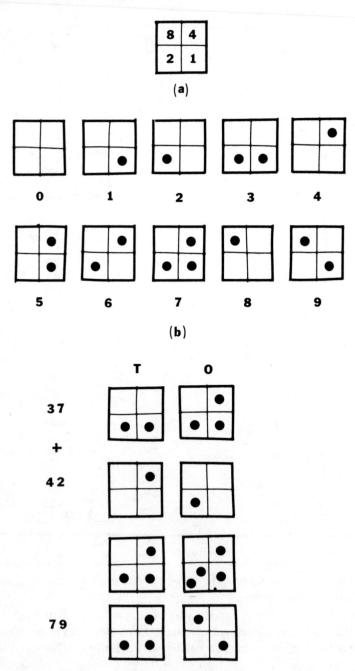

Figure 4-7 Using Number Lines and Base Ten Pieces for Multi-Digit Addends

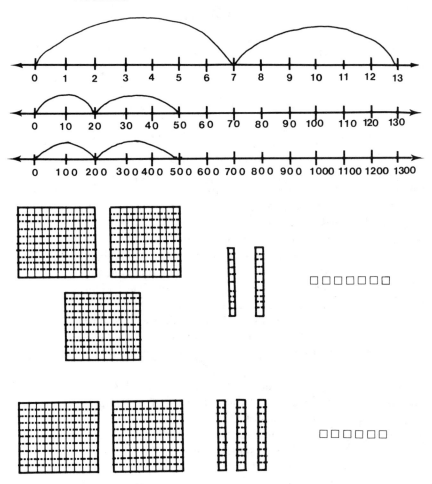

recting the left-to-right tendency as well as teaching the correct regrouping procedures. A second alternative is to teach a correct left-to-right algorithm. The steps are outlined in Figure 4-8.

Subtraction

Mathematically speaking, subtraction is defined in terms of addition. Hence, subtraction as a set of procedures and the practical situations in which subtraction is useful form the focus of instruction.

Figure 4-8 Addition from Left to Right

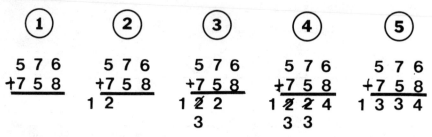

Subtraction is used to answer three different types of questions, and students must recognize its application in all three contexts. The first context is usually recognizable by the remainder question "How many are left?" or a variation thereof. The situation usually consists of a set from which a subset is removed.

The second setting is a comparative one. Two sets are under consideration. The questions to be answered concern themselves with the relative sizes of the two sets, and the magnitude of the difference.

The third setting is actually one of addition. One addend and the sum are known. The second addend is to be found.

The information to be analyzed is quite different from one situation to the next. The student should have many manipulative experiences with all three types of exercises, prior to and concurrent with translation into symbols.

1. Discuss with the students the three types of situations in which subtraction is appropriate. Cut out examples of simple problems of each type and paste the examples on cards. Ask the student to sort the cards into three piles, one for remainder subtraction, one for comparative subtraction, and one for additive subtraction.

2. Write a number on the chalkboard. Ask the students to make up an example of remainder subtraction, making use of the number on the chalkboard. Repeat for comparative subtraction and additive subtraction.

3. Suggest a theme around which problems are to be composed: sports, science, popular music, or the like. Ask the students to make up simple problems for remainder subtraction, comparative subtraction, and additive subtraction around the theme suggested. If the dynamics allow it, ask the students to role play the problems.

The conventional subtraction algorithm is based on the principle that one group of ten can be renamed as ten ones. A sequence of instruction is illustrated by the order of the examples in Figure 4-9. Again, examine the difference from one example to the next.

Figure 4-9 A Sequence of Instruction for the Conventional
        Subtraction Algorithm

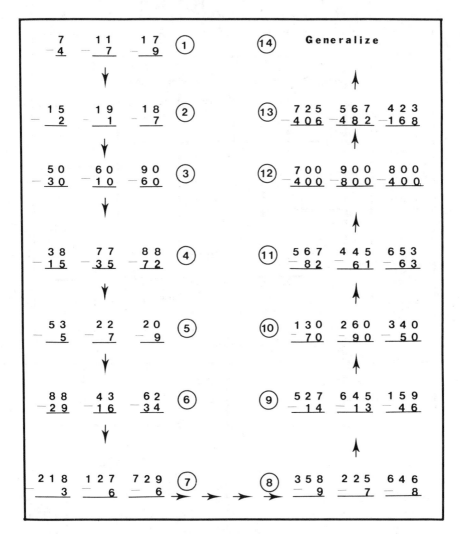

The conventional algorithm has as its chief recommendation the ease with which it can be represented manipulatively. Students attempting to master the subtraction algorithm need experience with such manipulation as well as practice with the algorithm itself, if mastery is to occur.

1. On a large piece of cardboard draw a game board as illustrated in Figure 4-10. Provide each student with an abacus or some other means of

Figure 4-10 A Game Board

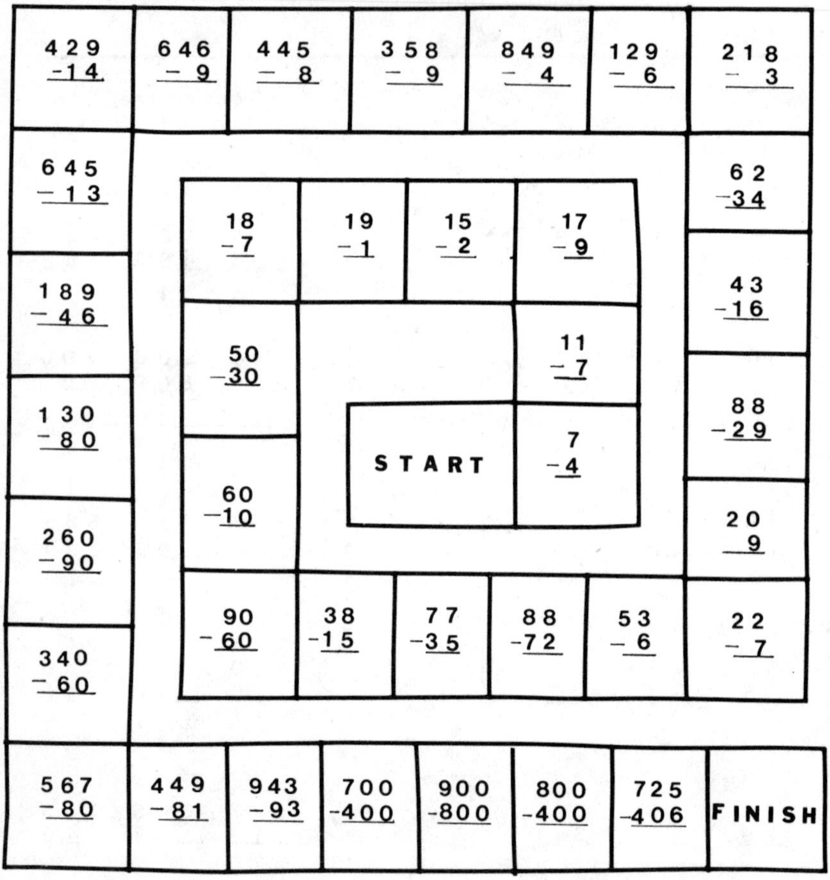

429 −14	646 − 9	445 − 8	358 − 9	849 − 4	129 − 6	218 − 3

645 − 13				62 −34
189 − 46	18 −7	19 −1	15 −2	17 −9	43 −16
130 − 80	50 −30		11 −7	88 −29
260 −90	60 −10	START	7 −4	20 9
340 − 60	90 −60	38 −15	77 −35	88 −72	53 − 6	22 − 7

567 −80	449 −81	943 −93	700 −400	900 −800	800 −400	725 −406	FINISH

representing subtraction (dollars, dimes, and pennies, or facsimiles thereof are effective). Demonstrate to the students the procedure for representing an example. Ask a student to throw a die and to move a marker the specified number of squares. When a student lands on a square, he or she is to construct a representation of the subtraction expression written in that square. A correct representation earns the right for the marker to remain on the square. Otherwise the player must return to START. The first player to reach the last space or beyond is the winner.

2. Draw a maze as illustrated in Figure 4-11. Ask the student to start at the arrow and to compute the answer to the first example. Explain that the next move is to the example having as its top number the answer to

Figure 4-11 A Maze

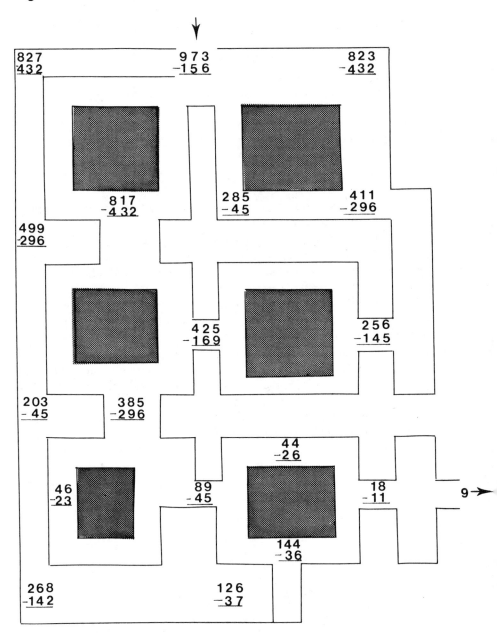

the previous subtraction example. The student is to continue on in this manner until out of the maze.

3. Computing age and the amount of time elapsed since particular events occurred can afford practice in subtraction. The contexts of such explorations into history are several—science, literature, automobile technology, photography, sports, and many others.

Inappropriate algorithms for left-to-right subtraction also make their appearances in students' work. The choice that exists with respect to instruction in addition can be exercised with respect to subtraction also. The left-to-right algorithm for subtraction is outlined in Figure 4-12.

Multiplication

Multiplication is frequently described and taught as repeated addition. The more traditional representations of multiplication, equivalent sets, arrays, and the number line depend on this interpretation for their efficacy. Although it is often the most efficient way to find the sum of a number of repeated addends, such a purpose does not define multiplication as an operation in mathematics.

To examine the mathematical definition of multiplication, let us imagine ourselves with four containers of ice cream, one of vanilla (V), one of coffee (C), one of maple walnut (M), and one of pistachio (P). Suppose also that we have available three different toppings: hot fudge (H), strawberry (S), and butterscotch (B). If we were allowed only one kind of ice cream and one kind of topping per sundae, what is the maximum number of different sundaes we could make?

The drawing in Figure 4-13 illustrates the solution to the problem. Each kind of ice cream must be crossed with each kind of topping. The points of intersection represent the different sundaes, and there are twelve in all.

Suppose we let A be the set of different kinds of ice cream. The cardinal property of A, n(A), is four. Likewise, if B is the set of different kinds of

---

Figure 4-12 Subtraction from Left to Right

①	②	③	④	⑤
1 3 3 4	1 3 3 4	1 3₁3 4	1 3₁3₁4	1 3 3 4
− 7 5 8	−7 5 8	−7 5 8	−7 5 8	−7 5 8
	6	6̶ 8	6̶ 8̶ 6	5 7 6
		5	5 7	

Figure 4-13 A Model for Multiplication

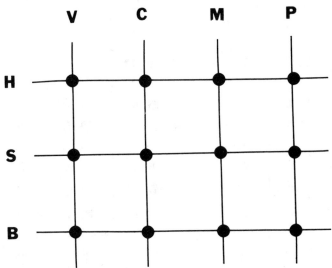

toppings, then n(B) is three. The product 4 × 3 is defined as the cardinal property of A × B, that is, the set formed when each and every member of A is matched with each and every member of B.

In symbols the words say

$$n(A) \times n(B) = n(A \times B)$$
$$4 \times 3 = 12$$

Students should have experiences with the representation of multiplication as an efficient way to do "repeated addition" and as a means for finding the cardinal property of the cross-product of sets.

1. Teach the students how to represent a multiplication expression with an array. The first factor names the number of horizontal rows in the array; the second factor represents the number of items in each row. Provide each student with a large sheet of paper, felt-tipped pens and/or self-adhesive dots. Suggest that the students make a multiplication chart in which the products are represented by arrays. Figure 4-14 is an example of such a chart.

Discuss the patterns that emerge, noting that as one moves across the chart, the number of rows in each box remains the same. As one moves down the chart, the number in each row remains the same. Also note the square arrays, 1 × 1, 2 × 2, 3 × 3, and so on.

2. Provide examples of the cross-product definition of multiplication. Ask the students to draw pictures representing the situations you describe.

Figure 4-14 A Multiplication Chart

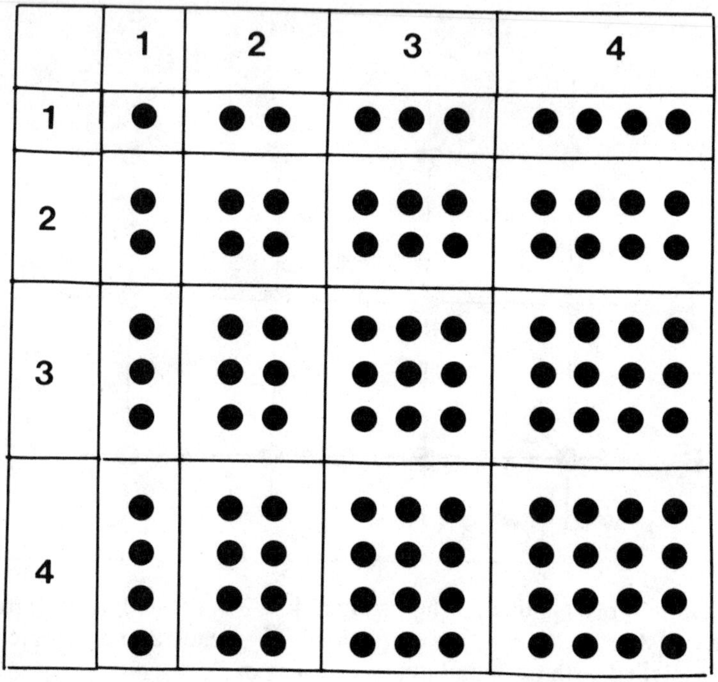

Examples: (a) a small town has four streets going north-south and six streets going east-west. How many intersections are there? (b) How many possible different outfits would you have if you had five shirts and four pairs of slacks, and each shirt could be worn with each pair of slacks? Encourage the students to make up their own examples.

Successful completion of the traditional multiplication algorithm requires that the student multiply every multiple of a power of ten in one factor by every multiple of a power of ten in the other factor. The total product is found by adding the results of those pairings. Once learned, much of the process is done mentally, with only the most necessary figures recorded on paper. Eves (1953) pointed out that such a process became necessary because until the latter half of the nineteenth century, paper was scarce and expensive. Hence algorithms that were efficient in terms of the space required for recording became more widely used. Teachers working with learning-disabled adolescents who have trouble with the multiplication algorithm should keep such a historical perspective in mind. There is nothing sacred about the traditional algorithm as such; it is merely a space saver.

A sequence for teaching the traditional algorithm is outlined in Figure 4-15. Suggestions for providing experiences related to some of the steps are listed below.

1. Ask the students to collect bottle caps from different containers to which they would have access. Assign a value to the caps from a given product. For example, caps from cola bottles might be assigned a value

Figure 4-15 A Sequence of Instruction for the Conventional Multiplication Algorithm

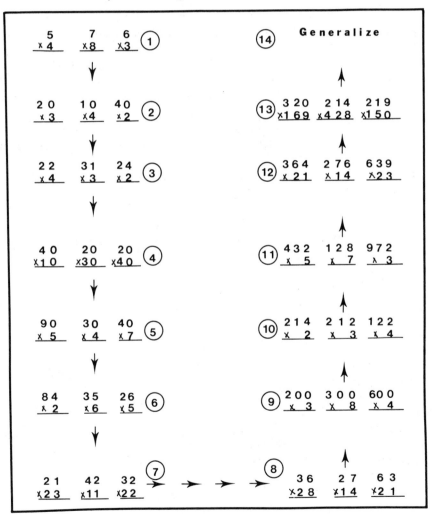

of ten. Represent different products of powers of ten with the bottle caps; ten cola caps would represent 10×10. Ask the students to name the products represented; $10 \times 10 = 100$.

2. Provide the students with wrappers for different types of coins. Discuss the use of coin wrappers and note the amount of money contained in each wrapper when it is full. Provide the students with coins or facsimiles of coins. Write multiplication expressions on the chalkboard. Ask the students to represent the expressions by filling the appropriate number of the coin wrappers involved. For example, 100×1 could be represented by two full penny wrappers.

3. Discuss the practice of saving trading stamps. Point out that trading stamps are a promotional technique used by merchants to encourage people to buy their goods. Show the students examples of trading stamps that may be popular in your area and the books in which the stamps are stored. Explain the rate at which stamps are given, usually one stamp per ten cents of purchase. Ask the students to figure out how much money was spent in order to get the following numbers of stamps: 10 stamps, 25 stamps, 750 stamps, 1,500 stamps, and the like.

4. Some learning-disabled students may need a structure to help them to line up the partial products in the appropriate rows and columns. Several strategies are available. Provide lined paper turned sideways for those students who have trouble keeping the columns straight. Provide one centimeter square graph paper for those students who have trouble keeping both rows and columns straight. In some cases you may have to outline the space occupied by the completed example. (See Figure 4-16.) Use whatever approach is necessary for a given student, gradually fading the organizational clues.

5. Some students may find the method of multiplication demonstrated in Figure 4-17 easier to learn than the traditional method.

Division

Like subtraction, division has no separate existence as a mathematical operation. From a functional perspective, the process called division is useful for finding answers to two types of questions. Students need experience with both kinds of division applications.

Recall that in a multiplication expression such as 2×4, the first factor is properly interpreted as naming the number of sets; the second factor tells how many members there are in each set. The complete multiplication sentence for the above expression would read $2 \times 4 = 8$.

The related division expressions are $8 \div 4$ and $8 \div 2$. The first expression might be the symbolic representation of the following situation: A carpen-

Figure 4-16 An Example of Organizational Cues

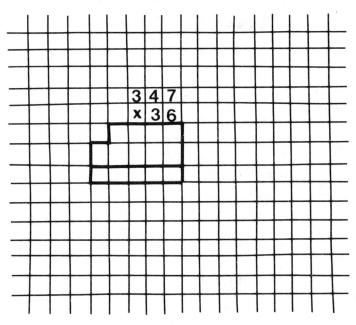

ter has an eight-foot long piece of plywood. She needs four-foot lengths of the plywood. How many such pieces can be cut from the eight-foot piece? Note that the size of each set is known (4 feet). What is required is the number of sets. ___ × 4 = 8. 8 ÷ 4 = ___. This type of example has been called measurement division. If you had to solve the problem without doing any computation, you would probably measure off four-foot lengths of plywood until there was no more wood to be measured.

The division expression 8 ÷ 2, derived from the sentence 2 × 4 = 8, might represent the following situation: A carpenter has eight nails. He wants to use them to strengthen two uprights. How many nails will he drive into each upright if he intends to divide the nails evenly between the uprights? The problem involves the partitioning of the whole set (eight nails) into subsets (the nails in the two uprights). The number of subsets is known; the number of elements in each set is not known. Such situations are examples of partitive division. To solve the problem without any knowledge of arithmetic, you would probably deal out the nails, one at a time to each upright, until the eight nails were all used.

Practice with the two types of division problems can include experiences like the following.

Figure 4-17 An Example of Matrix Multiplication

$$\text{Example:} \quad \begin{array}{r} 347 \\ \times\,36 \\ \hline \end{array}$$

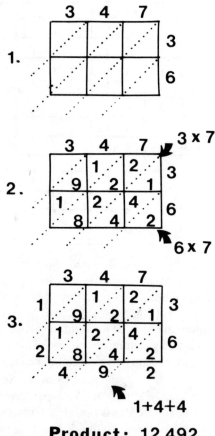

Product: 12,492

1. Present miniproblems for solution. (a) 64 yards of cloth. 8 yards per dress. How many dresses? (b) 5 bills to be paid. $75 in all. How much money can be paid on each bill? (c) 10 cups of flour. 2 cups needed for each batch of cookies. How many batches of cookies? Encourage the students to write the multiplication expression and the related division expression.

2. To emphasize the role of the remainder in division, discuss problems like the following with the students: Eighteen people who worked for the same company decided to form a car pool. Each of the available cars can hold only five people comfortably. How many cars are needed for the car pool?

The traditional division algorithm is one of repeated subtraction. In essence then, the algorithm represents measurement division only. A sequence for teaching the division algorithm is outlined in Figure 4-18. Note that the steps in the sequence are directly related to the sequence for multiplication outlined in Figure 4-15.

Since the algorithm is one of repeated subtraction, the teaching of the process begins with the use of repeated subtraction with no special effort to find shortcuts. When examples make the use of repeated subtraction of the divisor tedious, students are motivated to try to find shortcuts, which take the form of subtracting multiples of the divisor. After some experience with multiples, students are led to see the advantages of subtracting multiples of the divisor and ten, or when feasible, multiples of the divisor and one hundred. This particular method for teaching division is outlined in Figure 4-19.

One advantage to this method is found in examples like the following: $35\overline{)1085}$. Zeros anywhere in the dividend become no more troublesome than zeros in the top number of a subtraction example.

Likewise, teen divisors are no more troublesome than other two-place numbers. In other words, repeated subtraction as an approach to the traditional division algorithm does away with, or at least alleviates, some of the unnecessary distinctions between and among levels of difficulty with division examples.

CALCULATORS

As a tool for computation, the hand-held calculator has become both popular and necessary, superseding less convenient aids to computation such as the slide rule and common logarithms. Many parents and teachers, however, question the use of the hand-held calculator by school students. A surprisingly large number of college freshmen do not own calculators, despite the fact that prices start below $10, or if they do, they do not know how to operate them. They resist using the calculator, often expressing the belief that to do so is wrong; it is "cheating."

Such an attitude exemplifies the quandary in which many teachers find themselves. To be able to read, write, and do arithmetic has long been a minimal standard for being considered educated. To assign one of those

Figure 4-18 A Sequence of Instruction for the Conventional Division
Algorithm

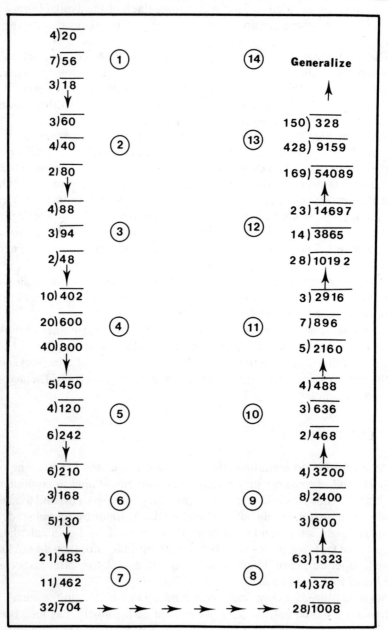

Figure 4-19 Division as Repeated Subtraction

Example: $32\overline{)664}$

Least efficient method	More efficient method	Most efficient method
	$5 \times 32 = 160$	$10 \times 32 = 320$
664		$20 \times 32 = 640$
−32	664	
632	−160 5×32	664
−32	504	−640 20×32
600	−160 5×32	24
−32	344	
568	−160 5×32	Shorthand:
−32	184	
536	−160 5×32	$20\dfrac{24}{32}$
⋮ 15	24	$32\overline{)664}$
more	20×32	−64
subtractions		24
56		
−32 20		
24 subtractions		
in		
all		

Answer: $20\dfrac{24}{32}$

---

capabilities to a machine, albeit a clever one, is to somehow lessen the quality of school learning. Yet the advantages of a product of technology that can so remarkably reduce the amount of effort spent on repetitive and time-consuming calculations cannot be ignored. In many school systems a compromise has been effected: hand-held calculators are not to be used until students have demonstrated competency with respect to the operations of arithmetic.

For many teachers of learning-disabled students at the secondary school level this compromise raises more questions than it answers. The young person who reaches secondary school with little or no computational skills presents a dilemma. Such a student has only a few years of formal school experience remaining to him or her. Is the amount of time required to develop computational skills justifiably spent on such an endeavor, when other areas of mathematics also require attention? The answer to such a question depends on individual circumstances and values, but for the teacher who wishes to minimize the time devoted to such instruction, a calculator can prove an invaluable aid.

In such cases, instruction in the use of a calculator must be designed to offset the problems the student quite often brings to the use of the tool. Basic number concepts, an understanding of place value and the meaning of each of the four operations of arithmetic, and some knowledge of the basic number combinations are prerequisites to the intelligent use of the calculator. Once the prerequisites have been achieved, formal instruction in the use of a calculator can begin.

Selection of a Calculator

The selection of a calculator depends on many factors. For some students the basic calculator that adds, subtracts, multiplies, divides, computes percent and square roots, and has simple memory capabilities is sufficient. Other students may require a calculator that prints out the operations as they are performed.

Calculators fall into two categories with respect to the type of logic used: arithmetic logic and algebraic logic. The latter type obeys the laws of algebra with respect to the order in which operations are performed: multiplication and division take precedence over addition and subtraction. To find out which type of logic governs a calculator, perform the following sequence: $9 + 6 \div 3 =$. If the display shows 5, the calculator operates on arithmetic logic. If the answer is 11, algebraic logic is the governing mode. Most basic calculators use arithmetic logic.

Other factors that enter into the selection of a calculator include the size of the calculator, the size of the buttons, and the source of the energy used. Many calculators being marketed today are solar powered. These have a special advantage for students (and teachers) who may forget to turn the tool off when finished with a task.

Learning To Use the Calculator

The use of a calculator involves both familiarity with the necessary procedures and the employment of behaviors that ensure accurate results. A certain amount of practice is necessary in both cases.

The best source of information on how to use a particular calculator to its fullest potential is the book of directions that accompanies the calculator. Such manuals often provide problems and examples. Once the operating procedures have been explained to the students, examples like those in the manual can be presented and used for rehearsal. Single-step problems should precede multi-step ones; the memory functions can prove quite helpful with the latter type of exercise.

Since a calculator operates only on the numbers presented to it, care must be taken to enter the correct numbers. Accuracy demands that each entry be checked before an operation button is pressed, and that each result be checked for appropriateness. Some students will have to check their results by doing an example twice. Others may be able to use estimation skills for this purpose. Whatever the strategy selected, students must form the habit of evaluating their answers in the light of the information given. With adequate caution, the calculator can prove an invaluable aid to the learning-disabled adolescent with limited computational skills.

MICROCOMPUTERS

The past few years have witnessed a growing use of microcomputers in the classroom for instructional purposes. Software packages abound, some offering instructional potential, others providing drill and practice exercises. Teachers wishing to take advantage of the opportunities afforded by the technology should be aware of some necessary cautions: (1) Not all software packages are accurate in their presentation of mathematics content. Care must be taken to avoid the rehearsal of inappropriate strategies. (2) Many software programs do little more than present examples on a screen. The student needs to work out the exercises on paper and then present the answer to the computer. Many programs offer a choice between a fixed (preprogrammed) selection of examples and sets of examples developed from randomly selected numbers. An instructor must be aware of the possible difficulty levels when numbers are randomly selected. (3) The methods students should use to report answers to the computer terminal differ from program to program. Students must be taught to follow directions exactly, or frustration will occur when correct answers are judged to be incorrect by the computer. Most potential problems can be avoided if the person in charge of computer-assisted instruction is familiar with all the programs in use.

ASSESSMENT IN THE ARITHMETIC OF WHOLE NUMBERS

The many gaps and faulty computational procedures accompanying the learning-disabled student to the secondary school level provide a special challenge to assessment practices. The limited number of school years left to such a youngster makes imperative a knowledge of how to instruct in the most efficient manner. An effective assessment instrument, then, must yield information about effective and efficient teaching modes, and must analyze algorithmic behaviors acquired over the years. Any instrument that does less than that is not serving the purpose for which it must be used. See Chapter 2 for a discussion of specific issues in the area of proficiency testing.

SUMMARY

In the preceding pages we have attempted to provide a rationale for decisions with respect to what and how much content in the area of the arithmetic of whole numbers should be taught to learning-disabled adolescents still in need of such instruction. With such a rationale as a background, an outline of content and some teaching suggestions were presented. The careful use of a calculator by those students with weak computational skills was viewed as one alternative to spending much time in such instruction. Criteria for assessment techniques appropriate and beneficial to the learning-disabled adolescent further handicapped by the lack of computational skills were mentioned briefly. A sense of balance and a spirit of ingenuity on the part of teachers of learning-disabled adolescents will have as their effect the diminishment of this added handicap.

REFERENCES

Cowan, R.E., & Clary, R.C. (1978). Identifying and teaching essential mathematical skills-items. *The Mathematics Teacher, 71,* 130–33.

Eves, H. (1953). *An introduction to the history of mathematics.* New York: Rinehart.

Fitzmaurice Hayes, A. (1984). Curriculum and instructional activities: Grades 2 through 4. In J.F. Cawley (Ed.), *Developmental teaching of mathematics for the learning disabled.* Rockville, MD: Aspen Systems.

Grob, Bernard. (1977). *Basic electronics.* New York: McGraw-Hill.

Huth, H.C. (1979). *Practical problems in mathematics for carpenters.* Albany, NY: Delmar.

Kreh, R. (1976). *Masonry skills.* Albany, NY: Delmar.

Suydam, M.N., & Reys, R.E. (1978). *Developing computational skills.* Reston, VA: National Council of Teachers of Mathematics.

Swadener, M. (1979). What mathematics skills hiring officials want. *Mathematics Teacher, 72,* 444–447.

Touzel, S.W. (1978). Secondary LD curricula—A proposed framework. *Learning Disability Quarterly, 1,* 53–61.

Chapter 5

Fractions, Decimals, Percentages

Anne M. Fitzmaurice Hayes

An introduction to fractions marks the student's initial contact with a set of numbers that has great potential for aiding humankind in its efforts to quantify its surroundings. To provide a picture of the relationships between and among the different sets of numbers, a brief survey of the real number system forms the beginning of this chapter. A scope and sequence of content in fractions, decimals, and percent and suggested teaching activities compose the remainder of the chapter.

FROM 1, 2, 3, TO THE SQUARE ROOT OF 3

The concept of number exerts a dual enchantment. When it uncovers the rich relationships between pure magnitudes to the scientist, it fills him with the satisfaction of intellectual insight; . . . . For others it exerts a fascination by its deep interconnection with the daily life of the people. Is it not true that every tribe spoke and noted down numbers, that every tribe had to calculate whenever it faced life on this planet? Did man's relationship to his environment not also necessitate his relationship with numbers? (Menninger, 1969, p. v)

Most of us recognize more familiarly the second aspect of the dual enchantment about which Menninger wrote. However, an outline of the relationships between and among the different sets of numbers with which we work requires some of the mathematician's thinking as well. One necessary concept is that of *closure*. In mathematics, if a set of elements is said to be *closed* with respect to an operation, we know that whenever the operation is performed on any two members of the set, the result is

115

also a member of the set. With that definition in mind, let us proceed to examine different sets of numbers and the operations we perform on their members.

Human beings in all probability first used numbers to count sets of discrete items. Hence the counting numbers, or the natural numbers, form the initial set of numbers for our purposes. They are represented by the dots in line (a) of Figure 5-1.

In time it became necessary to include among number names a designation for nothing, or zero. This new number joined to the set of counting numbers forms the set of whole numbers, illustrated in line (b) of Figure 5-1.

A moment's reflection will convince the reader that under the operations of addition and multiplication, the counting numbers and the whole numbers are closed sets. However, since $3 - 5$ and $3 \div 5$ cannot be written any simpler if we have only the whole numbers from which to choose, the sets are not closed with respect to subtraction and division. Likewise, since $\sqrt{2}$, the number which when used as a factor twice gives two, is not found in the whole numbers, the set is not closed with respect to the operation we have called "rooting." The first two columns of Figure 5-2 represent the closure properties of the counting numbers and the whole numbers.

By joining to the set of whole numbers a negative counterpart for each counting number (also called an additive inverse), we form the set of integers, shown in line (c) of Figure 5-1. Not only do these new numbers

---

Figure 5-1 From the Counting Numbers to the Real Numbers

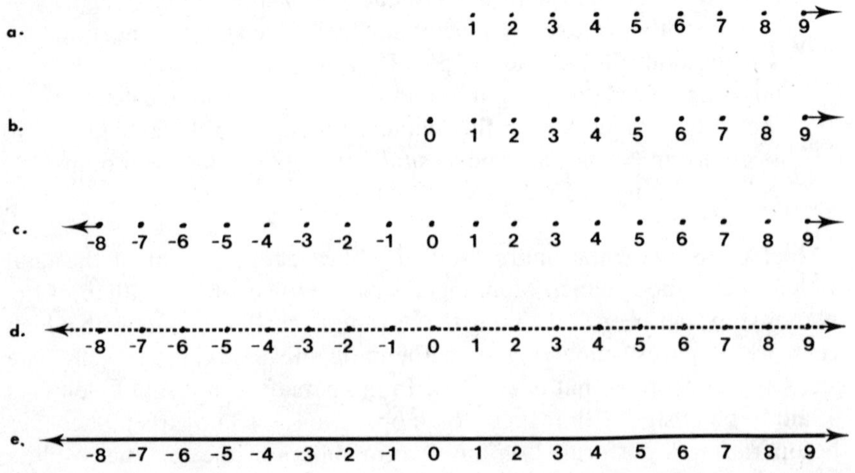

Figure 5-2 Closure Properties of Sets of Numbers

	Counting numbers	Whole numbers	Integers	Rational numbers	Real numbers
$+$	▨	▨	▨	▨	▨
$\times$	▨	▨	▨	▨	▨
$-$			▨	▨	▨
$\div$				▨	▨
"Rooting" *					▨

*Rooting here refers to roots of positive even numbers and positive and negative odd

have practical purposes as a means of expressing temperatures below freezing, being "in the hole" or in debt, but they also provide closure with respect to subtraction. Within the set of integers, $3 - 5$ can be as written -2.

As Figure 5-2 indicates, the integers are closed with respect to the operation of subtraction, but not division or rooting. We still do not have a place for $3 \div 5$ or $\sqrt{2}$. However, if we join to the set of integers the set of numbers formed by the quotient of any two integers, we arrive at a set of rational numbers. Our number line begins to look like that shown in line (d) of Figure 5-1, but, of course, the dots represent only a very small portion of the set of rational numbers. It is within this set that the numbers commonly called fractions are found.

The set of rational numbers does more than provide closure for division. We noted earlier that the set of counting numbers furnished the means for quantifying sets having individual members. Early man also found a need to quantify continuous quantity: length, mass, area, volume, capacity, and the like. Such quantification, ordinarily called measurement, requires the selection of a unit of measure and the determination of how many times that unit can be superimposed upon the dimension to be measured.

A problem occurs almost immediately. It is by no means necessary that a unit be used an integral number of times in a given instance. That is, if the unit measure of length is taken as the width of a hand, then the length of a desk or the height of a room may require expression in terms of so many hand widths plus a part of a hand width. Without fractions, measurement requires the use of very, very small units, and, therefore, very large numbers, or else it yields measures that are quite inexact in most cases. Although all measures represent an approximation to the true measure, the availability of numbers to designate parts of units serves to lessen the degree of approximation. A glance at a textbook in carpentry, masonry, electronics, or the like soon convinces one of the usefulness of the set of rational numbers, and specifically the numbers we traditionally call fractions, decimals, and percent, in very practical contexts.

Observe that there are still some gaps in line (d) of Figure 5-1. Also, Figure 5-2 indicates that even the set of rational numbers is not closed with respect to the operation designated as "rooting." There are many numbers, for example, two, three, and five, whose square roots (and other roots) cannot be written as a fraction. However, these roots exist as irrational numbers, and we can locate them on a number line. Proofs for the above statements are outside the scope of this text but can be found in mathematics textbooks at the secondary school level or beyond. The irrational numbers are mentioned here to complete the present discussion of the real numbers, and because learning-disabled adolescents may come across these numbers in algebra classes or drafting courses.

Line (e) in Figure 5-1 represents the entire set of real numbers. Every real number can be placed in one and only one position on the number line, and every point on the number line can be named by one and only one real number. As Figure 5-2 shows, the set of real numbers is closed for all the operations under consideration here.

Figure 5-3 illustrates the containment relationships among the sets of numbers we have examined. The numbers in each ring represent those numbers present in that set but in none of the contained sets. That is, the set of whole numbers contains the set of counting numbers and zero; the set of integers contains the set of whole numbers plus the additive inverses, and so on.

Figure 5-3 Relationships Among Sets of Numbers

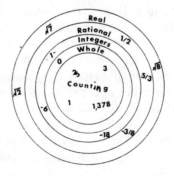

Most of the foregoing discussion was intended to provide background for the reader. The decision to include formal instruction in such content in the mathematics program of a learning-disabled adolescent must be made on the basis of the student's goals. Certainly, a youngster hoping to attend college will need to know the relationships as they have been outlined. For other students such content might be presented only as necessary.

RATIONAL NUMBERS: WHAT TO TEACH? WHEN? HOW MUCH?

Few, if any, educators would question the need to provide all students with basic skills in dealing with fractions, decimals, and percent. The emphasis during the past years on the usefulness of metric units of measure has led some to question the traditional sequence of instruction: fractions, decimals, percent. One can argue quite strongly the advantages of reversing the order of fractions and decimals, or at least teaching both kinds of notation concurrently. For purposes of simplicity we have chosen to discuss fractions first, decimals second, and percent last. We will, however, when treating decimals, mention procedures for teaching decimals before formal instruction in fractions.

Exhibit 5-1 lists a set of objectives. Some students should meet all the objectives; others may not. The list represents a reasonably sized universe from which goals and objectives can be selected for a specific learning program.

FRACTIONS

Basic concepts

In too many cases, instruction in fractions is confined to representation by symbols, except at the initial stages. To thoroughly understand fractions and the rules for computing with them, students must have many and continuing experiences with representation through manipulatives and pictures. Most of the activities in this section contain suggestions for using such aids.

Manipulatives or fixed displays useful for teaching fractions can usually be assigned to one of three categories—those based on parts of geometric regions, those based on sets, and those based on the number line. Students should have an acquaintance with fractions in all three contexts.

Exhibit 5-1 Secondary School Content Objectives—Fractions, Decimals, Percent

I. Fractions
    A. Basic concepts
        1. Proper fractions
           a. Can represent proper fractions with some type of appropriate manipulative device or by drawing a picture.
           b. Can write and state the name of a proper fraction represented by manipulatives or by a picture.
           c. Writes proper fraction names on dictation.
           d. Reads proper fractions named by numerals.
           e. Reads fraction words: *half, third, fourth, quarter,* and so on.
           f. Can identify numerator, denominator.
        2. Improper fractions and mixed numerals
           a. Recognizes the number *one* when written as $\frac{2}{2}$, $\frac{3}{3}$, $\frac{4}{4}$, and so on.
           b. Can represent improper fractions with some type of appropriate manipulative device or by drawing a picture.
           c. Can write and state aloud the name of an improper fraction represented by manipulatives or by a picture.
           d. Can convert an improper fraction to a mixed numeral and vice versa.
           e. Distinguishes between proper fractions and improper fractions.
        3. Equivalence classes
           a. Knows that every fraction has many names.
           b. Can demonstrate by way of manipulatives or pictures equivalence statements such as $\frac{1}{2} = \frac{2}{4}$, $\frac{6}{8} = \frac{3}{4}$, and the like.
           c. Given a fraction in standard form (lowest terms), can write any desired equivalent form of the fraction.
           d. Given a fraction in nonstandard form, can write the standard form of that fraction (can reduce a fraction to the lowest terms).
        4. Given any two fractions, can determine which is the greater (or smaller).
    B. Adding fractions
        1. Can represent the addition of fractions with some type of manipulative device.
        2. Can find common denominators efficiently.
        3. Can find sums of mixed numerals when renaming in the sum is necessary, for example, $4\frac{5}{6} + 13\frac{1}{4}$.
    C. Subtracting fractions
        1. Can represent the subtraction of fractions with some type of manipulative device.
        2. Can find differences between mixed numerals when renaming is necessary, for example, $13\frac{1}{4} - 4\frac{5}{6}$.
    D. Multiplying fractions
        1. Can represent the multiplication of fractions with some type of manipulative device or by a picture.
        2. Can find the product of mixed numerals, both factors less than ten.
    E. Dividing fractions
        1. Can represent division of a whole number by a fraction, or a fraction by a fraction when the divisor is smaller than the dividend, with some type of manipulative device or by a picture.
        2. Can divide one mixed numeral by another, both numbers less than ten.

Exhibit 5-1 continued

II. Decimals
    A. Place value
        1. Can label and name the value of any digit in tenths place, hundredths place, and thousandths place.
        2. Can rewrite a number given in standard form in a modified form of expanded notation. For example, $79.325 = 7 \times 10 + 9 \times 1 + 3 \times .1 + 2 \times .01 + 5 \times .001$.
        3. Knows that the function of the decimal point is to mark the location of units place.
        4. Can round off numerals having up to four digits to the right of the decimal point.
    B. Fraction notation/decimal notation
        1. Can convert any decimal numeral of up to three places to fraction notation.
        2. Can convert any fraction to a decimal.
        3. Knows from memory basic fraction-decimal equivalences, for example, $\frac{1}{2} = .5$, $\frac{1}{4} = .25$, $\frac{1}{5} = .2$, and so on.
        4. Can use appropriate manipulative devices or pictures to demonstrate fraction-decimal equivalences.
    C. Addition
        1. Can represent the addition of decimals or mixed numerals with some type of manipulative device.
        2. Can find sums of decimals or mixed numerals with addends having up to three decimal places.
        3. Can estimate sums to a reasonable degree of accuracy.
    D. Subtraction
        1. Can represent the subtraction of decimals or mixed numerals with some type of manipulative device.
        2. Can find differences between any two decimals or mixed numerals having up to three decimal places.
        3. Can estimate differences to a reasonable degree of accuracy.
    E. Multiplication
        1. Can represent products of multiples of tenths with some type of manipulative device or picture.
        2. Can find products of factors having no more than three decimal places.
        3. Can estimate products with a reasonable degree of accuracy.
    F. Division
        1. Can represent the division of a whole number by tenths with some type of manipulative device or picture.
        2. Can find a quotient when the divisor is a mixed numeral or a decimal with no more than three digits in all and the dividend is a decimal or a mixed numeral with no more than five places in all.
        3. Can estimate quotients to a reasonable degree of accuracy.
III. Percent
    A. Basic concepts
        1. Understands that percent is another name for any fraction with 100 as the denominator.
        2. Can represent a given percent using an appropriative manipulative device or pictures.
        3. Knows that the symbol % is used as shorthand for the word *percent*.

Exhibit 5-1 continued

   4. Understands the meaning of such quantity designations as 112%, 230%, 7½%, .15%.
   5. Can write any percent as a fraction and vice versa.
   6. Can write any decimal as a percent and vice versa.
   7. Knows from memory such equivalences as ½ = 50%, ¼ = 25%, ⅓ = 33⅓%, and so on.
   B. Computations based on percent
      1. Given the sentence A% of B = C, can find C when A and B are known (can find a percent of a given number).
      2. Given the sentence A% of B = C, can find A when B and C are known (can find what percent one number is of another).
      3. Given the sentence A% of B = C, can find B when A and C are known (can find a number that a given number is a given percent of).
      4. Can apply above skills to problems calling for them.
IV. Scientific notation
   A. Given a number written in scientific notation, can rewrite the number in decimal notation.
   B. Given a number written in decimal notation, can rewrite the number in scientific notation.

Activities

The following activities are based on fractions seen as names for parts of continuous wholes.

1. A personal set of fractional parts of geometric regions, cut from construction paper, can be very helpful to the student. Figures 5-4 to 5-6 provide illustrations of how such sets can be made.

Below are some guidelines, gleaned from teachers' experiences, for obtaining maximum benefit from the sets of fraction pieces.

- Whenever possible, students should participate in the making of the sets. Most of the parts can be obtained by folding. Where folding is insufficient, the teacher can provide patterns.
- Most teachers prefer to work on one denominator at a time. That is, they begin by cutting out and discussing the unit, or 1. They move on to cutting out and examining the halves of the different shapes, and the fact that in the case of the square and the rectangle, halves can be easily represented in more than one way. They then proceed to thirds, fourths, and so on.
- All pieces should be labeled with the name of the fraction represented.
- Whenever possible, provide paper of different colors to represent successive fractions such as ⅕ and ⅙, and ⅑ and ¹⁄₁₀.
- From the beginning, develop the concept that every fraction has many names. Begin by noting that 1 can be named ²⁄₂, ³⁄₃; ½ can be named

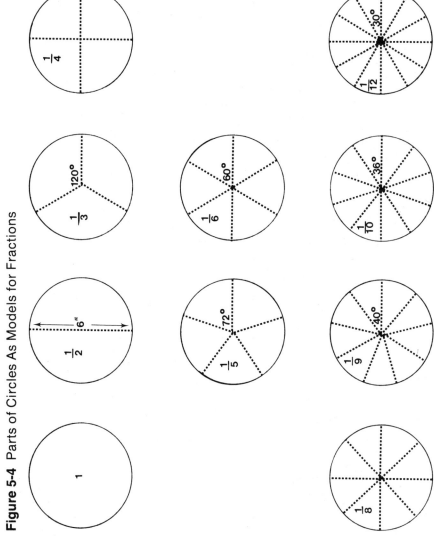

Figure 5-4 Parts of Circles As Models for Fractions

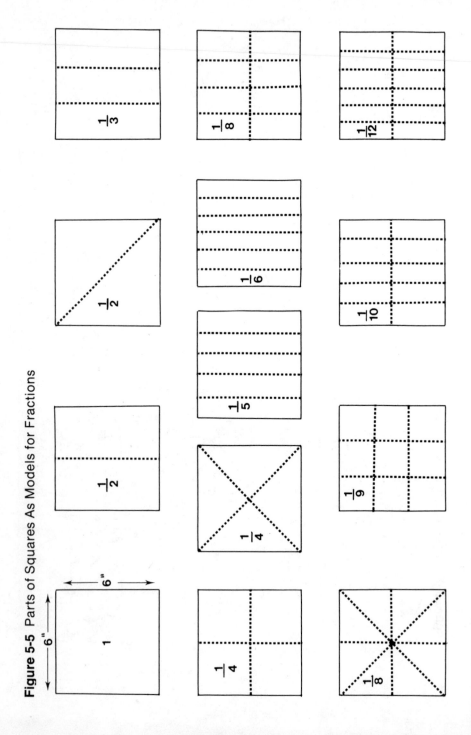

Figure 5-5 Parts of Squares As Models for Fractions

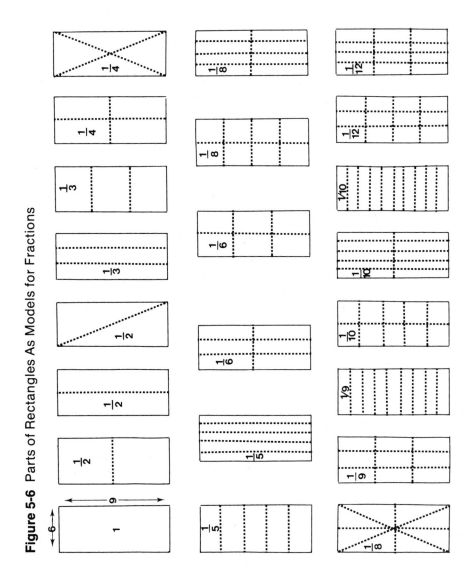

Figure 5-6 Parts of Rectangles As Models for Fractions

as ¼, ⅜, and so on. A record of the different names for a unit fraction (a fraction with 1 in the numerator) can be written on one side of the fraction pieces.

- Assign students to work with partners or in groups when the topic is improper fractions or mixed numerals.

- Building sets of fraction pieces take time, but teachers who have used this approach have found it a very effective way to build solid fraction concepts.

2. An alternative or supplement to sets of fraction pieces is illustrated in Figure 5-7.

Each 1″ x 12″ strip should be cut out and labeled with its fraction name. The student should also have a 1″x12″ strip of cardboard. Different fractions can be represented on each strip, as illustrated in Figure 5-8(a). Equivalent fractions can be examined by placing the appropriate strips so that one is below the other. See Figure 5-8(b).

3. Fractions are frequently depicted by a shaded area of a geometric figure. Van de Walle and Thompson (1980) suggested an alternative to such representation that is both efficient and, when properly interpreted, effective. The following is a modification of their approach.

Ten boxes, each partitioned into a different number of congruent parts, are illustrated in Figure 5-9. The boxes are arranged so that relationships between and among the different fractions can be observed and discussed. All ten boxes, each of length 6 cm and width 4 cm, can be easily drawn on an 8½″ x 11″ sheet of paper.

Each student should have a copy of such a reproduction and, if possible, a transparency identical to the paper copy. The only other material necessary is a supply of markers—small chips, dried kidney beans, or the like. By placing a marker in a part of a box, the student represents the shading of that area of the box.

The use of the markers is shown in Figure 5-10. The first row of the figure illustrates the representation of proper fractions. Although not necessary from a mathematical point of view, establishing rules for the placement of markers can be helpful to some learning-disabled students. That is, when a box is partitioned only in the vertical direction, markers should be placed from left to right. When a box is partitioned in the horizontal direction, markers should be placed from top to bottom. When a box is partitioned in both directions, either rule can prevail, but one should be agreed upon. Needless to say, all rules can be broken when the situation warrants, as in the case of the representation of ⁴⁄₆, which more clearly shows the relationship between ⁴⁄₆ and ⅔.

Figure 5-7 Paper Strips As Models for Fractions

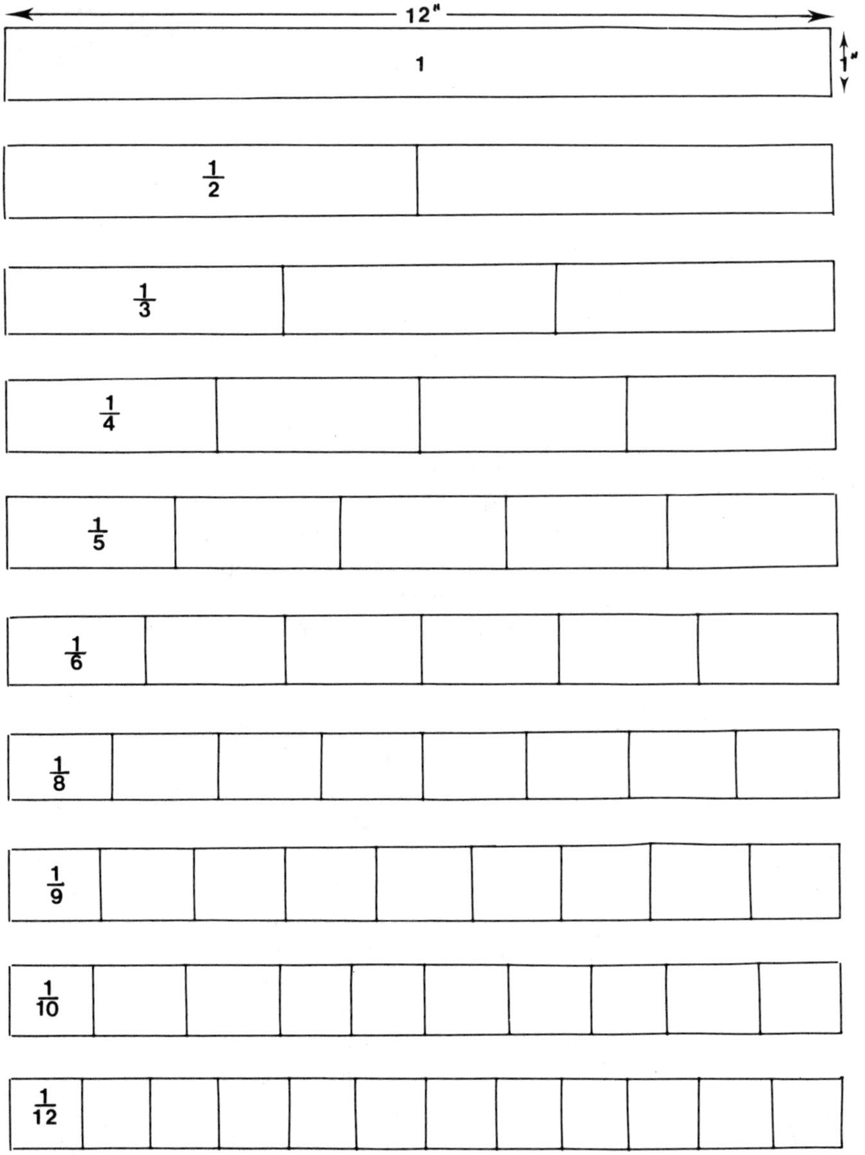

Figure 5-8 Using Paper Strips As Models for Fractions

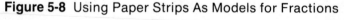

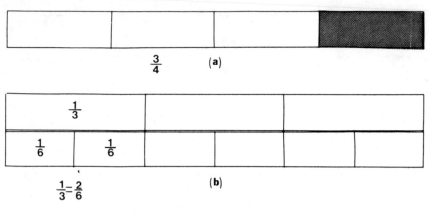

$$\frac{3}{4} \qquad \textbf{(a)}$$

$$\frac{1}{3} = \frac{2}{6} \qquad \qquad \textbf{(b)}$$

Improper fractions and mixed numerals are represented in Figure 5-10(b). One marker in each partition of a box means the unit is represented once; two markers in each partition indicates that the unit is represented twice, and so on. Left over markers represent the proper fraction portion of the mixed numeral. Some teachers fear that this representation might be confusing. In that case, more than one box of each type could be used just as well.

The use of the boxes and markers to represent pairs of equivalent fractions is illustrated in Figure 5-10(c). Transparencies can also be useful in this context. By superimposing the transparent boxes over the boxes drawn on paper, or on another transparency, families of equivalent fractions can be observed and discussed (see Van de Walle & Thompson, 1980). Note that a common denominator for a pair of fractions can be found by superimposing the boxes representing the denominators under consideration over other boxes until an appropriate match is found. For example, the *half* box and the *fifth* box can be superimposed on the *tenth* box, at the same time, with no extra lines showing. The *fourth* box and the *sixth* box can similarly be placed on the *twelfth* box.

Finally, although the topic is beyond the present discussion, the use of boxes to represent the addition of fractions with like denominators is shown in Figure 5-10(d). The procedure for representing the addition of fractions with unlike denominators is a bit more complicated, but with the basic concepts well developed through the use of the materials, many students can rely less on them, and move on to more symbolic and mechanical forms of computation, and they can do so with better understanding of the exercises and the results.

Figure 5-9 Fraction Boxes

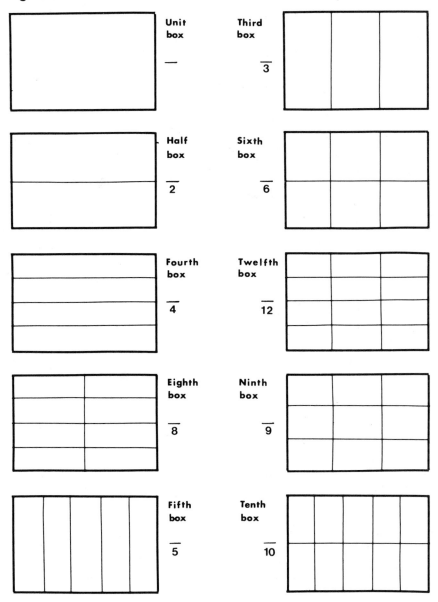

Figure 5-10 Using Fraction Boxes

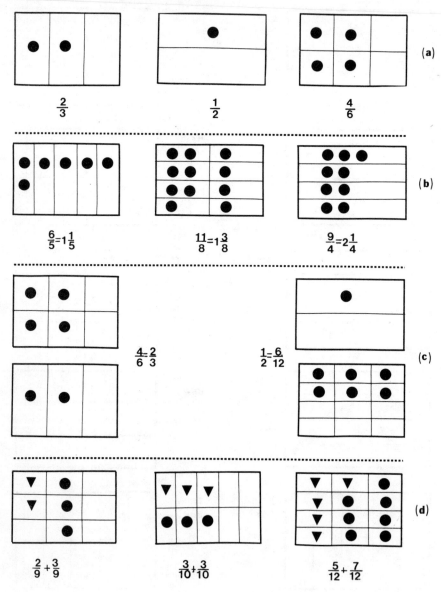

Fractions are also used to quantify parts of sets. "Seven out of ten people prefer Mrs. Antanoli's Salad Dressing." "Two-thirds of our employees have been with us for five years or more." "The horse came in a winner in eight out of his last eleven starts." This use of fractions is part of general conversation. Students should be familiar with the concepts being communicated.

As models of fractions, however, sets of discrete elements are quite limited in their capacity to represent improper fractions and mixed numerals. Further, while most students have no trouble representing or identifying one-fourth of a set of four, one-fourth of a set of eight, twelve, sixteen, and so on seems to be handled better through division of whole numbers. Although not impossible, to represent the addition of ½ and ¼ with sets requires a prior recognition of the equality between ½ and ²⁄₄. Hence, the use of sets to develop an understanding of the need to rename ½ and ²⁄₄ presents something of a dilemma in instructional sequencing. For all these reasons, students' experiences with sets and fractions should be limited to the representation of proper fractions by parts of sets and the development of familiarity with the use of language denoting parts of sets in everyday parlance.

Students can participate in a search for such uses of language in newspapers, advertisements, sports coverage, and the like. Each student must document each incident of fractions used to name parts of sets. These examples and the documentation can form the focus of a bulletin board display.

The move to represent fraction concepts through the use of the number line involves the corresponding greater use of symbols. Caution is necessary, then, to ensure that less abstract models have preceded the introduction to the number line representation. With such care taken, the number line can be used effectively to expand students' understanding of the basic fraction concepts.

As demonstrated by Figure 5-11, the number line can quite clearly portray sets of equivalent fractions. The use of different colors for each set emphasizes the equivalence relationship.

The number line can also be a useful tool for aiding students to properly sequence fractions. By writing fraction names below the number line and mixed numerals above the number line, the instructor can show the equality between improper fractions and mixed numerals. In addition to its value in teaching fractions, frequent reference to a number line can be very beneficial to the secondary school student in a college preparatory program, since the number line finds frequent use in algebra classes. Properly used, the number line can serve many purposes, and hence should be an integral part of a student's experience with fractions.

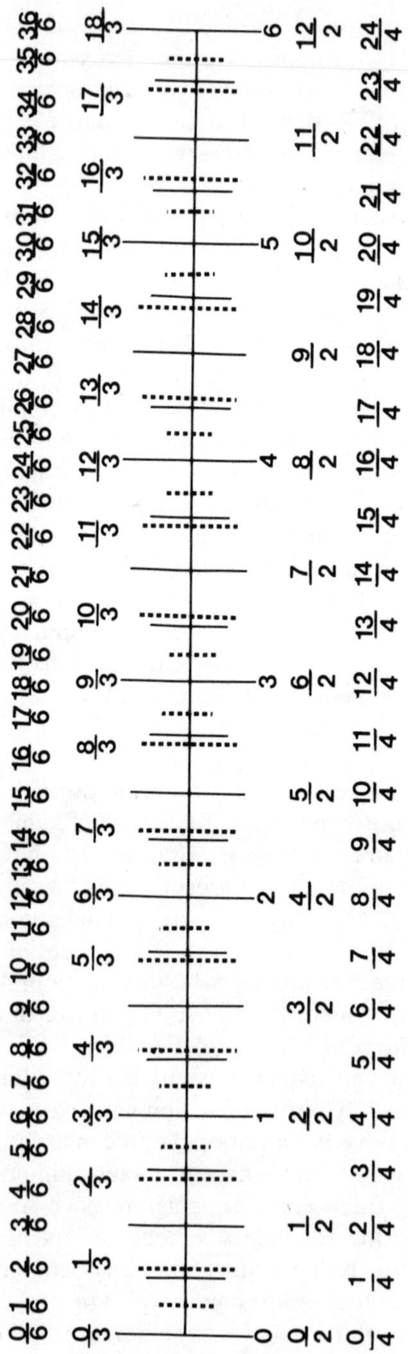

Figure 5-11 The Number line and Fractions

Adding and Subtracting Fractions

Figure 5-12 shows a sequence of instruction for developing competency in adding fractions. A similar sequence for subtraction is presented in Figure 5-13. It will be useful to work out each set of examples to determine the new behavior to be learned at each step.

The manipulatives and displays described in the preceding section can be used with the same facility and equally good results for demonstrating the concepts necessary for understanding the algorithms and notation employed in adding and subtracting fractions. For that reason we will concentrate here on the mechanics of computation.

Many students, when adding fractions, make the error of adding the denominators as well as the numerators. That error seems to stem from a lack of understanding that the denominator is nothing more than a label and must be treated as such. Good instruction in basic concepts will offset any tendency to treat denominators as addends; good remedial instruction will make use of models to correct misconceptions. When adding or subtracting fractions with like denominators, students can be encouraged to copy the denominator in the answer, *before* doing any computation at all. Some teachers preface instruction in adding fractions by a lesson or two in which fractions with nonsense denominators are used. They provide practice in using the denominators as labels only: one squiggle plus two squiggles equal three squiggles. Such a relatively simple strategy can do a great deal to prevent students from rehearsing inappropriate behaviors when the addition format is introduced.

The major challenge facing most students when adding or subtracting fractions is, of course, finding common denominators when necessary, and the lowest common denominator for purposes of efficiency. Most mathematics programs rely on the strategies outlined in Exhibit 5-2 and Exhibit 5-3. In Exhibit 5-2(a) the prime factors of the denominators are found, using a factor tree. Recall that a prime number is a whole number that has two and only two factors, itself and one. Exhibit 5-2(b) shows the staircase method for finding prime factors. This latter method has the advantage of a greater structure; the student always starts by trying 2 as a divisor and working up through the prime numbers until 1 appears at the top of the staircase. The lowest common denominator is found by taking each prime factor in the two sets the greatest number of times it appears in either set and finding the product of all the resulting prime factors (Exhibit 5-2(c)). The method can be used for any number of denominators.

In Exhibit 5-3, several consecutive nonzero multiples of each denominator are listed. The lists are then examined to determine if the same multiple shows up in both sets. The smallest of such common multiples is

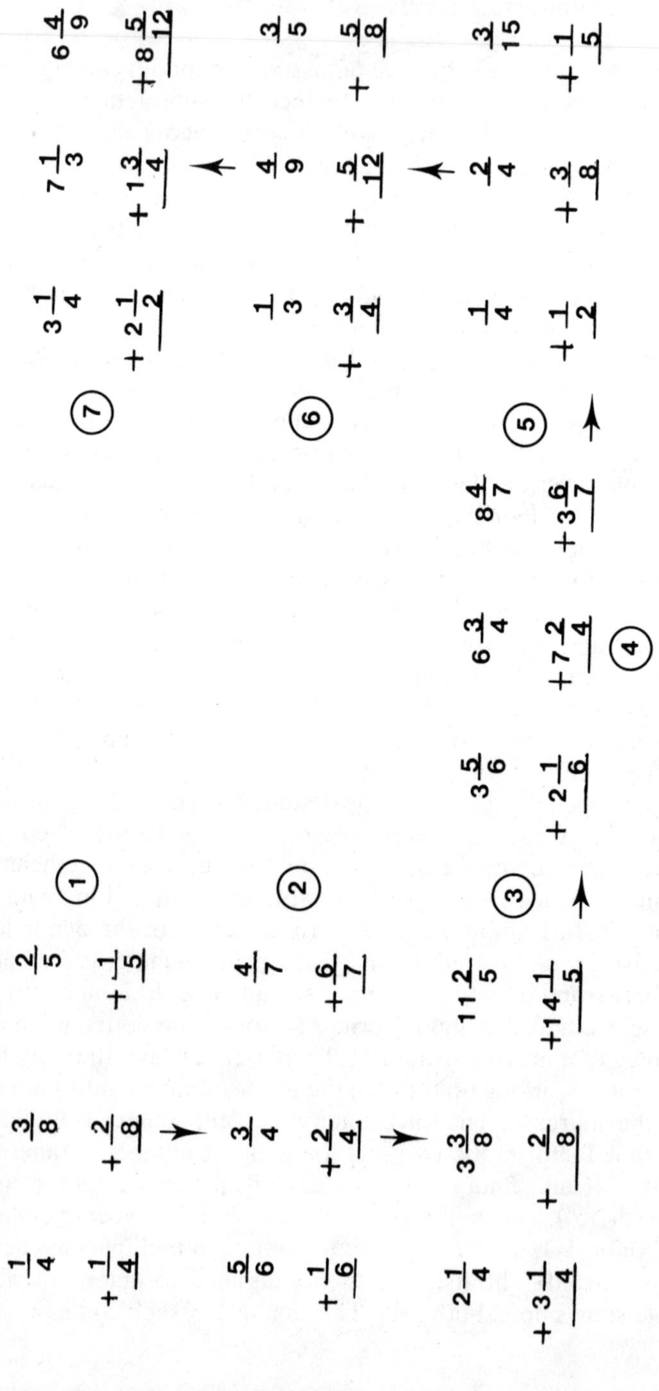

Figure 5-12 Scope and Sequence for Addition of Fractions

①
$$\frac{1}{4} + \frac{1}{4} \qquad \frac{3}{8} + \frac{2}{8} \longrightarrow \qquad \frac{2}{5} + \frac{1}{5}$$

②
$$\frac{5}{6} + \frac{1}{6} \qquad \frac{3}{4} + \frac{2}{4} \longrightarrow \qquad \frac{4}{7} + \frac{6}{7}$$

③
$$2\frac{1}{4} + 3\frac{1}{4} \qquad 3\frac{3}{8} + \frac{2}{8} \qquad 11\frac{2}{5} + 14\frac{1}{5}$$

④
$$3\frac{5}{6} + 2\frac{1}{6} \qquad 6\frac{3}{4} + 7\frac{2}{4} \qquad 8\frac{4}{7} + 3\frac{6}{7}$$

⑤
$$\frac{1}{4} + 1\frac{1}{2} \qquad \frac{2}{4} + 3\frac{3}{8} \qquad \frac{3}{15} + 1\frac{1}{5}$$

⑥
$$\frac{1}{3} + \frac{3}{4} \qquad \frac{4}{9} + \frac{5}{12} \qquad \frac{3}{5} + \frac{5}{8}$$

⑦
$$3\frac{1}{4} + 2\frac{1}{2} \qquad 7\frac{1}{3} + 1\frac{3}{4} \qquad 6\frac{4}{9} + 8\frac{5}{12}$$

Figure 5-13 Scope and Sequence for Subtraction of Fractions

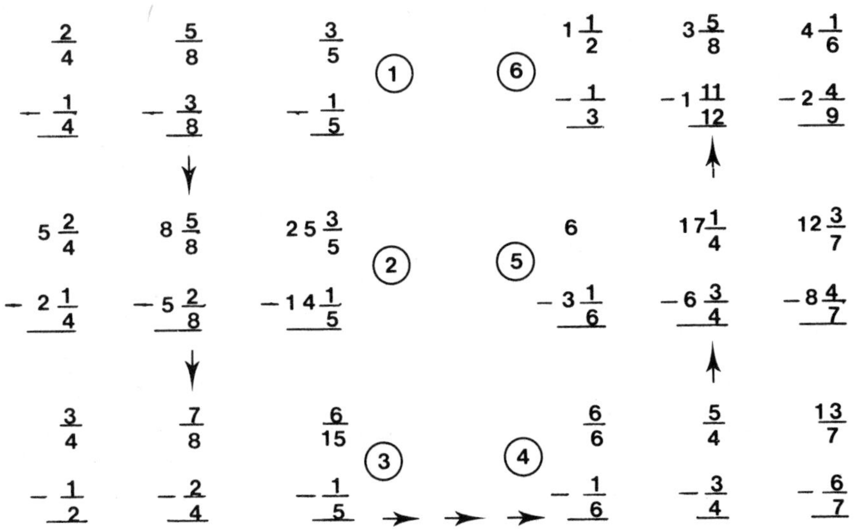

$$\frac{2}{4} \qquad \frac{5}{8} \qquad \frac{3}{5} \qquad ① \qquad ⑥ \qquad 1\frac{1}{2} \qquad 3\frac{5}{8} \qquad 4\frac{1}{6}$$
$$-\frac{1}{4} \qquad -\frac{3}{8} \qquad -\frac{1}{5} \qquad\qquad\qquad -\frac{1}{3} \qquad -1\frac{11}{12} \qquad -2\frac{4}{9}$$

$$5\frac{2}{4} \qquad 8\frac{5}{8} \qquad 25\frac{3}{5} \qquad ② \qquad ⑤ \qquad 6 \qquad 17\frac{1}{4} \qquad 12\frac{3}{7}$$
$$-2\frac{1}{4} \qquad -5\frac{2}{8} \qquad -14\frac{1}{5} \qquad\qquad\qquad -3\frac{1}{6} \qquad -6\frac{3}{4} \qquad -8\frac{4}{7}$$

$$\frac{3}{4} \qquad \frac{7}{8} \qquad \frac{6}{15} \qquad ③ \qquad ④ \qquad \frac{6}{6} \qquad \frac{5}{4} \qquad \frac{13}{7}$$
$$-\frac{1}{2} \qquad -\frac{2}{4} \qquad -\frac{1}{5} \qquad\qquad\qquad -\frac{1}{6} \qquad -\frac{3}{4} \qquad -\frac{6}{7}$$

the lowest common denominator. Once again, the method can be used for any number of denominators.

Some learning-disabled youngsters find trouble with both of the procedures described above. For some of these students the fraction bars described by Mercer and Mercer (1981) may provide assistance. Other students find the strategy outlined in Exhibit 5-4 helpful. A variation of the prime factorization process, the method of Exhibit 5-4 eliminates the need to examine separate sets of prime factors.

As illustrated, the student writes the denominators in question on a horizontal line. To the left the student draws a vertical line. The student examines the denominators to determine which is the smallest prime number to divide evenly into any one, some, or all of the denominators. That prime number is written to the left of the vertical line, and the quotient(s) of that prime number and the denominator(s) divisible by that prime number are written below the denominator(s). When division is not possible, the denominator is simply copied below itself. This procedure is continued until only ones are to be found written horizontally. The prime numbers written along the vertical line are the prime factors of the lowest common denominator. Study the examples given in Exhibit 5-4 and try the method for the denominators 8, 15, and 18. The lowest common denominator for those three numbers is 360.

Exhibit 5-2 Finding the LCD Using Prime Factorization

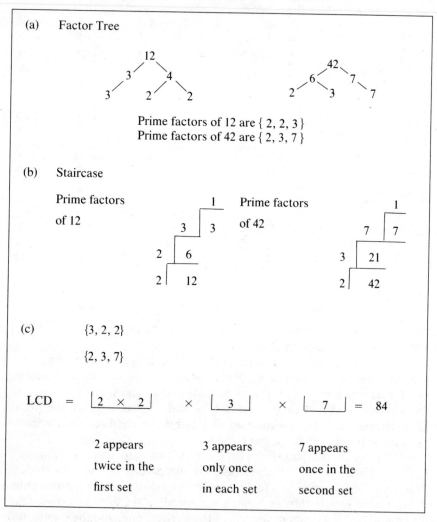

(a)   Factor Tree

Prime factors of 12 are { 2, 2, 3 }
Prime factors of 42 are { 2, 3, 7 }

(b)   Staircase

Prime factors of 12

Prime factors of 42

(c)   {3, 2, 2}

{2, 3, 7}

LCD = | 2 × 2 | × | 3 | × | 7 | = 84

2 appears twice in the first set

3 appears only once in each set

7 appears once in the second set

For all practical purposes, the denominators used in everyday life are limited to a very few, and the occasions on which we need to add fractions with unlike denominators are even fewer. For some students, then, the investment of a great deal of time in teaching methods for obtaining lowest common denominators will yield little interest, both actually and figuratively.

Exhibit 5-3 Finding the LCD Using Common Multiples

Problem: Find lowest common denominator for 12 and 42.
 Multiples of 12 are {12, 24, 36, 48, 60, 72, 84, 96 . . .}
 Multiples of 42 are {42, 84, 126, . . .}
 84 is the lowest common multiple, therefore the lowest common denominator.

Exhibit 5-4 Finding the LCD Using Prime Factors

Problem: Find lowest common denominator for 12 and 42.

		12	42
	2	6	21
	2	3	21
LCD = $2 \times 2 \times 3 \times 7 = 84$	3	1	7
	7	1	1

Problem: Find lowest common denominator for 4, 15, and 18.

		4	15	18
	2	2	15	9
	2	1	15	9
LDC = 180	3	1	5	3
	3	1	5	1
	5	1	1	1

There is nothing sacred about the lowest common denominator. Its use represents an effort toward efficiency, since the sum obtained will be in the simplest form, if the addends were originally in simplest form. A common denominator can always be obtained by finding the product of the denominators of the addends. For many students this method is preferable. In some cases, its use results in a sum not in simplest form. The student, then, when the context demands it, should rewrite the sum in the simplest form.

The learning-disabled student in a college preparatory program and the learning-disabled student in a vocational educational program, however, need to be able to add and subtract fractions with unlike denominators with fluency. The behaviors used to find lowest common denominators in algebra are like those described in this section. Their mastery will aid the transfer to the algebra context. Textbooks in carpentry, masonry, and electronics, to name but a few areas, abound with fractions and the operations on fractions. Students in these areas will miss the concepts involved if they get bogged down with the mechanics of the computation. As always, the educational plan of the individual student must guide the determination of which objectives are most valuable.

Multiplying Fractions

A sequence of instruction in multiplication of fractions is outlined in Figure 5-14.

The multiplication algorithm itself is perhaps the easiest to learn, and most students seem to master the skill. Few students, however, when requested to do so, can demonstrate with pictures or manipulatives the meaning of expressions such as $3 \times \frac{1}{2}$, $\frac{3}{4} \times 8$, $\frac{1}{3} \times \frac{1}{5}$, and many students are puzzled about the size of the product of $\frac{1}{2}$ and $\frac{1}{4}$ when viewed in relationship to the size of the two factors. In other words, most students do not understand what a multiplication expression means when one or both factors are fractions.

The pictures in Figure 5-15 illustrate the meaning of expressions like those mentioned above. Since the multiplication algorithm has little resem-

Figure 5-14 Scope and Sequence for Multiplication of Fractions

$$\text{(1)} \quad \frac{1}{3} \times \frac{1}{2} \qquad \frac{2}{5} \times \frac{3}{7} \qquad \frac{15}{3} \times \frac{1}{4}$$

$$\downarrow$$

$$\text{(2)} \quad 9 \times \frac{1}{2} \qquad 6 \times \frac{2}{3} \qquad 2 \times \frac{3}{8}$$

$$\downarrow$$

$$\text{(3)} \quad \frac{1}{2} \times 4 \qquad \frac{2}{3} \times 6 \qquad \frac{3}{5} \times 2$$

$$\downarrow$$

$$\text{(4)} \quad 2\frac{1}{2} \times \frac{2}{3} \qquad \frac{1}{2} \times 7\frac{3}{4} \qquad 9\frac{1}{3} \times \frac{3}{8}$$

$$\downarrow$$

$$\text{(5)} \quad 4\frac{1}{2} \times 2\frac{1}{4} \qquad 7\frac{1}{3} \times 3\frac{2}{5} \qquad 1\frac{1}{6} \times 4\frac{1}{3}$$

Figure 5-15 Representations of Multiplication Expressions

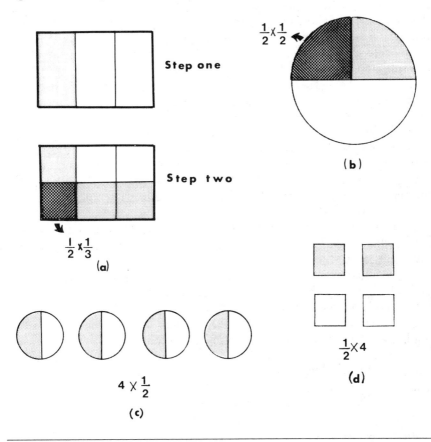

blance to what we would do physically to represent the multiplication of fractions, the algorithm cannot be presented as a shorthand way of writing down what we do. Rather it must be presented as a procedure that gives us the same results symbolically as we get when we perform the operation manipulatively. Hence, the algorithm must be preceded by many illustrations such as those presented in Figure 5-15.

The drawings portray for fractions the discussion of multiplication found in Chapter 4.

Dividing Fractions

Youngsters and adults alike find demonstrating the meaning of a division expression involving fractions quite difficult. If the material on division presented in Chapter 4 has been mastered, the representation becomes much simpler. The incomplete sentence $4 \div \frac{1}{2} = ?$ can be interpreted in the following way: "How many pieces $\frac{1}{2}$ of a unit in size can be found (or removed from) a 4 unit piece?" The corresponding multiplication incomplete sentence is $? \times \frac{1}{2} = 4$. Recall that we have here an example of measurement division. Likewise the incomplete sentence $\frac{1}{2} \div \frac{1}{3} = ?$ can be interpreted as "How many pieces $\frac{1}{3}$ of a unit in size can be removed from a piece that is $\frac{1}{2}$ of the same unit in size? The corresponding multiplication sentence is $? \times \frac{1}{3} = \frac{1}{2}$. Since $\frac{1}{3}$ is less than $\frac{1}{2}$, the answer will be 1 and a little more.

So far, so good. But what about the division expression $\frac{1}{3} \div \frac{1}{2}$? To be consistent, we must translate it as "How many pieces $\frac{1}{2}$ of a unit in size can be removed from a piece that is only $\frac{1}{3}$ of a unit in size?" A bit difficult to think about perhaps, but the answer must be less than one, since $\frac{1}{2}$ is greater than $\frac{1}{3}$.

Note that each of the examples given represents the type of division we have called measurement division. That is because in each case, partitive division becomes very contrived, if not meaningless altogether. However, if we look at the sentence $\frac{1}{2} \div 4 = ?$, an interpretation in the partitive division context becomes reasonable: How much would each person get if $\frac{1}{2}$ of a pie were to be divided among 4 people? In this case the number of sets is known, four, but the number in each set (the amount of pie) is not known. The corresponding multiplication sentence is $4 \times ? = \frac{1}{2}$.

Students should have experience with many examples like those given above before the division algorithm is introduced. Only then can they bring any degree of understanding to the symbolic representation.

The traditional algorithm for division is based on the "invert the divisor and multiply" rule. This procedure stems from the nature of division in mathematics as nothing more than multiplication of the dividend by the multiplicative inverse of the divisor. That is, $8 \div 2$ is actually $8 \times \frac{1}{2}$.

Unfortunately, most students learn the rule for dividing fractions before they develop an understanding of multiplicative inverses. For these students the rule becomes another entry into long-term memory storage, often without many cues to aid retrieval, in spite of the often elaborate procedures taken to justify the rule.

Recently, another approach has achieved some recognition. Recall that denominators play the role of labels. As such, they do not have much significance in a division expression such as $\frac{8}{3} \div \frac{2}{3}$. The expression has the same value as each of the following expressions: $8 \div 2$, $800 \div 200$, $80 \div 20$, $8{,}000{,}000 \div 2{,}000{,}000$, $.8 \div .2$. Hence, if we rewrite any division expression involving fractions so that each term has the same denominator, the denominators need no longer be considered. The quotient of the numerators is the answer to the original expression. Such is the rationale behind the algorithm presented in Figure 5-16. The algorithm lends itself to measurement, and where appropriate, partitive interpretations.

The algorithm merits consideration for at least three reasons. First, it is based on two skills students have already acquired: finding common denominators and dividing whole numbers. Second, once the two fractions in a division expression have been renamed in terms of a common denominator, representation of the division by way of manipulatives is somewhat more feasible. Third, the procedure can be transferred to division of algebraic fractions as easily as the invert and multiply rule. These three considerations offer a strong argument in favor of the less widely used algorithm. The sequence of instruction presented in Figure 5-17 reflects this algorithm.

Figure 5-16 Division Algorithm—Common Denominators

Example: $\dfrac{1}{2} \div \dfrac{1}{3}$

$= \dfrac{3}{6} \div \dfrac{2}{6}$

$= 3 \div 2$

$= 1\dfrac{1}{2}$

Example: $\dfrac{2}{3} \div 4$

$= \dfrac{2}{3} \div \dfrac{12}{3}$

$= 2 \div 12$

$= \dfrac{1}{6}$

Example: $3 \div \dfrac{3}{5}$

$= \dfrac{15}{5} \div \dfrac{3}{5}$

$= 15 \div 3$

$= 5$

Example: $4\dfrac{1}{2} \div 2\dfrac{3}{4}$

$= \dfrac{9}{2} \div \dfrac{11}{4}$

$= \dfrac{18}{4} \div \dfrac{11}{4}$

$= 18 \div 11$

$= 1\dfrac{7}{11}$

Figure 5-17 Scope and Sequence for Division of Fractions

① $\dfrac{3}{4} \div \dfrac{1}{4}$ $\dfrac{6}{9} \div \dfrac{3}{9}$ $\dfrac{8}{12} \div \dfrac{2}{12}$

② $\dfrac{1}{4} \div \dfrac{3}{4}$ $\dfrac{3}{9} \div \dfrac{6}{9}$ $\dfrac{2}{12} \div \dfrac{8}{12}$

③ $\dfrac{1}{2} \div \dfrac{3}{4}$ $\dfrac{5}{6} \div \dfrac{4}{9}$ $\dfrac{3}{5} \div \dfrac{4}{3}$

④ $4 \div \dfrac{5}{6}$ $\dfrac{9}{10} \div 3$ $7 \div \dfrac{5}{7}$

⑤ $3\dfrac{1}{3} \div 4\dfrac{1}{3}$ $7 \div 3\dfrac{1}{2}$ $4\dfrac{1}{3} \div 3\dfrac{1}{2}$

DECIMALS

Basic Concepts

Most students are introduced to decimals by way of fractions. Decimals are presented as a special notation for fractions with denominators that are powers of ten. In such a context, the types of manipulatives and displays suggested for teaching the basic concepts of fractions are quite suitable for decimals. The use of such materials will also help to familiarize students with the common fraction-decimal equivalences quite early in their experience with decimals.

Since the basic concepts of decimals flow from an understanding of fractions, decimal notation forms the bulk of new learning. To develop competence in the use of decimal notation, activities like the following can be helpful.

Activities

1. Make available representations of units, tenths, and hundredths like those illustrated in Figure 5-18.

Dictate or present in written form numbers such as five, two tenths, three hundredths, thirty-six hundredths. Ask the students to use the materials to represent each number in the most economical way. If necessary, point out the relationship between thirty hundredths and three tenths.

2. Display a chart like that illustrated in Figure 5-19. Explain that the decimal point serves to locate units or ones place. Once we know which digit is in ones place, tens and tenths are on either side of it, hundreds and hundredths border tens and tenths, and so on.

List a sequence of numbers on the board, for example, 247925. Place the decimal point thus: 2479.25. Ask the students to name the digit in ones place, tens place, tenths place, and so on. Erase the decimal point and write it elsewhere. Repeat the exercise. Note: The use of the decimal point to locate the unit is a strategy we frequently observe. If the penny is the unit, then thirty-seven cents is written 37¢, with the decimal point understood as being to the right of the 7. However, if the dollar is the unit, thirty-seven cents becomes $.37. Likewise, if the dollar is the unit, the national debt might look something like $2,220,330,472,625. However, if a trillion dollars becomes the unit, then the national debt is expressed as $2.2 trillion.

Figure 5-18 Decimal Representations

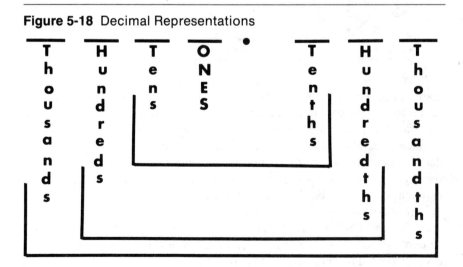

Figure 5-19 Decimal Places and Labels

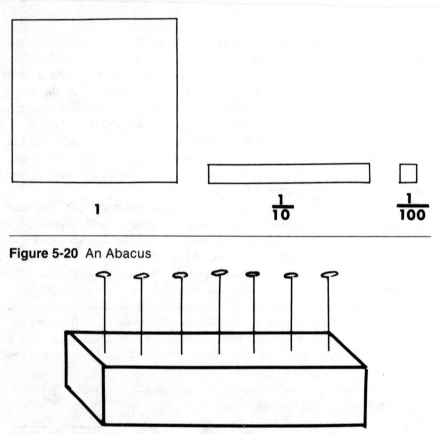

Figure 5-20 An Abacus

3. A simple abacus can be made by placing dowels of the appropriate diameter into the edge row of holes on a peg board, or by driving a row of seven four-inch nails into a narrow strip of plywood or a two-by-four, as illustrated in Figure 5-20. Life savers or washers make good counters.

Place a number of counters on each nail. Place a dot representing a decimal point between any two of the four nails on the right-hand side of the abacus. Ask the students to name the value of the number represented on each nail of the abacus, beginning with units place. Move the decimal point to another position. Repeat the question.

Activities like those listed above can also be helpful when introducing students to decimal notation before formal work with fractions has been encountered. The decimal point is presented as the marker for units place.

The name (label) we use for the digit to the right of the decimal point is tenths. The label for the digit two places to the right of the decimal point is hundredths, and so on. Ten hundredths equal one tenth; ten tenths equal one unit. By convention we use the word *and* when reading decimal numbers aloud to alert the listener to the position of the decimal point, and hence, to the position of the unit. The basic rule governing our base ten number system is maintained. Reference to the parts of the whole can be avoided.

Reading and Writing Decimals

Many students experience trouble with reading and writing decimal fractions. When we listen to the names of whole numbers, we wait for the first group name (millions, thousands, ones (usually unspoken))to determine how long the number will be. When listening to the decimal portion of a number, we must do the same. Students must learn to hold the number in memory until the label has been added. For some learning-disabled students this can be troublesome. One solution is to teach the student the following association: tenths .__; hundredths .__ __; thousandths .__ __ __. The student listens to the number being dictated and writes it down as he or she hears it. The student then listens for the label and beginning from the right of the number written down, he or she writes the number of dashes that corresponds to the label, one under each digit that has been written. If there is a dash with no digit, a zero is written above that dash. Finally, a decimal point is placed to the left of the dashes. An actual sequence might look like the following:

Teacher says	Student writes
"Thirty six	36
thou-	.036
sandths"	

The process works in reverse when the student reads decimal fractions. The student reads the number named by the digits, and then counts the number of (invisible) dashes before adding the label.

There are many suggestions for other strategies for teaching decimal notation in any collection of issues of *The Arithmetic Teacher,* a journal published by the National Council of Teachers of Mathematics.

Operations with Decimals

Students with a good understanding of place value who have mastered an addition algorithm and a subtraction algorithm seldom have trouble adding or subtracting decimal fractions. Since we add only like powers of ten, students need to be reminded to line up the addends so that each column contains only like powers of ten. This is most easily accomplished, of course, by writing the addends so that the decimal points fall one under the other.

Most youngsters have little difficulty learning and remembering the rule for placing the decimal point in the product of two factors that are decimal fractions. The reason for the rule can be demonstrated by representing products as illustrated in Figure 5-21. Students can then be asked to draw representations of other products.

The conventional division algorithm, when used in examples where the dividend is a decimal fraction, actually makes use of the common denominator algorithm for division with fractions. Hence $.5\overline{)4}$ is treated as $4 \div \frac{5}{10} = \frac{40}{10} \div \frac{5}{10} = 40 \div 5 = 5\overline{)40}$. The example is easily illustrated by dividing four strips of paper of equal length into ten units apiece, and counting the number of groups of five in the entire collection. The process is usually referred to as "moving the decimal point." Students who have mastered the conventional algorithm need only apply this new rule when the divisor is a decimal fraction.

Students who have learned division as a process of repeated subtraction (see Figure 4-16) can use the method with or without moving the decimal, as demonstrated in Figure 5-22. Because of the amount of work involved, these students may prefer to use a calculator or master the conventional algorithm.

Figure 5-21 Model for Representing Multiplication with Decimals

.1

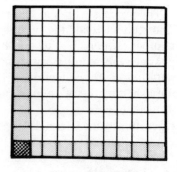

.1×.1= .01

Figure 5-22 Repeated Subtraction When the Divisor Is a Decimal

$$
.36\overline{\smash{)}720} \quad \begin{array}{r} 2000 \\ \hline \end{array}
$$

```
        2000
.3 6) 720          .36×10     = 3,6
     −720          .36×100    = 36
        0          .36×1000   = 360
                   .36×2000   = 720
```

PERCENTAGES

The word "percent" or its symbol % is one that we encounter nearly every day. An understanding of the concept is imperative if students are to function well as consumers in our society. Yet many students, and adults as well, find percent a difficult topic.

Percent is simply another name for a fraction with 100 in the denominator. An introduction to percent can be facilitated through activities like the following.

Activities

1. Duplicate copies of a worksheet like the one shown in Figure 5-23. The students are to write both the fraction and the percent describing the portion of each grid that is occupied by shapes of one kind or another.

2. Provide each student with a sheet of graph paper. Show the students how to draw squares of 100 units each on the paper. Write several percents on the chalkboard. Ask the students to shade in a portion of a grid to correspond to each percent on the board. Also ask the students to write under each grid the correct sentence equating the percent with a fraction the denominator of which is 100, and the correct decimal fraction.

3. Provide each student with a list of sentences mentioning the word "percent," culled from science books, advertising circulars, newspapers, or other reading matter. Example: ". . . iron meteorites are 10 percent nickel and 1 or 2 percent cobalt. . . ." (Asimov, 1981, p. 125) Distribute graph paper on which 100-square grids are drawn. Ask the students to illustrate each sentence on a 100-unit grid. For the example given above, the student would think of the grid as a meteorite, shade in 10 square units to represent nickel, and shade with another color 1 or 2 square units to represent the cobalt.

4. Distribute graph paper as described in the two previous activities. Ask the students to shade in one-half of one of the 100-unit squares. Then

Figure 5-23 Representations of Percent

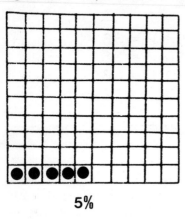

5%

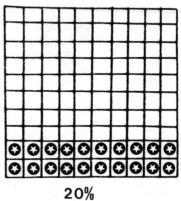

20%

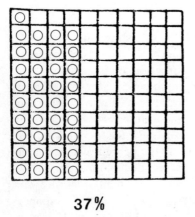

37%

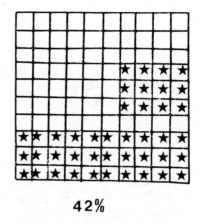

42%

ask the students to count the number of units shaded and to write ½ as a percent and as a decimal fraction. Repeat for other common fractions.

Many activities like those described above are necessary if students are to develop a firm understanding of percent. Until such a foundation has been laid, few, if any, youngsters can begin to grapple with computing answers to problems involving percent. When such problems are introduced, the encounter should take place in as concrete a manner as possible, using 100-unit squares as a help in translating the words of the problem into percent expressions.

As with the other topics, there is an abundance of material in this area in *The Arithmetic Teacher*.

SUMMARY

The preceding discussion has provided a survey of content in the areas of fractions, decimals, and percent. The suggested teaching activities are designed to help students achieve an understanding of the material, as well as master the concomitant skills. The large proportion devoted to fractions reflects the conviction, based on experience, that time spent in developing a firm grasp of fractions bears fruit during later experiences with decimals and percent. For learning-disabled adolescents, as for all students, mastery in these areas is most important, if students are to progress in mathematics.

REFERENCES

Asimov, I. (1981). *Change! Seventy-one glimpses of the future.* Boston: Houghton Mifflin.

Menninger, K. (1969). *Number words and number symbols.* Cambridge, MA: M.I.T. Press.

Mercer, C.D., & Mercer, A.R. (1981). *Teaching students with learning problems.* Columbus, OH: Charles E. Merrill.

Van de Walle, J., & Thompson, C.A. (1980). Let's do it. Fractions with counters. *The Arithmetic Teacher, 28*(2), 6–11.

Chapter 6

Geometry Concepts and Skills

Robert A. Shaw

Geometry has been in the secondary school mathematics curriculum for many years and it continues to receive emphasis. In a 1981 publication of the National Council of Teachers of Mathematics (NCTM), *Priorities in School Mathematics,* four goals for geometry received over 80 percent support in the preference survey: (1) to develop logical thinking ability, (2) to develop spatial intuitions, (3) to acquire the knowledge for further study, and (4) to learn to read and interpret mathematical arguments. Strong support was given to the inclusion of three geometric topics in the secondary school curriculum for *all* students: (1) properties of triangles and rectangles (94 percent), (2) properties of circles (84 percent), and (3) similar figures (85 percent). In terms of developing new curriculum materials 47 percent of the individuals surveyed stated that adequate materials for geometry already exist. Assuming that this conclusion is true, then what remains is to adapt the content, strategies, and methods to serve the needs of learning-disabled individuals; that is the purpose for this chapter.

GEOMETRY—OPTIONS AND STRUCTURE

It should be noted that the "standard" plane geometry of the secondary school is basically Euclidean geometry and that Euclidean geometry is one of the several geometries. This geometry is one of the most restrictive geometries in that precise relationships and measurements are determined within the confines of a plane (within two dimensions—on a flat surface). The position of Euclidean geometry in a hierarchy of geometries was best described by Meserve (1967) and is represented in Figure 6-1.

From Figure 6-1 we can see that in school mathematics we move into other geometries as we study properties of similar figures (similarities), vanishing points and perspective drawing (projective), or a globe (spheri-

151

Figure 6-1 From Topology to Euclidean Geometry

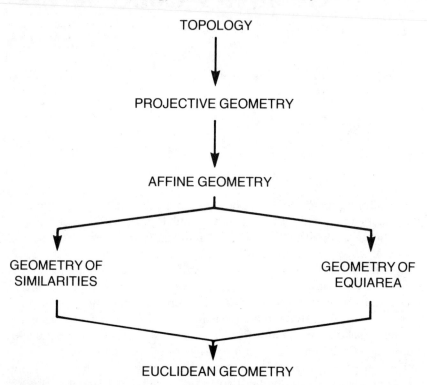

cal). The early elementary school child's geometric experiences are in the area of topology as he or she is led to understand such concepts as *open* and *closed*. From grades 1 through 8 or 9 we foreshadow the organization and structure of the geometries. It is well to keep in mind Meserve's statement: "Awareness that many geometries exist underlies the genuine understanding of any geometry" (p. 2).

The Report of the Commission on Mathematics of the College Entrance Examination Board, *Program for College Preparatory Mathematics* (1959), served to define a sequence for secondary school geometry that is still relevant today. The report contains descriptions of six units: (1) informal geometry, to serve as a connecting link between junior high or middle school geometry and the secondary program, (2) deductive reasoning, to introduce the idea of proof, (3) sequence of theorems culminating in the Pythagorean Theorem, (4) coordinate geometry, (5) additional theorems and originals to include circles, and (6) solid geometry (which serves an enrichment function in most cases). We will use part of this organizational pattern in discussing the geometric concepts and skills of this chapter.

EXPECTED PERFORMANCE OF LEARNERS

When learners enroll in a geometry course at the secondary level, it is assumed or determined that they have had success in learning the fundamentals of arithmetic and (in most cases) algebra. They are expected to function in the "formal operations" stage of cognitive development and to (1) read and develop an understanding of the concepts that are presented within the textbook for the course, (2) listen to the presentation of the instructor, take notes, participate in class, and do assignments successfully, (3) organize the concepts into meaningful relationships and generalizations, and (4) study and demonstrate knowledge and skills in an oral and written manner. The skills of listening, reading, studying, thinking, drawing diagrams, speaking, and writing become essential for the development of an understanding of geometry and to demonstrate to instructors that the understanding is present.

These are skills essentially defined in Public Law 94-142 and represent the areas where disorders begin to appear in individuals who are classified as learning disabled. Since each skill is a processing skill of either inputting, using, or outputting information, the instructional strategy appears to be one of providing alternative ways for giving information to the learners and preparing for alternative responses.

Instructors of geometry cannot expect an individual with a learning disability to perform in the same manner as everyone else or even in a manner like another individual who has a different learning disability. On the other hand, they cannot lower their expectations of final achievement for learning-disabled individuals. Under these circumstances we have two premises: (1) a learning disability is independent of intelligence and (2) since a learning disability may be incurable, we must help the learners to develop compensating skills.

Only after instructors have (1) acquired an awareness of specific learning disabilities in such areas as attention disturbances, figure-ground pathodology, dissociation, memory dysfunction, sequencing, discrimination, spatial disorientation, (2) participated in formal and informal assessment/ evaluation procedures, and (3) learned of the different content strategies and methods will they be able to help learners develop compensating skills. Since it is impossible to develop a mathematics program with all possible strategies built in, the instructor must assume the responsibility of trying to obtain the optimal match among content, strategies, methods, and the abilities of the learners. Emphasis must be placed on success.

SOME GENERAL GUIDELINES

Getting started in the approach to working with learning-disabled learners is often difficult as we must plan ahead so that any teaching and learning situation will contain no (or very few) surprises for either the learner or the teacher. Cohen (1979) gave a helpful list that can be adapted to the secondary school situation. Using Cohen's list the following guideline was produced:

1. Structure the units of work and the class presentations.
   - Develop objectives, content overviews, and reviews, so that you may present them in both oral and written form.
   - Develop brief and specific sets of directions for homework and assessment situations.
   - Organize presentations so that only a small amount of material is before a given learner at a given time. Consider alternative courses of action.

2. Demonstrate, discuss, and summarize content topics.
   - Use objects and models to simplify and explain a given concept.
   - Give the learner prepared notes or outlines of the material.
   - Keep your pace at an appropriate rate and your voice at a moderate even rate and level.
   - Use praise and give credit for what has been successfully completed.
   - Allow the learners to work at a comfortable pace.
   - Help the learners to think about the content and get started on assignments.

3. Provide alternatives.
   - Allow learners to present homework and take tests orally.
   - Simplify worksheets.
   - Use a mask to cover material that is not being used on a given page.
   - Allow learners to work alone or in groups, whatever way is most productive for the learners.
   - Provide feedback as soon as possible.

ADAPTING GEOMETRY TO MEET THE NEEDS OF LEARNING-DISABLED STUDENTS

Following the outline set forth by the CEEB Commission on Mathematics (1959), the first unit of secondary school geometry should be concerned with informal geometry—that geometry that has already become a part of a learner's experience. This geometry deals with points, lines, line segments, angles, polygons and their relationships. Geometry of this form is sets of points. Prerequisite concepts for this beginning include geometric vocabulary and concepts of relative position, relative size, patterns, and open and closed paths.

If the development of content in geometry has been followed since the time the youngster entered school, such concepts as open and closed paths should be familiar to them (as early as kindergarten); however, this development may have been delayed because of poor sequence in geometric content and activities, some disability on the part of the learner, or the absence of such material in the program. Whatever the reason an instructor should determine where the learners are in the development and continue from this point. Some tenth-grade learners may not have these concepts of open and closed and thus should be given an introduction.

While geometric ideas of the elementary school were developed in a deductive manner—from general three-dimensional figure to specific details—the ideas of the secondary program should be developed inductively—from specific ideas to general concept—with formal proofs still in the deductive framework. While this general plan will govern the development, we should not fail to use realistic situations whenever possible.

To illustrate what is meant by the preceding material of this chapter, sample lessons with annotations will be presented. The purposes of these lessons are to (1) illustrate various strategies and methods of instruction, (2) demonstrate that the type of lesson depends, to a large degree, on the material to be presented and the types of learners, and (3) tell how the learners may be led toward involvement in the many different types of instructional approaches. The dashed lines are used to set off individual frames that we might present to the learners at any one time. If they are not separated, then a mask should be used for parts not being discussed at a given time. Selected answers are given with the lessons to assist the instructor.

AN INTRODUCTORY LESSON

Lesson Overview

Lesson I is an example of a lecture-discussion lesson that might be used to introduce a unit or a course in geometry. The programmed format will serve as a guide to the teacher in conducting the lesson and as the text material for a student. It could also be used independently by a learner who misses the presentation. Instructions in brackets are for the student using the material by himself or herself.

Some general instructional objectives for this lesson are

1. To introduce the students to the kind of thinking involved in studying geometry
2. To explore the geometric background that each student possesses
3. To set the pace for the study of geometry

Some performance objectives sought in this lesson are that the students should be able to

1. Tell why point, line, and plane are accepted as undefined terms in geometry.
2. Outline some basic relationships between points, lines, and planes, such as
   a. Two points determine a line.
   b. Through one point an infinite number of lines may pass.

Exploration and a Review

To begin this course let's imagine a situation. Suppose that you are in a boat on the middle of a lake during a moon- and starlit night. As you look into the sky several different views appear: stars, some small and some large; a full moon; and a shooting star.

The next day you meet a friend. You want to tell him or her about what you saw. Without thinking, your mind *tries* to *see* the sights of the night. A mental picture is formed. Your immediate problem becomes one of describing this picture to your friend. How would you do it? [Outline an approach in the space below or think of what you will tell your friend.]

In some manner you tried to tell him or her about the picture that you saw in your mind. You probably thought that if you had a sheet of paper, this would help you in your explanation. What might you draw? [Explain by a diagram.]

O   .   *   *   *
          .   *
                    *
                      .
               *   .

Would your diagram be more accurate than your ideas?
___ Yes ✓ No. Why? _The diagram is only a_
representation of your ideas.

At this point your friend might begin to create his or her own mental picture. Would it be the *same* as your mental picture? Why? or Why not?

No, because we form mental pictures with different
backgrounds and experiences.

Now, can you tell what we have just outlined?
[See information below.]

To help you, we have used a process of thinking called *association*. From the scene of real objects, the stars and the moon, you developed a mental picture. You attempted to relate this picture by a *verbal description*, and perhaps, to assist you, you made a *diagram* using certain symbols to stand for the moon and the stars.

Someone might say that *dots* were used to represent stars; that a *circle* was used to represent the moon; and a *line* to represent the "shooting star."

Suppose that a certain group of stars was present, for example, the constellation that most people know as the "big dipper." How can you tell one star from another in the "big dipper?"
[See information below.]

The "big dipper" consists of seven distinct stars, each in a certain position relative to the others; therefore, we distinguish each star by its relative position.

You have used points (or dots) to represent the stars. Are these points the same size? _No_ Are the stars the same size? _No_. In all probability no two stars and no two points are the same size; we can't tell. Since a point is a symbol for some object, and only the relative position is important, the size is not that important. As a concluding statement one can say that a point has neither length, width, nor depth—a point is not measured.

Diagrams are very helpful, but we should realize that they are only diagrams and not the real objects they represent. Let's look at a possible diagram that you might have drawn.

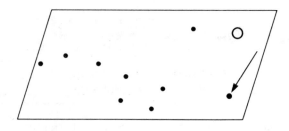

What kind of symbols were used? __*Points*__

Points are distinguished by their positions.

The stars can be called points (or dots) of light in the sky with each one being located by its *relative position* to one basic star, the North Star. If you know, tell how you can locate the North Star.

_____*[See information in Diagram 2]*_____

Perhaps the diagram that follows will help you.

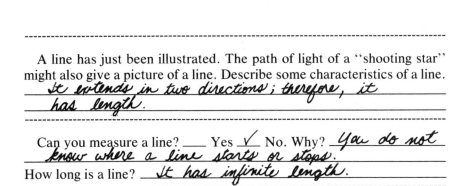

A line has just been illustrated. The path of light of a "shooting star" might also give a picture of a line. Describe some characteristics of a line.

It extends in two directions; therefore, it has length.

Can you measure a line? ___ Yes _✓_ No. Why? *You do not know where a line starts or stops.*

How long is a line? *It has infinite length.*

A line is also a symbol for an idea. You *cannot* measure a line since you cannot identify the beginning or the end of a line. The symbol for a line on a sheet of paper is only a partial symbol.

Lines and points are *undefined* terms since we make no attempt to define them. They are only described by position and relationships.

Use the space below to describe some possible relationships between points, between lines, and between points and lines.

[See information below.]

A possible list might be:

Two points determine a line.

There are points on the same line (collinear points) and points not on the same line (noncollinear points).

Lines can be parallel (they never meet) or intersect (cross over each other in a plane).

What is a plane? __*A flat surface*__

Is plane an undefined term also? __✓__ Yes ___ No.
Why? __*We describe condition for a plane but we cannot measure a plane.*__

An equivalent symbol for a plane might be a flat surface. Again we describe but don't define. Plane geometry is concerned with points, lines, and relationships within a plane.

The diagram of the sky represented a plane; therefore, from this small beginning will evolve a course in plane geometry. You will be asked to describe, associate, define, distinguish, and prove geometric conditions and relationships. Diagrams will be your ally.

To begin thinking geometrically state at least six specific relationships of points, lines, and planes and draw a diagram to illustrate. The following is one example.

Diagram 3 illustrates that the intersection of two lines is at most one point. Lines l_1 and l_2

Plane U

or

Discussion of the Lesson

As stated in the overview of the lesson one purpose was to explore the geometric background of the learners. Using a lesson model such as this one an instructor can assess the most favorable functioning mode of the learners. Does each learner respond to *verbal* input, *symbolic* or *graphic* input, *written* material, or some combination of these input modalities? Is each learner able to respond verbally, draw diagrams, and write explanations? From such lessons as this we gain information that will enable us to plan other lessons.

POINTS, LINES, AND PLANES

All geometric figures are sets of points and all geometric figures are subsets of a plane in Euclidean geometry. We do not measure points, or lines, or planes, but specific subsets made from these sets of points (for example, a line segment). We need at least two points in order to discuss specific relationships. Two points exist in relative position to each other. The beginning vocabulary of geometry can be reviewed by using two models (for example, golf balls) for points and placing one to the right of, over, beside, north of, etc., to demonstrate relative position. Such an activity can be demonstrated using an overhead projector. With this step the objects become restricted to a plane (the screen) and you have a natural step to move to the pictorial mode.

Using pencils we can describe portions of lines and how the lines can relate to one another in a plane. The lines can be either parallel or intersecting. The intersection contains at most one point, but many lines may pass through the same point. Toothpicks in a Styrofoam ball can serve as a model for this discussion.

The first general truth (axiom) that we should develop for the learners is that *every line contains at least two distinct points*. The line should be a *straight* line. Also, any two points determine a line. We should develop models for all situations that we describe and, after the learners are able to verbally describe the situation and give a real-world example (for example, as the corners of a room serve to define a portion of a line where two walls meet), we should introduce the symbol for a line ($\leftrightarrow$). This general approach from modeling to symbolizing should continue for parallel lines, intersecting lines, line segments, and rays. Line segments are essential for introducing polygons and measurement and rays play a major role in angle development.

The concept of betweenness serves to introduce a line segment since a line segment is defined as two end points and all points between these two end points that are on the same straight line. From this distinction we define collinear sets of points (points that are on the same line) and non-collinear points.

Other concepts that can be modeled are that points separate a line into three parts—the two half lines and the point—and a line separates a plane into three parts—two half planes and the line. These are essential if we plan to discuss interiors of angles and polygons in the geometric development.

By introducing axioms and theorems that learners can discuss into the geometric development we contribute to an introduction to proof. A key idea to remember is that the learners must be able to *see* the relationships and theorems being developed.

MEASUREMENT: THE CONNECTING LINK

While measurement is the topic of the next chapter, we must include it in this chapter so that the concept of congruence may be introduced. Another example lesson should serve to make the connection.

MEASURES OF SEGMENTS

Lesson Overview

Lesson II is an example of a guided-discovery lesson that might be used to introduce a student to formal measurement in geometry and to an approach to axiom development. The format used is a narrative, which will serve as a guide to the sequence of the lesson. The sequence is very important in a guided-discovery approach.

Some instructional objectives for this lesson are

1. To introduce the students to a more formal type of geometry than was previously introduced
2. To introduce the students to the discovery approach to learning
3. To encourage the students to use self-initiated discovery with new situations.

Some performance objectives for this lesson are that the student should be able to

1. Develop the additive property of measures
2. Distinguish between segment (a set of points) and the measure of a segment (a numerical value)

I am giving you a sheet of paper with symbols of line segments drawn to some particular scale. Note line segments of lengths a, b, and c.

	$m(\overleftrightarrow{XY})$	$m(\overleftrightarrow{YZ})$	$m(\overleftrightarrow{XZ})$
M_a	$\approx 3\frac{5}{6}$ $\approx 3.83\overline{3}$	$\approx 5\frac{3}{4}$ ≈ 5.750	$\approx 9\frac{7}{12}$ ≈ 9.583
M_b	6.50	9.75	16.25
M_c	2.0	3.0	5.0
M_d	1.0	1.5	2.5

$\approx$ approximately

Use the line segment of length "a" to construct along one edge of a sheet of paper a scale marked in a-units.

Procedure:
1. Draw a line segment (with a ruler) along the bottom edge of the paper and locate some point near the left end.
   (NOTE: If some learners have difficulty here, give them a prepared sheet. Perhaps different levels of completeness should be available.)

2. Take a compass and use it as a divider by placing the point on one end of the line segment of length "a" and the pencil point on the other end.

3. Using this length "a" construct a scale marked in a-units on the line segment on the paper.
   (Demonstrate on chalkboard.)

4. Number the marks beginning with "zero" with the first one on the left, "one" for the second one, etc.

Questions? (Check to see if everyone understands.)

Turn the paper to another edge and use length "b" to construct a scale marked in b-units.

On another edge do the same thing with length "c."

On the fourth edge construct a scale using a length that you make up. Call this a scale marked in d-units.
(Make sure that everyone is at the same point, with four scales, one on each edge of the paper.)
(NOTE: Do what is necessary—even providing a complete sheet—to get the learners to this point.)

Everyone should have four scales each beginning with number zero.

Will someone please explain the measuring process? *Place the zero point of the measuring device on one end of the line segment, with the ruler along the line segment read the scale value that matches the other end of line segment.*
Summarize by emphasizing end of line segment matching to zero and ruler along line segment so that you can read measure.

Now look at the table that you have on the sheet with the units. I want you to record the results of measuring line segments XY, YZ, and XZ by using the different scales on this table. Down the left side let's record the scale used as:

a-unit as m_a (measure using the a-scale)
b-unit as m_b (measure using the b-scale)
c-unit as m_c (measure using the c-scale)
d-unit as m_d (measure using the d-scale)

Across the top let's record the measure of the line segment as:
$m(\overleftrightarrow{XY})$; $m(\overleftrightarrow{YZ})$; and $m(\overleftrightarrow{XZ})$.

Now use your scales and complete the table. If you have any questions, I'll be coming around the room to help you. Remember to make each measurement and don't jump to conclusions just yet.

(Fill in a reproduced chart on the board and explore the relationships.)
The c-scale is 2, 3, and 5 units; the b-scale is 6.50, 9.75, and 16.25; and the a-scale is the most difficult 3⅜, 5¼, and 9½.
(Have someone give a value for $m(\overleftrightarrow{XZ})$ with respect to his or her d-unit.) Now can we complete the table?
(Complete the table and ask for questions.)

Suppose a d-unit with $m(\overleftrightarrow{XY})$ = 1 is selected as a standard unit. The c-unit would be equivalent to a *two*-standard unit, an a-unit, a _3⅜_ standard unit, and a b-unit, a _6.5_ standard unit.

Now looking at the table what conclusions can you draw about the measures of the line segments?
[We can add them and the whole is equal to the sum of its parts.]

In a generalized form this becomes:
$$\forall_x \forall_y \forall_z [Y \in \overline{XZ} \Rightarrow m(\overleftrightarrow{XY}) + m(\overleftrightarrow{YZ}) = m(\overleftrightarrow{XZ})]$$

(NOTE: Different symbols may be present in different texts. Be consistent.)

This implies that Y is between X and Z. How can we strengthen this so that Y can be either = X, or = Z, or between X and Z?
Include the end points.

With this we can formulate the development into an axiom.

$$\forall_x \forall_y \forall_z [Y \epsilon \overline{XZ} \Rightarrow m(\overrightarrow{XY}) + m(\overrightarrow{YZ}) = m(\overrightarrow{XZ})]$$

Discussion of the Lesson

This activity provides the opportunity for the learners to construct a ruler and to be introduced to a first measurement axiom. The procedure used here may be used to develop a *greater than* relationship involving noncollinear points and angle measure.

INTRODUCTION TO PROOF

In order to systematically study geometry we must derive theorems about geometric figures from axioms that we adopt. In addition, since measures are numbers, we must use elements from algebra as we develop formal proofs. This implies that certain allowable "gaps" will appear as we introduce proof since it will be impossible to prove every algebraic relationship and to do the proof would distract from the geometric structure. What we must be careful to include are a precise logic and sound structure to a proof. One way to do this is to introduce proof through the geometric framework by letting the rules of logic be developed as the need arises to extend a set of theorems. The relationships between sets of points and sets of numbers—the measurement process—present an excellent opportunity to function in this framework. Zero can be introduced, units along a number line (ruler) can be developed, and points between end points of a number line may be defined in formal theorems while introducing rules of logic, for example: the replacement (or substitution) rule and the deduction rule.

While proof may take many forms, from a two-column format to a paragraph, learners should be able to follow a diagram of a proof; therefore, the proof should be so organized as to allow for diagramming. A theorem should be viewed as a tentative hypothesis obtained from observation of a diagram, a symbolic representation, or a verbal description that specifies a possible relationship. A learner should somehow *see* the relationship and have the necessary prerequisites to attempt a logical argument to prove the hypothesis. For example, a learner should be able to see that if two end points exist so that a line segment exists, then the measure of the line segment is a number greater than zero and that there is only one real number to represent the answer. From this we can develop the ideas of midpoints.

INTRODUCTION TO ANGLES

The study of angles allows us to return to real-world models and to use such materials as wire to construct models of a more abstract nature. Another sample lesson will serve to introduce this idea.

Lesson Overview

Lesson III is also an example of a guided-discovery lesson. Note the difference in format in this lesson. The student is led to make a decision and to judge the correctness of his or her decision. Very seldom are the answers given directly. Again, the sequence is very important.
Some instructional objectives for this lesson are

1. To introduce the students to various relationships between sets and subsets in geometry
2. To encourage the students to develop analogies
3. To encourage the students to think of geometry as a mathematical system

Some performance objectives for this lesson are that the student should be able to

1. Recognize the separation postulates
2. Define an angle
3. Determine the degree measure of an angle

You have studied points, lines, parts of lines, and planes, along with some relationships between these sets of points. For example, if A is a point of some line 1, then the complement of {A} with respect to line 1 is

_____ *two half lines.* _____

We say that {A} separates line 1 into two half-lines. The half-lines do not have any points in common (intersection is empty). Describe a situation in which two half-lines do have something in common (intersection is not empty).

When the two half-lines go in the same direction they have something in common.

Draw a diagram to illustrate this situation.

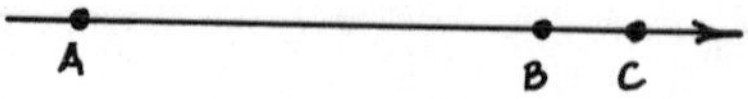

$\overrightarrow{AB}$ and $\overrightarrow{AC}$ have a portion of the line in common, as does $\overrightarrow{AC}$ and $\overrightarrow{BC}$.

Can you describe another situation, unlike the one you just did, such that the intersection of two half-lines of the same line is not empty. ✔ Yes ___ No. Consider the direction of the half-line.

Half-lines may go in different (or opposite) directions and have something in common.

Draw a diagram to illustrate this situation.

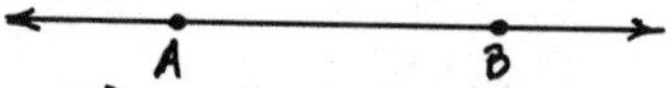

$\overrightarrow{AB}$ and $\overrightarrow{BA}$ have something in common.

Describe a situation in which the union of two half-lines will represent the entire line. The diagram above satisfies this condition.

Draw a diagram to illustrate this situation.

[Same as the one above.]

Let's see what we can do with rays. Like half-lines, rays can be on the same line with the intersection of two such rays being either empty or not empty.

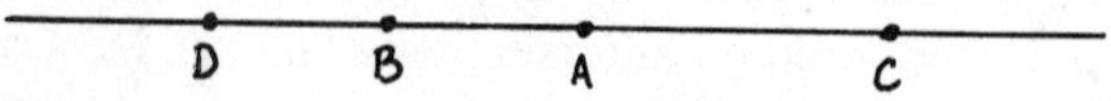

Also, the union of two rays can be the line, such as $\overrightarrow{BC} \cup \overrightarrow{AD}$ in Diagram 4.

Suppose that we have two rays that are not subsets of one line. What relationships can the two rays have? Illustrate by diagrams.

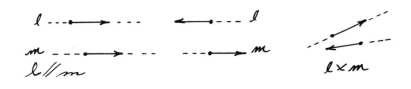

The two rays may be part of two parallel lines, and are thus parallel,

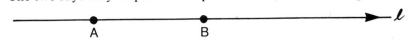

or parts of two intersecting lines:

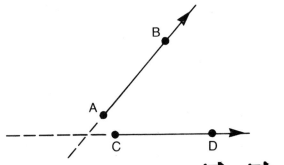

I'm sure that you will agree that the union of $\overrightarrow{AB}$ and $\overrightarrow{CD}$ would produce a set of points.

Suppose A = C, that is, A and C correspond to exactly the same point of the set. The set of points represented could be pictured as follows:

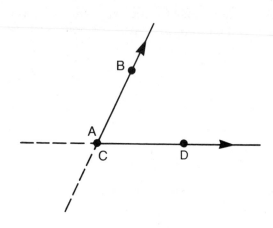

Describe how this set of points would differ from the following set.

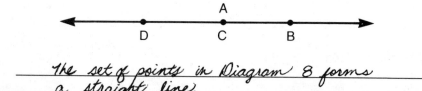

The set of points in Diagram 8 forms a straight line.

The quality of uniqueness is present in the first diagram (7). We can say that there is no question about the vertex point, A, where in the second diagram (8), A could be located anywhere along the line and the diagram would be the same.

The first set _(diagram)_ we define as an _angle_. It is the union of two noncollinear _rays_ that have the same _end point_.

The rays are the sides of the angle, and their common vertex is the vertex of the angle.

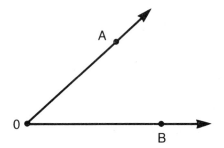

In Diagram 9 $\angle AOB$ = $\overrightarrow{OA}$ ∪ $\overrightarrow{OB}$ or $\overrightarrow{OA}$ ∪ $\overrightarrow{OB}$ or $\overrightarrow{OA}$ ∪ $\overrightarrow{OB}$.
Just as in the case of segments, we shall find it convenient to assign
measures to angles. Using the protractor, determine the degree measure
of the angle in Diagram 9 and explain the measuring process used in
determining the degree measure of an angle.

*Place arrow of protractor on vertex of angle and
straight edge of protractor along one ray. The
other ray should cross the protractor at its
degree measure (the measure of the angle.)*

Indicate several ways of representing this measure.

40° or m (∠AOB) =° 40

Discussion of the Lesson

From this development of angles we develop the degree measure of the
angles and define interiors and exteriors of angles, supplementary angles,
right angles, complementary angles, vertical angles, adjacent angles. After
the introduction to angles we can (and should) introduce the idea of congruence for both segments and angles. Angles are said to be congruent if
and only if they have the same measure. Segments are said to be congruent
if and only if they have the same measure.

TRIANGLES

Triangles, congruence, and corresponding parts constitute a major portion of the work in geometry and the second major unit defined by the
CEEB Commission on Mathematics (1959); therefore, a lesson that ties
these together will be given.

Lesson Overview: An Introduction to Congruence

Lesson IV is a lecture-discussion lesson in which the ideas are presented and the students are asked various questions to check their understanding. The format for this lesson is changed somewhat from the other examples as a script is provided.

Some instructional objectives for this lesson are

1. To introduce the students to congruence relations
2. To formalize a congruence definition
3. To help the students develop an intuitive feeling of corresponding parts of congruent figures

Some performance objectives for this lesson are that the student should be able to

1. Label the corresponding parts of congruent polygons
2. Determine various minimum conditions to produce a congruence relationship

Start the class by drawing a picture like the one in Diagram 10 on the board as the students are entering the room or have one already drawn on poster board.

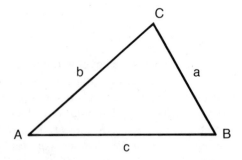

After the routine procedures, such as attendance taking, have been completed conduct a review session.

[REVIEW]
    "Let's review the parts of a triangle."
    Questions and statements to be used in assessing prerequisite knowledge: (If students do not know the answers, the ideas involved will have to be developed.)

[PAUSE] [Write VERTEX on the board].
"Name a *vertex* of the triangle . . . , _A_; another vertex . . . , _B_; another vertex . . . _C_."
[Write SIDE]
"Name a *side* of the triangle . . . , $\overleftrightarrow{AC}$."
"Can you name the same side in another way . . . , $\overleftrightarrow{CA}$?"
"Name another side in either way . . . , $\overleftrightarrow{AB}$."
"Another side . . . , $\overline{BC}$."
[Write ANGLE]
"Name an *angle* of the triangle . . . , ∠CAB"
"Can you name the same angle in another way . . . , ∠A ?"
"Name another angle in either way . . . , ∠B."
"Another angle . . . , ∠C."
"Who can write the definition of a triangle on the board?"
Obtain the definition in the following form: $\overline{AB} \cup \overline{BC} \cup \overline{CA}$ where A, B, and C are three noncollinear points.
"Name the side that is *opposite* vertex _A_." a
"Name the vertex that is *opposite* side _b_." B
Repeat until the students have an idea of *opposite*.
[DEVELOPMENT]
"Now we want to establish some relationships between various parts of triangles. First consider two groups, one with three males and one with three females. The females have challenged the coach of the track team because they want to participate with the track team. The coach agrees to give them a chance. He selects three of his runners at random and tells the females that if each one can tie or beat two of the three males in a 100-meter race, then he will let them participate with the team. How many races are necessary if each female is to race each male and if you consider only the result of each pairing as in each race all six can run?"
[Help students to diagram Race 1]

Race 1:   Males   Females

Males		Females					
A	⟷	D	A	⟷	E	A	⟷ F
B	⟷	E	B	⟷	F	B	⟷ D
C	⟷	F	C	⟷	D	C	⟷ E

"Therefore, there are three winners or three ties or a combination of these two. Now determine the other conditions."
Three races are sufficient.
"In order to think about this type of relationship consider a cable with three wires."
[If possible find such a cable or have a prepared diagram similar to the following diagram.]

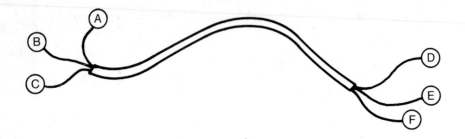

"At one end of the cable three wires are tagged A, B, and C and at the other end they are tagged D, E, and F.

The wires are twisted together in the cable so that you can't tell which of the wires are the same. One possible arrangement is:

the A wire is the E wire

the B wire is the D wire

the C wire is the F wire or ABC ↔ EDF

What are the other possible arrangements?"

ABC↔DEF , ABC↔FED

ABC↔EFD , ABC↔FDE , ABC↔DFE

Help the students obtain the other five possible arrangements as you develop the intuitive idea of order.

"Now let's consider two triangles."

[Draw diagrams similar to those in the following diagram on the board.]

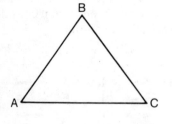
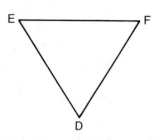

"How many different ways could we match △ABC to △DEF by drawing lines from each vertex of one triangle to only one vertex of the other triangle?" [Same answers as above.]

Help the students obtain the matchings and illustrate that some of the matchings are the same, such as ABC ↔ DEF and BCA ↔ EFD, and, therefore, cannot be counted as separate matching.

"Consider triangle GHI and triangle LJK:

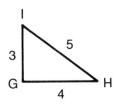

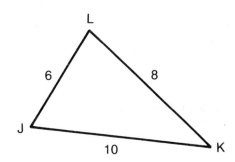

Since $\overleftrightarrow{LJ}$ is twice as long as $\overleftrightarrow{IG}$, try to match in this way.

L ↔ I

J ↔ G   therefore H ↔ K

and we have: IGH ↔ LJK.

but LK is not twice as long as IH.

This doesn't seem to work. What is the 'correct' matching? IGH ↔ JLK.''

This implies that with some triangles we must be careful in our matching. Scalene triangles are such triangles whereas with equilateral triangles six matchings are possible.

For convenience we usually select a possible matching, even with equilateral triangles, so that we can label corresponding sides and corresponding angles of the triangles. Corresponding sides are sides with matching end points and corresponding angles are angles with matching vertices. For example:

ABC ↔ EFD   A ↔ E
            B ↔ F
            C ↔ D

[CLOSURE]

The learners should now be given exercises to develop matchings and the following definition: A first triangle is congruent to a second triangle if and only if there is a matching of their vertices for which corresponding parts are congruent (Beberman & Vaughan, 1965).

Discussion of the Lesson

Upon this will be built the triangle congruence theorems and formal proof and the completeness of this lesson should indicate the detail and possible alternatives that we should consider in designing lessons for learning-disabled individuals.

BEYOND DEVELOPMENT OF TRIANGLES

Since space does not permit extensive sample lessons for all sections of geometry we will discuss what comes next in the content sequence and suggest that the reader examine the sample lessons for ideas.

After the section on triangle congruence we have some options regarding the direction that we could go in our development. Some might suggest that we introduce transformation in the plane since we now have the prerequisite for such a distance-preserving motion. Others would suggest that we introduce inequalities, parallel lines, similar polygons, and conclude with circles. Following the recommendations of NCTM (1981) we should include rectangles, circles, and similar figures. Let's discuss the recommended topics.

Rectangles

The complete development of polygons should extend from the development of paths and closed paths. By defining a simple closed polygonal path as the union of a finite number of segments with the following conditions:

1. Each end point of any of the given segments is an end point of just one other.
2. No proper subset of the given set of segments satisfies 1.
3. Each point common to two of the given segments is an end point of both.

We can develop the ideas of polygons by adding another condition:

4. No two of the given segments that have a common end point are collinear.

A rectangle is a member of the family of quadrilaterals. It is a quadrilateral with right angles; also, a rectangle is a special case of a parallelogram and a square is a special case of a rectangle. Vertices, sides, diagonals, and their relationships should be illustrated by models, diagrams, and verbally described. Laboratory activities may be introduced through constructions. If desirable, the family of quadrilaterals may be used to explore necessary and sufficient conditions of an implication.

Similar Polygons

The study of similar polygons extends the Euclidean geometry and brings ratios and proportions into the geometric framework. Using the same approaches as with congruence we can define a similarity by matching of vertices to produce corresponding congruent angles and corresponding proportional sides. We can prove the proportional segments theorem of parallel lines, similarity triangle theorems, and end with a proof of the Pythagorean theorem.

Circles

One reason that circles should be introduced is to provide learners with the concept of locus of points. The circle is defined as the set of all points that are equidistant from a point called the center. Since the circle is a conic section, its locus-of-points definition should help learners understand other conic sections such as parabola and hyperbola. A unit on circles that also makes use of measurement and laboratory activities can be introduced to demonstrate such concepts as tangency. Constructions should also play a major role.

SUMMARY

In this chapter we have discussed geometry options and structure as they relate to the learning-disabled student at the secondary level. Some general instructional guidelines were listed. Sample lessons that served to illustrate the content and sample the guidelines were detailed in an attempt to adapt geometry to meet the needs of the learning-disabled individuals. The lessons and discussions between the lessons served to define the scope and sequence of a possible geometry course of study for learners at the ninth or tenth grade levels.

REFERENCES

Beberman, M. & Vaughan, H.E. (1965). *High school mathematics, course 2.* Boston: D.C. Heath.

Cohen, L. (1979, September/October). Suggestions for teachers in helping children with learning disabilities. *ACLD Newsbriefs, 128,* 12.

Meserve, B.E. (1967, January). Euclidean and other geometries. *The Mathematics Teacher, 50,* (1), 2–11.

Priorities in school mathematics: Executive summary of the PRISM project. (1981). Reston, VA: National Council of Teachers of Mathematics.

Program for college preparatory mathematics: Report of the Commission on Mathematics. (1959). New York: College Entrance Examination Board.

Chapter 7

Measurement Concepts and Skills

Robert A. Shaw

Unlike many of the content strands of mathematics the measurement strand is not treated in a separate course or large unit. Measurement is a part of many courses with the major ones being mathematics and science. What happens often is that no one assumes responsibility for measurement instruction. As a result learners may find measurement concepts new and strange to them. This situation is occurring at a time when, according to Osborne (1979), "The pervasive orientation to mass production and uniform consumerism has established measurement as a critical component of American industry. The measurement units and procedures are an essential tradition of the mass-production, assembly-line techniques that characterize our technological, industrial society" (p. 107).

Teachers are often confused about the reasons for teaching measurements. A scientist uses measurements to describe reality—to build a model of reality—while a mathematician is concerned with the correctness within the reasoning of the model. The model is reality for the mathematician. Since measurement is a process in either situation and requires certain skills or performance levels, learners do need to know the procedures and acquire the necessary skills to function in mathematics and science.

By its very nature measurement provides instructional opportunities for multiple strategies and methods to be used; therefore, we have an ideal topic with which to work with individuals who have learning disabilities.

THE MEASUREMENT FUNCTION

Since measurement is a process, let's describe it mathematically (from what we already know from Chapter 6). Measurement is a part of Euclidean geometry since measurement is that rule that assigns a numerical value to a set of points. For example, $\overleftrightarrow{AB}$ is the symbol for a line segment—a set of points. Some number represents the distance from point A to point B.

The rule that assigns that number to the distance is a measurement rule. The symbolic representation of this process is:

1. $\overrightarrow{AB}$ a line segment AB (a set of points)
2. $m(\overrightarrow{AB})$ [or just AB] the linear measure of line segment AB (a function)
3. $m(\overrightarrow{AB}) = n$ by measuring we produce a number

The measurement function also possesses certain properties that give strength to the function. Symbolically, they are (1) $m(\overrightarrow{AB}) = m(\overrightarrow{BA})$, (2) if $m(\overrightarrow{AB}) = 0$, then $A = B$, (3) if B is between A and C, then $m(\overrightarrow{AB}) + m(\overrightarrow{BC}) = m(\overrightarrow{AC})$, and (4) if $\overrightarrow{AB} \cong \overrightarrow{CD}$, then $m(\overrightarrow{AB}) = m(\overrightarrow{CD})$, and conversely. These ideas of linear measure are presented to provide an example of how formal the idea of measurement may become. We should realize that similar structures also exist for area, volume, and other measures. This chapter will enable us to lay the groundwork for such formal development.

PREREQUISITES AND CONDITIONS

The prerequisite concepts and skills for measurement include time, temperature, use of ruler and protractor, relative size, and using arbitrary units to develop the measuring process and the need for a standard. The formal development of length (linear measure) follows a basic understanding of whole numbers and fractions and experiences with line segments. In this chapter we will be concerned with length (linear measure), angle measure in the plane, area, volume, mass (weight), and measurement in the sciences.

Lesson II in Chapter 6 serves to define the connecting link between geometry and measurement. The process of measurement is defined with this connection as sets of points are related to sets of numbers by defining a relationship (function) called measurement. In Lesson II we assumed that all learners knew how to measure. This may not be a valid assumption for some learners; therefore, we will begin this section with some suggestions for introducing measurement and building a ruler. The procedures used in this chapter will be to consider the topics in order and describe possible instructional strategies instead of detailed lessons as in Chapter 6.

LENGTH

While the first type of measurement in geometry should be of line segments, these segments should be represented as parts of real objects (for example, the edge of a cracker box). Before the measurement process can begin the learners should have an understanding of the particular units that will be used in measurement. In addition, the first measures should result in whole number answers instead of decimal or other fractions. This situation implies that we should begin with a measuring device that represents some standard length and contains no other markings.

Decimeter

A strip of paper a decimeter in length is a good device with which to begin the measuring process since it can easily be used to build other units in the metric system of measurement.

Each learner should be given a portion of a blank index card that is one decimeter in length. We should define the length as "1 decimeter," show the proper labeling, 1 dm, and ask the learners to use the edge of the strip of paper to draw line segments that are one decimeter in length. Labeling of each line segment should be encouraged. A template with a slot one decimeter long may be constructed and used if some learners have difficulty in using the strip.

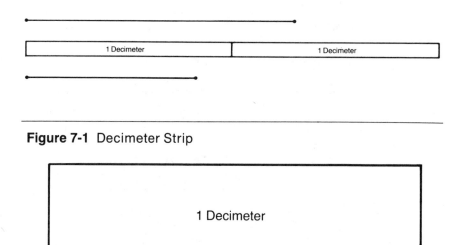

Figure 7-1 Decimeter Strip

Line segments one decimeter long should be drawn in horizontal positions (in reference to a sheet of paper), vertical positions, and slanting positions so that we can foreshadow perimeter development. If some learners construct a broken line or an equilateral triangle we are ready to develop polygons. The learners should also be asked to develop a list of objects that are approximately one decimeter in length. This activity will serve to introduce estimation and rounding. Sample elements for the list might include: a light switch cover (width), a piece of new chalk (length), a wallet (width), or a playing card (width).

The next set of activities should be involved with using the decimeter strip or template to determine lengths that do not necessarily result in an exact whole number answer. The learners should be asked to record answers to the nearest whole number. For example: would both be recorded as 1 dm if rounded to the nearest whole number. This type of activity should indicate to the learners that an error equal to one-half of the smallest unit being used is possible in any measurement. For a line segment being measured by a decimeter strip, the length could vary from 0.5 dm to 1.50 dm and still be labeled as 1 dm if no other units are being introduced. Mathematically, this condition is called the greatest possible error (GPE). The learners should have extensive practice with whole number answers that need to be rounded, including using string to determine the length of curved line portions. The string is placed along the curve, cut to match the length of the curved section, and then matched to the decimeter strip to determine the length. The decimeter strips may be attached end-to-end to produce a longer measuring device. Ten decimeter strips placed end-to-end produce the meter length. (This device may be used to determine width and length of a room.)

A Geometric Activity To Develop Centimeter Unit

The estimation and rounding activities should imply that a more accurate instrument is needed to measure the line segments. After studying parallel lines, especially sets of parallel lines that are the same distance apart, we have the necessary tools to build a centimeter scale.

Give each learner a lined sheet of paper. Ask the learners to count eleven lines on the paper that are the same distance apart. Next, place the decimeter strip so that an edge will fit between the first line and the eleventh line (see Figure 7-2).

By making a small mark on the decimeter strip at every intersection—where the lines of the paper touch the edge of the strip—we can produce the centimeter unit (see Figure 7-3).

Figure 7-2 Construction of a Ruler

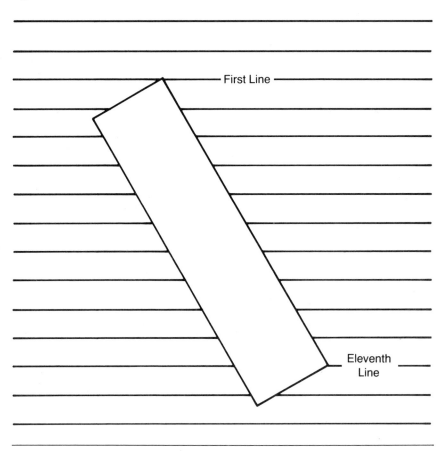

You should have ten sections and eleven lines (counting both ends). Each section is one centimer (1 cm) long. Label the centimeters as 1 (at first mark), 2, 3, 4, 5, 6, 7, 8, 9, and 10 (one end). Now we can measure line segments to the nearest centimeter. The measurement results should be within 0.5 cm (one-half of the smallest unit used) as we round to the nearest centimeter.

The learners should be asked to draw line segments of length equal to one centimeter (1 cm) in different positions on a sheet of paper. After the drawing activity, a list of objects that have some measure equal to one centimeter (1 cm) should be developed. Such a list might include the width of a fingernail, the width of a paper clip, or the diameter of a piece of chalk. The next activity is to measure objects or pictures of objects that

Figure 7-3 Construction of a Ruler

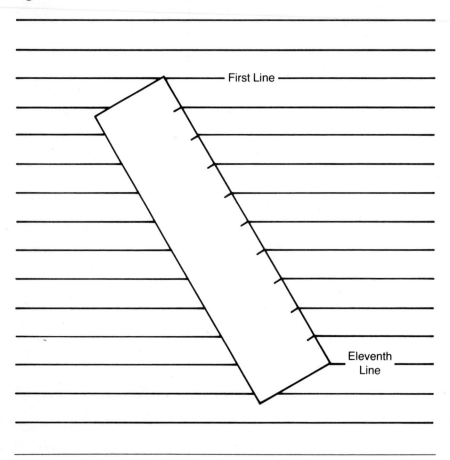

are in true (or real) size (see the sample worksheet in Figure 7-4). Worksheets such as this can be developed and used to get the learner to estimate the answer, measure, and label the result.

A Metric Ruler

After the development of the centimeter unit, the learners should be given a metric ruler; that is, a ruler scaled in centimeters and the next smallest unit, millimeters. The millimeter unit can be represented by the thickness of a paper clip. Using the metric ruler the learners should be asked to repeat all previous measures and record the answers in (1) milli-

Figure 7-4 Sample Worksheet

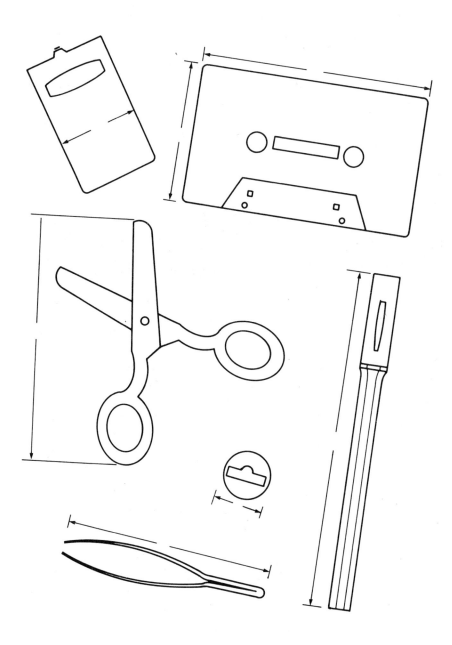

meters, (2) centimeters, (3) decimeters, and (4) meters. The relationships in Table 7-1 should be established.

A measure equal to 32.5 cm is also equal to 325 mm or 3.25 dm or 0.325 m. Other tables with such results as 32.5 cm should be constructed for learners to complete.

Another activity involves reading measures and asking the learners to draw line segments that are equal in length to the measures that you read. For example, "Draw a line segment that is 3.5 dm long."

Inches, Feet, and Yards

Until we decide what measurement system we are going to use in the United States it is the responsibility of the school mathematics program to include as many as possible of the common units of linear measure. We should define the inch and build the foot ruler by adding the inch units together. (One of our axioms of geometry tells us that we can do this.) The subdivisions are obtained by the geometric construction procedure of bisecting each unit. Bisection of the inch units produces the one-half-inch units. Continuing to bisect we get the one-fourth-inch units and one-eighth-inch units. Again, students should construct each unit, learn about the unit, and use the unit before going on to the next unit. After we have developed the one-eighth-inch unit, we can place three foot units together to generate the yard. Learners need to understand the subdivisions of each measuring device before they are asked to use the devices as tools in other activities. For example, if asked to cut a piece of copper tubing to a length of 5-7/8 inches, they must understand what 5-7/8 inches represent on a ruler before measuring the tubing to be cut. They must not only know how to measure a given line segment but also be able to construct a line segment of a given length before going on to more complex operations.

Table 7-1 Metric Relationships

1 meter(m)	=	10 decimeters(dm)	=	100 centimeters(cm)	=	1000 millimeters(mm)
0.1 m	=	1 dm	=	10 cm	=	100 mm
0.01 m	=	0.1 dm	=	1 cm	=	10 mm
0.001 m	=	0.01 dm	=	0.1 cm	=	1 mm

Perimeter, Circumference, and Addition of Measures

The concept of perimeter should follow the development of polygons because the perimeter means the total length of the line segments that constitute a polygon. To introduce the idea of perimeter take a piece of wire (perhaps a coat hanger), straighten the wire, and determine (measure) its length. The wire should then be bent to form a triangle as the two ends touch. Ask the learners if the length of the wire changed. After they have been convinced that the length is the same, bend the wire to form a square. To extend this concept provide the learners with preconstructed polygons and a flexible measuring device (a tape measure or string). Ask them to determine the perimeter (the distance around). If a rigid measuring device is used, it will be necessary to add the lengths of the line segments that are used to build the polygon. This concept will lead into approximate number operations. The major concept is that the result can be no more precise than the least precise measure. For example, if four sides of a rectangle have the following measures: 2.54 cm, 1.8 cm, 3.732 cm, and 2.37 cm, then the preciseness of the answers will be dictated by 1.8 cm since it is only to one decimal place. To add or subtract numbers arising from approximations (measures), round each number to the unit of the least precise number and then perform the operation. In the example given, 2.54 cm becomes 2.5 cm; 3.732 cm becomes 3.7 cm; and 2.37 cm becomes 2.4 cm; and 2.5 cm + 1.8 cm + 3.7 cm + 2.4 cm = 10.4 cm for the perimeter of the rectangle.

The distance around a circle, the circumference, should be measured with some flexible measuring device. If circular objects are being used, the student may identify a point on the circle, place this point on the zero point of a measuring device, roll the object along the measuring device, and identify the number value to which the point corresponds as it is rolled around to touch the measuring device again.

The concepts and skills obtained in measuring circumference and diameter (the distance from a point on a circle through the center to another (opposite) point on the circle) of circles can serve as an opportunity for a problem-solving, discovery activity. By providing the learners with several different circular shapes (for example, coffee cans, rings, basketball rims, etc.), asking them to determine (measure) the diameter and circumference of each shape, and having them complete a table like the one shown in Table 7-2, they should be able to discover a unique number relationship.

The measure of the circumference (c) divided by the measure of the diameter (d) produces similar answers for the different circular shapes. The result is an approximation for the number pi (TI).

Table 7-2 Circumference and Diameter Relationships

Shape	Circumference (c) [dist. around]	Diameter (d) [dist. around]	c + d	c − d	c × d	c ÷ d
1.						
2.						
3.						
4.						
5.						
6.						

ANGLE MEASURE

Angle measure is more abstract than linear measure because it is difficult to identify angles to measure with respect to real objects. Choices are limited. Right angles are readily available; however, a true representation of an obtuse angle is more difficult to find. As a result, we often depend upon models for angles, and thus we make them more abstract. In addition we introduce a new measuring instrument—a protractor—and a new measuring procedure.

In working with angles we must not forget the function concept. An angle is a set of points; degree measurement is a function that maps (assigns) a real number to the measure for the set of points. Since angles may be defined in many different ways, let's use the set idea. An angle is a set of points made of the union of two noncollinear rays with the same end point. In this definition we recognize acute angles (degree measure (°m) greater than zero but less than 90), right angles (°m = 90), and obtuse angles (90 < °m < 180). Perhaps right angles should be introduced first since they can be seen as corners in a real-world sense. We can define the measure of a right angle as 90° and use a corner of a sheet of paper to demonstrate this relative size. The edges of a quarter (¼) section of a circular region match the edges at the corner of the sheet of paper (see Figure 7-5).

If we fold the quarter section of the circular region so that the edges correspond we produce two acute angles with the edges and the folding line that have a measure of 45° (see Figure 7-6).

Students should become familiar with this degree measure of 45 since it is very common in real-life situations and in mathematics, as well, for example, in trigonometry. Folding a quarter section of the circular region

Figure 7-5 A Right Angle

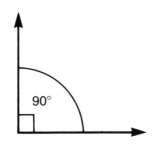

Figure 7-6 Producing a 45° Right Angle

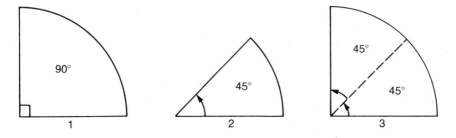

as you fold a letter (into three sections) produces other common angles, the 30° angle and 60° angle (see Figure 7-7).

Plaster or oaktag models of the 30°, 45°, 60°, and 90° angles might be beneficial to some learners. From activities such as these we can convince students that angle measures are additive, as were the measures of line segments.

We can now introduce the protractor (see Figure 7-8) and formalize the angle measuring process. Note that the first protractor should have only one set of numbers labeled in a counterclockwise manner.

To use the protractor place the center (point 0) on the vertex on the angle to be measured and let one ray of the angle be in line with the straight edge of the protractor, through the zero point. The other ray of the angle should cross the semicircle of the protractor somewhere between zero and 180 (see Figure 7-9).

Students should be asked to measure and label, construct, and sketch angles of various sizes. Adjacent angles, supplementary angles (two angles with total degree measure of 180), complementary angles (two angles with total degree measure of 90), and congruent angles should be introduced

Figure 7-7 Producing 30° and 60° Angles

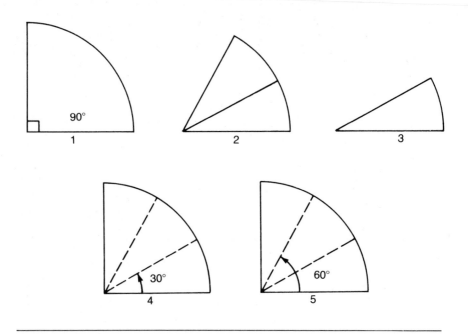

Figure 7-8 A Protractor

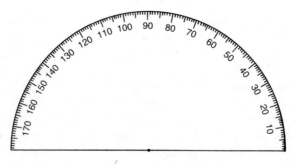

and used. Analytical proof may be developed as learners discover interior and exterior angles to the extent that they measure the interior angles of any triangle (or polygon). They can be led to discover that the total degree measure of the interior angles of a triangle is 180. An appropriate activity is to have the students draw any triangle, cut off each vertex section, and

Figure 7-9 Measuring an Angle

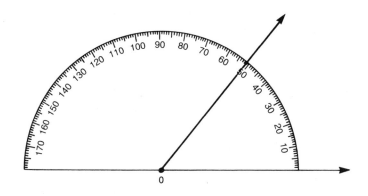

Figure 7-10 Interior Angles of a Triangle

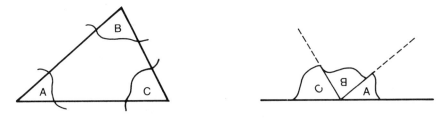

see if all of the angles can be placed together to form a total of 180° (see Figure 7-10).

Working with angles can become an excellent laboratory activity involving tracing paper. The student can check to determine if angles are congruent by tracing an angle on the paper and placing the copy over other angles to determine if they match—are congruent. This simple activity foreshadows geometric transformations.

AREA

The concept of area is mathematically similar to the concept of length in that some number is assigned to a set of points to name the amount of flat surface covered; however, this concept of area should come much later in the mathematical development.

Since area involves the concept of multiplication and results in different kinds of units, the potential is present for difficulties to arise in the teaching-learning process. Every opportunity should be taken to "show" the learner what square units mean. Cutting, drawing, and measuring activities are essential. Development should start with a square region, perhaps one with an area of one square decimeter (1 dm²). Using this model students should be asked to estimate the area of various surfaces (for example, a sheet of paper) and record the answer to the nearest whole number and in *square* units. Following this activity they should be given a square decimeter region that is made of acetate and contains square centimeter regions (100 square centimeter regions). This acetate model may be placed over small irregular regions to enable the learners to estimate the area of each region by counting square centimeter regions (see Figure 7-11).

Regions may also be placed on square centimeter graph paper and traced to determine how many square centimeter regions were covered. Portions of 100 cm² (1 dm²) may be cut from the graph paper and used to develop area formulas. Students can readily see that the square region that contains 100 square centimeters has the length of each side equal to 10 cm. The

Figure 7-11 Approximating Area

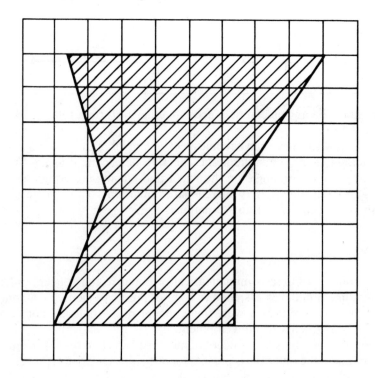

length of one side times the length of an adjacent side (10 cm × 10 cm) is equal to the area (100 cm²) or S · S = A$_\square$. Exploration with square regions of different sizes should lead the learners to generalize that the formula, A$_\square$ = S · S (or S²), is true for any square region.

If one of the square decimeter regions is cut from the midpoint of one side to the midpoint of the opposite side and the two pieces are placed end-to-end, a rectangular region is formed that has the same area as the square region. The length of the rectangle is 20 cm and the width is 5 cm. Again, a general formula may be generated from graph paper models: A$_\square$ = bh (area of a rectangle is equal to length of base times the height). As the concept of area is developed, all figures should be in true size to enable students to measure the lengths and widths. In addition, they should be asked to draw squares and rectangles of the appropriate size, label the sides with appropriate units, and determine the area of the enclosed regions. A simple problem is to describe a rectangle with a given area (for example, 48 cm² (square centimenters)) and ask them to sketch and label rectangular regions that could have the given area (for example, a rectangle with b (or length) = 8 cm and h (or width) = 6 cm would be one example). Given any two of the three number values required to complete the area formula of a rectangle, students should be able to determine the third.

Careful development from a square, to a rectangle, to other polygons should be followed using regions that have lengths and widths represented by whole numbers instead of fractions. Following the rectangle we should introduce parallelograms so that students can cut and construct rectangles (if necessary) to obtain the area (see Figure 7-12). Students should discover that area formulas for rectangles and parallelograms are the same if the height is used for both.

The perpendicular concept is now used and plays a major role in area of triangles. Triangular regions constructed from square and rectangular regions serve to introduce the area of triangles, A$_\triangle$ = ½ bh where b is the length of the base and h is the height. The geoboard can be a useful device

---

Figure 7-12 Area of a Parallelogram

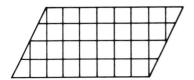
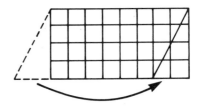

at this point in area development since squares and rectangles may be constructed along with the triangles in each. On a geoboard, as on graph paper, it is not difficult to determine the height of a triangle even though it is in the exterior of the triangle.

After students have learned how to estimate and then verify the areas of given square, rectangular, and triangular regions, composite figures should be presented to introduce the idea that areas (or numbers that represent areas) are, like linear measures, additive (see Figure 7-13).

Such enrichment topics as tesselations may be introduced as students get involved in covering surfaces. The general problem is, What figures (regular polygons) may be used to cover a given surface with no overlap and no open spaces? Equilateral triangular regions present one solution and square regions another solution. There are others.

Figure 7-13 Area of an Irregular Figure

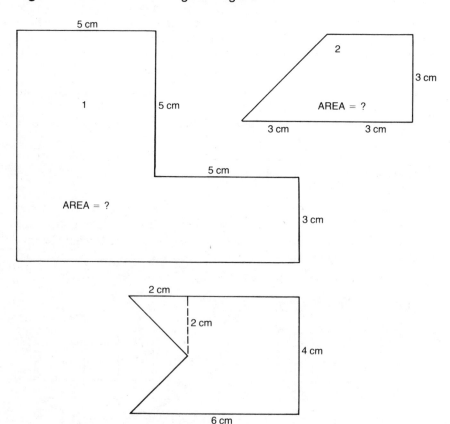

Area should be extended to a trapezoid by combining a rectangular region and two triangular regions, and to a hexagon by combining six, triangular regions. This also provides students with a procedure for determining the area of irregular polygon regions. By dividing the regions into rectangles, squares, and triangles they can determine the total area.

Introducing students to the area of a circular region is somewhat more difficult because you cannot divide the region into exact squares, rectangles, and triangles; however, we should not miss the opportunity to introduce approximation. From the circumference development students obtained the information that the ratio of the circumference (c) to the diameter (d) was the same regardless of the size of the circle. This ratio represented how many times the diameter would fit around the circle.

As the area of a circular region is being developed, give students circular regions and ask them to trace the regions onto paper. Have students construct two diameters for the circle that are perpendicular to each other (see Figure 7-14). Now, have students connect the end points of the diameters to form a square. This square region is inside the circle. Using the sides of the square as diagonals of four smaller squares will produce a large square so that it contains the circle.

Figure 7-14 Approximating the Area of a Circular Region

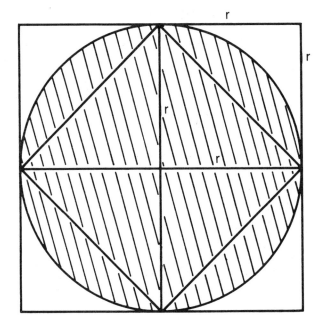

The area of the square region inside the circle is the sum of the four triangle regions, each with an area of $\frac{r^2}{2}$; therefore, the total area of the enclosed square regions is $4\frac{r^2}{2}$ or $2r^2$. The large square has each side equal to 2r; therefore, its area is $4r^2$. Since the circular region falls between the two square regions, an average of the areas of the square regions is a good approximation for the area of the circular region: $4r^2 + 2r^2 = 6r^2$ and the average is $3r^2$. Further experimentation and measurement will produce $3.14r^2$ as an approximation for the area and we can define the area of a circular region as $A_o = \pi r^2$.

The connecting link between area and volume involves developing two-dimensional patterns for three-dimensional figures—patterns that may be traced on cardboard, cut out, and folded to produce a model for a geometric solid (for example, a cube, see Figure 7-15). In developing such patterns we must remember to include tabs so that we can fasten the faces together.

The area concept can be extended to surface area. How much material is used to construct a pattern? How much wrapping paper is needed to cover a box? Soon we arrive at problem solving as we discuss the amount of material necessary to construct a certain container.

Figure 7-15 Pattern for a Cube

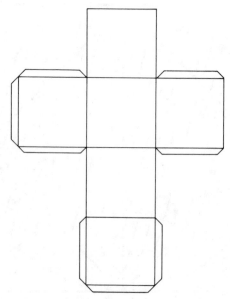

VOLUME

Volume is a more difficult concept than area, but it can be developed in a similar manner. The use of blocks (centimeter cubes or inch cubes) to build volumes in a manner similar to the use of area units as coverings for polygon regions serves to introduce the concept. Initially we should select or construct containers that hold an exact number of blocks.

One of the models that should be constructed is a cubic decimeter so that the instructor may use Dienes blocks to demonstrate to students that 100 cubic centimeters cover one base and that 10 layers of 100 cubic centimeters make the entire cube of 1,000 cubic centimeters (1,000 cm^3). This type of model can be used to demonstrate that if you find the area of a base section or any cross-section and multiply by the height, then you have the volume (the amount of space occupied) of the three-dimensional figure ($V = \ell wh$). Students should also discover that if some of the layers are moved, the volume is still the same because the same amount of space is occupied. Spatial relations can be studied by having learners predict how many cubes of a given volume are in a certain construction or containers. Rectangular prisms of various sizes should be constructed and measured. Emphasis should be placed on labeling answers with correct units.

Using solid geometric models of relative size, various dimensions can be determined and volume formulas developed. Another alternative is to use containers shaped like the solids. Use a plastic cubic decimeter container as a standard. Fill this container with sand and pour the sand into other containers to determine how much they hold. Table 7-3 represents the formulas that can be produced.

The volume for pyramid and cone can be generated by pouring the sand from a known container into the respective containers. When we discuss how much something will hold, capacity is the term that is most often used. The cubic decimeter will hold a cubic decimeter or 1,000 cubic centimeters of sand. This same container will hold 1,000 milliliters of water (liquid-volume concept). Of course, 1,000 ml is equal to 1 liter; therefore, students have the opportunity to extend the solid-volume concept to liquid volume. Two-liter containers have become common in our society and provide a physical model for liquid volume.

Students should be given the opportunities to estimate volume and to verify their estimations. In addition, by using some standard container they should use "throw-away" containers and develop their set of standard containers for 10 ml, 100 ml, 250 ml, 500 ml, 750 ml, 1,000 ml, or 1 liter, 1,500 ml, and 2,000 ml, or 2 liters.

Table 7-3 Volume Formulas

Shape	Area of Base	Volume	Example
Cube	$B = s \cdot s$ or s^2	$V = s \cdot s \cdot s$ or s^3	$10cm \cdot 10cm \cdot 10cm = 1000cm^3$
Rectangular Solid	$B = \ell w$	$V = \ell wh$ or Bh	$25cm \cdot 4cm \cdot 10cm = 1000cm^3$
Cylinder	$B = \pi r^2$	$V = \pi r^2 h$ or Bh	$3.14 \cdot (5.64cm)^2 \cdot 10cm \approx 1000cm^3$
Pyramid (Square base)	$B = s^2$	$V = \frac{1}{3}Bh$	$\frac{1}{3} \cdot 10cm \cdot 10cm \cdot 30cm = 1000cm^3$
Cone (Circle base)	$B = \pi r^2$	$V = \frac{1}{3}\pi r^2 h$	$\frac{1}{3} \times 3.14 \cdot (10cm)^2 \cdot 10cm \approx 1000cm^3$

The volume-capacity concepts provide the connecting link between mathematics and science. Before students begin to do experiments in the laboratory they should have some concept of liquid capacity.

MEASUREMENT IN THE SCIENCES

The measurement concepts of mathematics become the tools of the scientist since much of the work of the scientist is concerned with observation and measurement. Estimation and approximation play a key role in the activities of the scientist. Let's use the concept of mass (weight) to demonstrate.

MASS (WEIGHT)

To set the stage we need to say that although mass and weight are usually considered the same, they do differ. Mass is the amount of matter in an object. It is constant, no matter where the object is located, because it does not depend upon the force of gravity. Weight, on the other hand, changes as the force of gravity changes.

Understanding mass is more complicated than understanding length, area, and volume. Perception is the problem because holding two objects in your hands and saying which has the greater mass is difficult. Materials are necessary to enable the individual to "see" whether two objects have similar masses (weigh the same) or not. A balance beam (Figure 7-16) or a scale becomes a necessity. Objects placed on the ends of the balance

Figure 7-16 Balance Beam

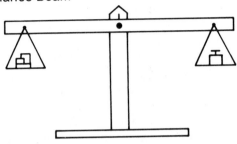

---

beam have the same mass (weigh the same) if the beam is balanced (level with the floor).

The concept of equilibrium is introduced here and involves perceptions of the objects being weighed that are not directly related to the objects. This fact in and of itself contains the rationale for including mass in the mathematics and science curriculum. Determining mass introduces the concept of indirect measure. As a result we may experience some degree of difficulty and be forced to examine mass (weight) in the following manner. Students should be given objects of pound and kilogram masses to handle. They should be asked to weigh these objects and find other objects that are heavier and others that are lighter. Each student should learn to read a scale to determine how much objects weigh. A good supplementary topic at this point is unit pricing, which involves weight.

If the metric system is being developed the kilogram mass should be studied as follows:

1. Build a cubic decimeter from heavy cardboard (10 cm × 10 cm × 10 cm).
2. Secure the sides together.
3. Put a liner of plastic in the cube.
4. Fill the cube with water. This defines a *liter* of water.
5. Weigh the cube with the water. If you ignore the mass of the cardboard cube, the mass of the water is one *kilogram*.

Just as with the other units, many comparisons should be made with the developed standards. As these comparisons are made students need to become more skilled in using the instruments. Observations become more precise and the skills of a scientist are developed. This measurement process and the skills learned enable a chemistry student to precisely mix amounts of substances to determine the results of chemical reactions and the physics student to construct experiments in physics to determine the results of physical reactions.

The arbitrary units concept used to introduce measurement in mathematics appears in science when an individual may have several units from which to choose but must select the most appropriate one. Estimation and approximation processes are other characteristics of both mathematics and science and serve to introduce the concept of error as a part of measurement. Perhaps the most important characteristics involve observations in science that lead to model building in mathematics and models of mathematics being used to predict behaviors of experiments in science.

Measuring activities provide the learning-disabled individual with multiple options to experience his or her world. These learners may listen as measurement is explained, they may read about measurement, they may do measurement, or they may watch as measurement is done by others. Activities of measurement form a multiple option curriculum—an ideal situation for the learning-disabled individual.

SUMMARY

In this chapter we have discussed measurement options as they relate to the learning-disabled student at the secondary level. A rationale and content overview was developed. The topics of length, angle measure, area, volume, mass, and measurement characteristics were presented in detail. Suggested classroom activities were also included. The theme of this chapter was the relationship of measurement in mathematics to measurement in science.

REFERENCE

Osborne, A.R. (1979). Metrication, measure, and mathematics. In *A metric handbook for teachers*. (pp. 107–137). Reston, VA: National Council of Teachers of Mathematics.

Chapter 8

Mathematics and Vocational Preparation for the Learning Disabled

John F. Cawley

The term *vocational preparation* is used in this chapter to refer to those aspects of school programs that stress a combination of academics, work experiences, and/or trade-related training. A more comprehensive term, *career education*, encompasses factors such as career awareness, vocational interests, and long-term career planning. Career education, although an important component of a complete program for the learning disabled, is not the primary consideration in this chapter. Rather, the emphasis is on mathematics and its implications for vocational preparation.

Vocational preparation programs vary according to interests, proficiencies, and curriculum requirements. Perhaps this can be illustrated by the following:

> During a recent visit to a vocational education program for the learning disabled, I observed one youngster using a hand calculator to determine values from Ohm's Law, another youngster measuring plywood sheets to determine the number of pieces of different sizes that could be cut from each sheet, and a third youngster measuring angles so as to produce a duct in sheet metal class. Each of these youngsters was performing calculations. Yet, none of them was computing.

These observations heightened an awareness of two points. One is that learning-disabled youths can and must be different in their mathematical proficiencies. The second is that vocational preparation programs for the learning disabled vary markedly.

EMPLOYMENT SETTINGS

The validity of vocational preparation programs will be established when each individual is provided with a free and appropriate public education such that he or she attains the highest level of training and the maximum employment opportunity possible. Different individuals will receive different levels of preparation, attain varying levels of employment, and work in different settings. Some of these settings are:

- Normal competitive employment setting
  Here the individual works with others on an equivalent basis. In these settings, the quality and rate of work is expected to be commensurate with the job description and job standards. Rewards and benefits are provided accordingly.
- Modified employment setting
  Here the individual works in a modified setting with support services. The individual functions at the highest possible level. These settings may provide both training and productivity conditions. Portions of the salary may be compensated for with tax relief or direct support to the employer.
- Productive sheltered setting
  Here the emphasis is on training. The individual may remain in this setting until certain skills are developed or specific social skills and habits are maintained. It is expected that the individual will move to a less restricted setting.
- Dependent sheltered setting
  This type of setting provides training and productive employment of a limited competitive level. In these settings, the rate of work may be substantially below that found in the normal competitive setting. Pay scales and other considerations are adapted.

The range of occupations the learning disabled can enter in the various settings will differ with the type and severity of the disability and the extent to which the individual is able to cope with or to compensate for the disabilities. This may be from the most highly professional (e.g., president of a corporation) to the less skilled (e.g., busperson in the corporate cafeteria). Neither of these individuals may be required to demonstrate exceptional levels of mathematics proficiency. The quantitative concepts and skills that one needs will differ from the other. The price of company stock and the current dividend will be of considerable importance to the busperson who is participating in a company-sponsored stock option plan.

Their meaning, however, will be different from that to the company president who is about to make a presentation at a stockholders meeting. Possibly, both the president and busperson might have met the school-based criteria for learning disability. Possibly, both might still be learning disabled.

VOCATIONAL PREPARATION

Vocational preparation is a process that begins early in the school years. With respect to mathematics and the learning disabled, this preparation starts with the decision as to what kinds of mathematics will be taught to the individual. If the emphasis is to be on computation with whole numbers, the decision maker must understand the long-term implication of this approach. Minimal attention to topics in measurement, geometry, and problem solving will soon create other problems for the learning disabled, particularly in vocational training and work settings where skill in these areas is needed. The learning disabled will then have to develop these skills in less time and with less prerequisite background than would be given to the nonlearning disabled. This burden may prove more than they can handle.

The more appropriate approach would be to recognize that a broad range of mathematics is encountered in vocational preparation, in employment settings, and in real life and that we should prepare individuals for these possibilities. In this instance, one would increase the total amount of time devoted to mathematics throughout the school years. The youngster would not be removed from instructional activities in the regular grades that are emphasizing problem solving in order to provide instruction in computation. Other arrangements would have to be made.

Prevocational education for the learning disabled can be viewed from two perspectives. In one perspective, the individual is enrolled in a program that emphasizes developmental training and it is expected that the individual will advance to higher and possibly more specific types of training at the upper grade levels. This perspective might be represented by the industrial arts programs in the junior high or middle school. The program is exploratory and each youngster may have a number of shop or trade-related experiences.

In the second perspective, the individual is enrolled in a terminal program. There is little expectancy that the individual will advance to the more highly demanding job areas. The experiences in such a program are ordinarily conducted in a self-contained setting and the stress is upon the development of social and survival skills through work experience activities.

The mathematical offerings at the prevocational level need to reflect the different perspectives. In some instances, the concepts may be similar (e.g., measurement: telling time, time to be on task, time to complete the task). In other instances there will be differences (e.g., measurement: determining the length of an item as 11¾ inches versus determining the length of an object to be as long as the red line painted on a workbench).

Vocational education for the learning disabled should also be viewed from at least two perspectives. One perspective is that commonly found in the comprehensive secondary school. The other is that found in the vocational-technical school.

The comprehensive secondary school programs tend to emphasize work experience and survival skills (e.g., interview techniques, social skills). Vocational experiences are often provided through generalized programs of industrial arts, home economics, and business education curricula.

The vocational-technical school stresses proficiency in one trade area. The purpose is to provide the individual with skills and knowledge that are associated with a specific job area. During the four years an individual spends in a vocational-technical school, about one-half the time is spent in trade areas and about one-half in academics. The vocational-technical school produces journeyperson-level entrants to the job market. Many will enter apprenticeship programs and will continue their education in collaboration with employer-sponsored programs.

The two perspectives have different implications for mathematics. The comprehensive secondary school is not as likely to require as much mathematics as the vocational-technical school. Nor will it demand as high a level of proficiency. In fact, many youngsters in comprehensive high schools may terminate their mathematics education after one or two years. This is not generally true in the vocational-technical school. Exhibit 8-1 shows the plan of study for a vocational-technical school.

On the basis of test scores, individuals are guided into programs appropriate to their levels of achievement. Some individuals enter Algebra 1 immediately, whereas others enroll in General Mathematics. In either case, a full program of mathematics is a requirement. In conjunction with regular course offerings, additional academic assistance is offered to students by the school's:

1. Basic Skills Improvement Program in reading, writing, math, listening, and speaking.

2. E.S.E.A. Title 1 Computer Assisted Instruction in Mathematics and Reading. This system supports a mainframe and approximately 100 terminals.

In addition to the above, the learning disabled receive services through an academic and/or vocational resource center. The former is equipped with computer terminals.

Learning-disabled youngsters in the comprehensive secondary school can also be the beneficiaries of four years of instruction in mathematics. All that need be done is to integrate the goals and objectives of mathematics into the Individualized Education Program. Supplemental support systems can be provided in a manner similar to that described above for the vocational-technical schools. For those youngsters with exceptional talent in mathematics, but who manifest specific learning disabilities in other areas, program modifications such as those described in Chapter 10 can be prepared. Special educators, mathematics educators, and vocational educators need to work together to provide these modifications or services.

Remedial mathematics needs to be interrelated with developmental mathematics, and each of these needs to be interrelated with applications. As a case in point, the character of mathematics can be examined as it might exist in a vocational-education program at the secondary level.

Figure 8-1 shows three facets of mathematics: the mathematics to be attended to by special education or remedial personnel, the mathematics to be attended to by mathematics teachers, and the mathematics to be attended to by trade area instructors. Here the role of the special education teacher is to assist the child to become proficient at the entry level for both the trade and mathematics programs. The special education teacher also assumes a degree of responsibility for maintaining the level of functioning of the child in the trade and classroom. The mathematics teacher works on the development of all the skills and concepts needed in the trade area and then extends the program to include the development of mathematical skills, concepts, and rules that are part of mathematics per se (e.g., explains why $3x + 4y$ works differently than 3 pears + 4 apples). The trade area teachers work on the applications of the skills, rules, and concepts of mathematics (e.g., congruence is the basis of interchangeable parts, a factor that enables educators to replace one part with another).

BASIC SKILLS AND APPLICATIONS

Osterman (1980) indicates that there is no convincing evidence that a youngster who goes through vocational training has any more success in finding a job than someone who doesn't. In addition, he indicates that a

Exhibit 8-1 Plan of study

Curriculum

The curriculum is divided into three separate units.

1. **Productive Application**—applying the technical knowledge gained in the classroom under the direction and guidance of a certified instructor in an environment that approximates that of industry.

2. **Related Technology**—the study of the mathematics, science, trade processes, drawings, and schematics used in the trade or technical field.

3. **Academic Subjects**—that lead to a high school diploma, those areas of study that assist in the development of the educated individual including english, mathematics, science, social studies, and physical education.

The school will provide a Track 1 program for those individuals who intend to terminate the formal portion of their education upon graduation from the 12th grade. It will provide a Track 2 program for those individuals who plan to continue their formal education beyond the 12th grade.

A typical four year program follows:

	Periods per 10 days	
Shop or Lab	40	
Related Technology	15	
Academic Subjects:		
English 1	8	*Math program determined by past
Social Studies	4	achievement and current test score.
*General Math 1		
or Algebra 1	8	
Physical Ed.	5	
	80	

Track 1	Periods per 10 days	Track 2	Periods per 10 days
Shop or Lab	40	Shop or Lab	40
Related Technology	15	Related Technology	15
Academic Subjects:		Academic Subjects:	
English 2	8	English 2	8
U.S. History	4	U.S. History	4
General Science 1	4	Geometry	8
General Math 2	4	Physical Ed.	5
Physical Ed.	5		80
	80		

Track 1	Periods per 10 days	Track 2	Periods per 10 days
Shop or Lab	40	Shop or Lab	40
Related Technology	15	Related Technology	15
Academic Subjects:		Academic Subjects:	

English 3	8	English 3	8
U.S. History	4	U.S. History	4
General Science 2	4	Algebra 2	8
General Math 3	4	Physical Ed.	5
Physical Ed.	5		80
	80		

Track 1	Periods per 10 days	Track 2	Periods per 10 days
Shop or Lab	40	Shop or Lab	40
Related Technology	15	Related Technology	15
Academic Subjects:		Academic Subjects:	
English 4	8	English 4	8
Democracy	4	Democracy	4
General Science 3	4	Physics	8
General Math 4	4	Physical Ed.	5
Physical Ed.	5		80
	80		

Source: Greater-Lawrence Regional Vocational-Technical School

Figure 8-1 Cooperative Education

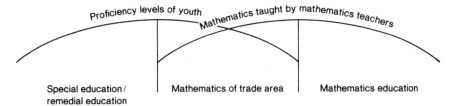

Proficiency levels of youth

Mathematics taught by mathematics teachers

| Special education / remedial education | Mathematics of trade area | Mathematics education |

Source: Reprinted from J.F. Cawley (1981), "Commentary." *Topics in Learning and Learning Disabilities, 1*(3): 89-94, © Aspen Systems, Rockville, MD.

good grasp of basic skills (reading, writing, and arithmetic) is more important than vocational training.

McMillan (1981) studied the relationships between drafting abilities and mathematical abilities of high school students in a first year drafting course. The data showed significant correlations between mathematical abilities and drafting, sufficient enough to predict that a student with an ability for mathematics would also have an ability for drafting. Drafting and blueprint reading are such important competencies for many technical areas that the lack of achievement in mathematics could seriously impede progress.

Some basic skills, acknowledging that the participating youngsters have the necessary prerequisites, can be quickly learned. McCabe (1981) studied the accuracy of linear measurement of individual students using English or metric systems. Junior and senior high school students were randomly assigned to English or metric measurement programs and provided with *one* hour of instruction in their respective systems. After one hour, each participant measured 40 different one- and two-dimensional shop materials. The objects were prepared so the lengths and widths measured were precise to the nearest millimeter or $\frac{1}{16}$ of an inch respectively.

The results showed that there were no combinations of statistically significant differences in measurement systems, IQ group, or grade level. McCabe concluded that students can quickly adapt to the measurement system without a loss in their rate of accuracy.

Surely, a good grasp of basic skills is an integral aspect of success in any field. The basic skills problem may result in a dual problem for the learning disabled. To begin with, if the learning disabled lack proficiency in these skills they are unlikely to succeed in getting a job and performing that job more than the nonhandicapped. Second, the learning disabled are likely to be excluded from many vocational schools and/or trade areas within these schools because their math scores are not "high enough" or their performance in needed math areas is inadequate.

Career Exploration for Handicapped Junior High School Students is an extensive document in use in the Jefferson County Public School System, Jefferson County, Colorado. Although the document makes specific reference to basic skills in mathematics and their application in real life, it relates these only to survival skills (e.g., making change). No reference is made to skill use in the job-related sense (e.g., reading a thermometer as part of the nurse assistant program). This particular document illustrates the problem in that there are general references to the need for proficiency in the basic skills and a need to apply these to real situations, but the real situations are not job specific.

Porter (1980) describes a "hands on" program in which students explored a variety of occupations and the impact of these experiences upon performance in academic areas. Significant differences were noted between participants in the "hands on" program and those who remained in the regular special class in reading and mathematics. Porter suggests that a major factor contributing to these differences was that the experimental group had to apply skills and concepts in order to carry out job tasks.

Not all authors are in agreement regarding the role of basic skills. A basic document, *Basic Skill Proficiencies of Secondary School Vocational Education Students* (Corman, 1980), raises a number of questions concerning performance in the basic skills.

To begin, Corman points out that although we have some information relative to the basic skills requirements of different occupations, the ratings provided in the *Dictionary of Occupational Titles* (DOT) permit only indirect inferences about reading and arithmetical reasoning. The matter might be further illustrated by a summary of a Canadian study of basic skills, which is cited by Corman as follows:

> While skill training has been developed and carried out as if every occupation or job had unique skill requirements, academic pre-vocational training has proceeded as if every job had the same academic requirements.

An analysis and comparison among vocational and nonvocational students in a number of different projects, none referencing the handicapped, led Corman to conclude:

> to date, no information exists on the extent to which job related tasks are reflected in measures commonly used in school and state assessments of basic skills.

Concern for the use of mathematics in business and industry has been expressed time and time again. Much of the early emphasis was generated under the leadership of Guy M. Wilson and is ably summarized in the text *Teaching the New Arithmetic,* which was published in 1951. Table 8-1 illustrates the decimal usage of over 68,000 workers in 89 industries. Wilson suggests that these data evidence the facts that (1) most decimal study is pursued for academic value rather than applied value, (2) decimals have little applicability, and (3) in most instances the average citizen needs only a reading knowledge of decimals. Have things changed in the years since Wilson did his work?

Phelps and Lutz (1977) adapted material to illustrate quantitative and numerical skills that ought to be included in basic skills modules for the handicapped. These materials are as follows:*

AREA: QUANTITATIVE AND NUMERICAL SKILLS

01	Counting and recording	Reads, counts, and/or records numerical information accurately.
02	Cardinal numbers	Reads, interprets, and writes cardinal numbers up to four digits.
03	Ordinal numbers	Reads, interprets, and writes ordinal numbers up to four digits.

---

*Source:*Material reprinted from L. Phelps & R. Lutz, *Career exploration and preparation for the special needs learner.* Boston: Allyn & Bacon, © 1977. Used with permission.

04	Addition/subtraction	Performs simple addition and subtraction computations accurately.
05	Multiplication/division	Performs simple multiplication and division computations accurately.
06	Measurement	Performs or interprets the following measurements correctly and accurately:

      a. distance-size
      b. weight-volume-balance
      c. liquids-solids
      d. time (measurement of)
      e. temperature-pressure-humidity
      f. torque
      g. electrical units
      h. vertical-horizontal
      i. degrees of a circle (angularity)

07	General numerical usage	Recognizes and affixes meaning to Zip codes, Social Security numbers, street addresses, etc.
08	Fractions	Reads, interprets, and uses common fractions, e.g., ½, ¼, ⅓, etc.
09	Money	Recognizes common denominators of coins and bills and can make change accurately.
10	Roman numerals	Reads, interprets, and writes common Roman numerals.
11	Approximations	Estimates and judges distances, height, weight, or size accurately.
12	Configuration	Discriminates differences in shape, form, texture, and size.

Exhibits 8-2 to 8-5 display samples of mathematics and mathematics-dependent items from a test of minimum vocational proficiency designed to assess the learning disabled. The directions to the item developers, who were trade specialists, stipulated that they were to develop items they felt represented a *minimum* capability for entrance into the specific trade area. In effect they were asked to prepare items such that a youngster who mastered the item would be acceptable in the trade area, regardless of other disabilities. Exhibit 8-2 shows the basic computation test. Note that it is not overly complex or lengthy. Note also that 12 of the 20 items were based on fractions.

Exhibit 8-3 displays test items for graphics communication technology. The computational requirements are minimal. In effect, the instructor did

Table 8-1 Extent of Decimal Usage

Census Classification	Total in survey Number	Number figuring decimals		Number reading decimals		Number not using decimals	
	Number	No.	%	No.	%	No.	%
1. Chemical industries	3,968	481	12.5	20	0.5	3,467	87.2
2. Food industries	1,403	121	8.6	129	9.1	1,153	82.3
3. Textile industries	2,353	77	3.2	6	0.2	2,270	96.5
4. Clothing	1,150	60	5.2	0	0.0	1,090	94.8
5. Fishing and forestry	160	0	0.0	2	1.2	158	98.8
6. Machinery-vehicle	33,790	4,133	12.2	2,586	7.7	27,071	80.1
7. Metal industries	1,660	422	25.4	178	10.7	1,000	63.9
8. Lumber and furniture ..	640	25	3.9	3	0.5	612	95.6
9. Paper industries	895	36	4.0	37	4.1	822	91.9
10. Leather industries	1,125	20	1.8	0	0.0	1,105	98.2
11. Miscellaneous manufacturing	11,483	3,817	33.0	4,503	39.2	3,163	27.6
12. Clay-glass-stone	3,484	58	1.7	25	0.7	3,401	97.6
13. Transport-communic ...	4,131	88	2.1	14	0.7	4,029	97.6
14. Trade	193	39	20.2	16	8.3	138	71.5
15. Wholesale-retail	49	1	2.0	3	6.0	45	94.0
16. Public Service	990	24	2.4	0	0.0	966	97.6
17. Domestic and personal	93	0	0.0	0	0.0	93	100.0
18. Mineral extraction	427	14	3.3	2	0.5	411	96.2
19. Building trades	......		4.0	....	0.0	....	96.0
20. Agriculture	47	1	2.0	1	2.0	45	96.0
Grand trades	68,043	9,417	...	7,525	.....	51,101	
Mean	....	....	7.4	....	4.6	....	88.2
Median	....	....	3.6	....	0.5	....	95.8

Source: Reprinted from G. Wilson, *Teaching the new arithmetic.* New York: McGraw-Hill, © 1951. Used with permission.

not want to place an undue burden on computation. Rather, the stress was on application and concepts, with considerable emphasis on measurement.

Exhibit 8-4 shows the pilot version of the test related to Culinary Arts. The test is entirely measurement related, a factor that further demonstrates the need to provide comprehensive programs in mathematics for the learning disabled. Computational requirements are minimal, as is true of the other tests. Item 1, "What would you do if you wanted to make 12 dozen bran muffins?" requires that the individual read the correct recipe and recognize that an increase in the number of items sought is associated with a need to increase the ingredients.

Exhibit 8-2 Arithmetic Computation Test

(41) $\begin{array}{r} 23 \\ +\ 16 \\ \hline \end{array}$	(42) $\begin{array}{r} 336 \\ +\ 407 \\ \hline \end{array}$	(43) $\begin{array}{r} 39 \\ -\ 24 \\ \hline \end{array}$	(44) $\begin{array}{r} 743 \\ -\ 407 \\ \hline \end{array}$
(A) 12　(B) 39 (C) 13　(D) 93	(A) 733　(B) 743 (C) 131　(D) 143	(A) 15　(B) 19 (C) 24　(D) 55	(A) 350　(B) 346 (C) 344　(D) 336
(45) $\begin{array}{r} 12 \\ \times\ 7 \\ \hline \end{array}$	(46) $\begin{array}{r} 236 \\ \times\ 16 \\ \hline \end{array}$	(47) $\begin{array}{r} 60.73 \\ +78.09 \\ \hline \end{array}$	(48) $\begin{array}{r} 6.073 \\ -2.345 \\ \hline \end{array}$
(A) 10　(B) 89 (C) 84　(D) 24	(A) 3776 (B) 2366 (C) 3876 (D) 1416	(A) 1388.2 (B) 130.06 (C) 138.82 (D) 136.57	(A) 4.032 (B) 3.728 (C) 4.738 (D) 4.052
(49) $\begin{array}{r} 243.4 \\ \times\ 2.7 \\ \hline \end{array}$	(50) $6\,)\overline{16}$	(51) $21\,)\overline{826}$	(52) $3.9\,)\overline{1.092}$
(A) 65.758 (B) 657.58 (C) 557.21 (D) 657.18	(A) 3　(B) 2^{R4} (C) 4^{R2}　(D) 2	(A) 93^{R7}　(B) 39^{R7} (C) 21　(D) 41^{R7}	(A) 28　(B) 3.9 (C) .28　(D) .38
(53) $\begin{array}{r} \frac{3}{4} \\ +\ \frac{4}{4} \\ \hline \end{array}$	(54) $\begin{array}{r} 1\frac{1}{3} \\ +4\frac{1}{3} \\ \hline \end{array}$	(55) $\begin{array}{r} \frac{8}{4} \\ -\ \frac{3}{4} \\ \hline \end{array}$	(56) $\begin{array}{r} 5\frac{3}{5} \\ -2\frac{1}{5} \\ \hline \end{array}$
(A) 15　(B) $\frac{7}{4}$ (C) $\frac{11}{4}$　(D) $\frac{12}{3}$	(A) $13\frac{1}{3}$　(B) 3 (C) $5\frac{3}{4}$　(D) $5\frac{2}{3}$	(A) $\frac{11}{4}$　(B) $\frac{5}{4}$ (C) $\frac{11}{8}$　(D) $\frac{5}{0}$	(A) $3\frac{2}{5}$　(B) $\frac{17}{5}$ (C) $7\frac{4}{5}$　(D) $3\frac{4}{5}$
(57) $\frac{1}{2} \times \frac{2}{4} =$	(58) $3\frac{1}{4} \times \frac{1}{5} =$	(59) $\frac{3}{4} \div \frac{1}{4} =$	(60) $1\frac{2}{3} \div \frac{1}{2} =$
(A) $\frac{2}{6}$　(B) $\frac{2}{8}$ (C) $\frac{3}{6}$　(D) 9	(A) $\frac{13}{20}$　(B) 14 (C) $3\frac{1}{20}$　(D) $3\frac{2}{9}$	(A) 12　(B) $\frac{3}{16}$ (C) $\frac{4}{8}$　(D) $\frac{12}{4}$	(A) $\frac{8}{5}$　(B) $1\frac{3}{5}$ (C) $\frac{10}{3}$　(D) $1\frac{3}{10}$

Exhibit 8-3 Task from Vocational-Technical Assessment—Graphics

TASK 12 In each frame, read the question and from the choices mark the correct answer.

1. A ream of paper contains 500 sheets. How many sheets of paper are there in two and one-half reams?
   ____ a. 750   ____ c. 1250
   ____ b. 1000   ____ d. 1500

2. Bond paper weighs 41 pounds per thousand sheets. How much would two thousand sheets weigh?
   ____ a. 8200 lbs.   ____ c. 4100 lbs.
   ____ b. 82 lbs.   ____ d. 41 lbs.

3. When processing litho-film, the film is washed in water for 10 minutes. This is 50 minutes less than the time for age paper. How long is age paper washed?
   ____ a. 40   ____ c. 100
   ____ b. 60   ____ d. 50

4. Printers have a special way to measure. The pica is an important unit of measure. It takes 6 picas to make an inch. How many picas would there be in one-half an inch?
   ____ a. 3   ____ c. 18
   ____ b. 12   ____ d. 6

5. A piece of paper is 11 inches long. How long would it be if you folded it in half?
   ____ a. 22 inches   ____ c. 5 inches
   ____ b. 2 inches   ____ d. 5 ½ inches

6. Slugs are metal strips that are used to space material between lines of type. Slugs are "6 prints" in thickness. How many slugs would it take to fill a space that was 18 prints wide?
   ____ a. 6   ____ c. 2
   ____ b. 3   ____ d. 8

7. How many pieces of 4″ × 6″ paper can be cut from a sheet that is 8″ × 12″?
   ____ a. 4   ____ c. 24
   ____ b. 10   ____ d. 2

8. A piece of paper needs to have a mark in the exact center. The paper is 8 inches by 4 inches. Where would the exact center be?
   48″   24″   2″   4″
   ____ a. 32″ ↓ ____ b. 12″ ↓ ____ c. 4″ ↓ ____ d. 6″ ↓

The test for Plant Maintenance, Exhibit 8-5, does not require any computation. The instrument is based entirely upon the ability to locate specific items and to read the given measurements.

Nearly every component of the mathematics of the vocational area involves direct application or problem solving. A guide, *Sample Practical*

Exhibit 8-4 Task from Vocational-Technical Assessment—Culinary

Read the two recipes and then answer the questions.

BRAN MUFFINS	BLUEBERRY MUFFINS
Approximate yield: 10 dozen	Approximate yield: 9 dozen
1 lb. granulated sugar	2 lbs. 8 ozs. cake flour
¾ oz. salt	1 lb. 4 ozs. shortening
6 ozs. powdered milk	2 lbs. 8 ozs. sugar (granulated)
10 ozs. shortening	1 ½ ozs. salt
1 lb. 3 ozs. honey and molasses	8 ozs. honey
8 ozs. whole eggs	½ oz. baking soda
3 lbs. water	½ oz. baking powder
1 oz. baking soda	1 lb. 4 ozs. buttermilk
8 ozs. cake flour	1 lb. 8 ozs. whole eggs
1 lb. 8 ozs. bread flour	2 lbs. blueberries (fresh or frozen)
1 lb. bran flour	
1 oz. baking powder	

1. What would you do if you wanted to make 12 dozen bran muffins?
   a.＿＿ add some buttermilk
   b.＿＿ add more bread flour
   c.＿＿ subtract some bran flour
2. Which of the following is *not* found in both recipes?
   a.＿＿ powdered milk
   b.＿＿ cake flour
   c.＿＿ salt
3. How much more salt is there in blueberry muffins than in bran muffins?
   a.＿＿ ½ oz.
   b.＿＿ ¼ oz.
   c.＿＿ ¾ oz.
4. What is the heaviest ingredient in bran muffins?
   a.＿＿ bread flour
   b.＿＿ cake flour
   c.＿＿ bran flour
5. How much less baking soda is there in blueberry muffins than in bran muffins?
   a.＿＿ 1 oz.
   b.＿＿ ½ oz.
   c.＿＿ ¼ oz.
6. If you put the cake flour, sugar and blueberries for the blueberry muffins in one pan, how much would they weigh altogether?
   a.＿＿ 6 lbs.
   b.＿＿ 7 lbs.
   c.＿＿ 8 lbs.
7. If you only wanted to make 5 dozen bran muffins, how much shortening would you use?
   a.＿＿ 10 ozs.
   b.＿＿ 8 ozs.
   c.＿＿ 5 ozs.

Exhibit 8-5 Task from Vocational-Technical Assessment—Maintenance

---

Look at the diagram of a baseball field. Answer the following questions by placing a mark next to the best answer.

---

1. How far is it from HOME PLATE to FIRST BASE?

    a. _____ 45'–0"
    b. _____ 90'–0"
    c. _____ 60'–60"

2. What is the distance straight across from FIRST BASE to THIRD BASE?

    a. _____ 127'–3⅜"
    b. _____ 90'–0"
    c. _____ 45'–0"

3. What is the difference from HOME PLATE to the PITCHER'S MOUND?

    a. _____ 90'–0"
    b. _____ 60'–0"
    c. _____ 60'–6"

4. How wide is the BASE PATH from THIRD BASE to HOME PLATE?

    a. _____ 6'–0"
    b. _____ 60'–0"
    c. _____ 60'–6"

5. What is the radius of the PITCHER'S MOUND? (R = radius)

    a. _____ 10'–0"
    b. _____ 9'–0"
    c. _____ 6'–6"

6. What letter shows the BATTER'S BOX to the right of home plate?

    a. _____ M
    b. _____ Y
    c. _____ A

7. What letter shows the CATCHER'S BOX?

    a. _____ T
    b. _____ C
    c. _____ L

Exhibit 8-5 continued

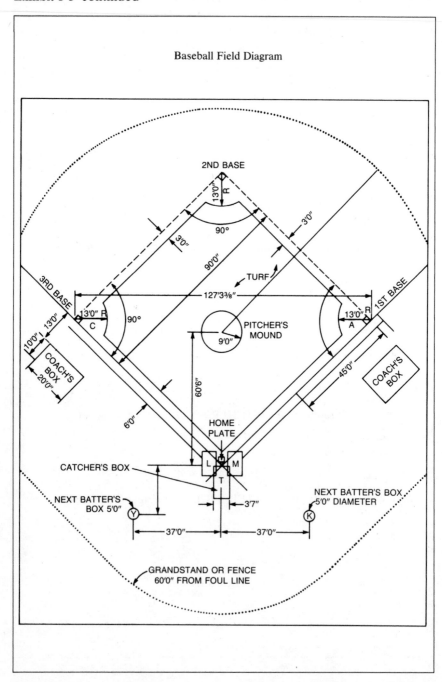

Baseball Field Diagram

Math Problems for Service Trades in Connecticut Vocational-Technical Schools, illustrates why the instructors who participated in the development of items for the tests shown previously emphasized the types of items they did.

Whole Numbers
Building:
A journeyperson working for a master painter put in 35 hours in one week. During this week she worked on four jobs. On the first job she worked 7 hours, the second 15 hours and the third 9 hours. How many hours did she put in on the fourth job?

Culinary:
How many loaves of bread can be sliced in 12 hours by a bread-slicing machine that handles 22 loaves per minute?

Graphics:
A printer can set 130 lines per hour. How many lines can he set in 5 eight-hour days?

Common Fractions
Building:
A painting contractor used white lead from a 100 lb. container in the following quantities: $4\frac{1}{4}$ lbs., $6\frac{1}{8}$ lbs., $2\frac{5}{8}$ lbs., $5\frac{5}{16}$ lbs. How much was used in all?

Culinary:
A pie was cut into 8 servings. What fractional part of pie remains after three servings are made?

Graphics:
If there are 6 picas to an inch, 1 pica is what fractional part of the inch?

Decimals
Building:
A master painter figured a job to cost $785.00. When the job was finished, the material cost amounted to $296.75 and the labor and overhead amounted to $345.45. How much profit did she make on the job?

Culinary:
If the profit on one piece of pie is .1325 cents, what is the profit on 25 pies if each pie is cut into 8 servings?

Graphics:
If an electrotype plate is .153 inch thick, what height would the electrotype base have to be in order to bring the plate up

to type high? (Type high = .918 inch). General Mathematics Curriculum in Vocational Education

Modifications in the college preparatory program are described in Chapter 10. This section will present one four-year general mathematics program from a vocational-technical school. Exhibit 8-6 shows the progression of mathematics expectancies across the four years of the secondary school. The complexity of the mathematics and the introduction of new concepts and skills takes place in the first three years. The fourth year is directed toward the application of mathematics and the use of mathematics in social experiences.

The program at the ninth-grade level reinforces and develops competence with the four operations on whole numbers, fractions, and decimals. It is not until the tenth grade that percents are introduced. At the tenth-grade level, we also find extensive reference to measurement and to geometry and this emphasis is carried into the eleventh grade. Notice that one entire term in the eleventh grade is devoted to formulae. These formulae are being used by the youngsters in their trade classes, a factor that extends their meaning and the opportunities for further practice.

This particular curriculum provides for both general and specific knowledge. It is an approach that recognizes both the commonalities among mathematics topics and the uniqueness of each in their application in the trade areas. Specific goals are established and it is anticipated that the youngster will attain them. Term II, year 3, is illustrative, as shown below:

Term II: Objectives
1. Learn how to use estimates in practical applications.
2. Calculate board feet.
3. Estimate distances.
4. Find pitch and rise of a roof.
5. Calculate work.
6. Calculate power.
7. Convert power to horsepower.
8. Calculate braking horsepower.
9. Calculate engine displacement.
10. Calculate rear-axle ratio.
11. Make calculations using Ohm's Law.
12. Convert horsepower to watts.
13. Make calculations using distance formula.

Exhibit 8-6 Course Outline for General Mathematics Sequence

GENERAL MATH I

TERM I
I.   Whole Numbers
   A. Reading and representing numbers
   B. Powers of ten
   C. Odd and even numbers
   D. Rounding whole numbers
   E. Adding whole numbers
   F. Subtracting whole numbers
   G. Multiplying whole numbers
   H. Dividing whole numbers

TERM II
I.   Fractions
   A. What are fractions?
   B. Reducing fractions
   C. Increasing fractions
   D. Least common denominator
   E. Mixed numbers
   F. Adding fractions

TERM III
I.   Fractions
   A. Subtracting fractions
   B. Multiplying fractions
   C. Dividing fractions

TERM IV
I.   Decimals
   A. What are decimals?
   B. Fractions to decimals
   C. Decimals to fractions
   D. Adding decimals
   E. Subtracting decimals
   F. Multiplying decimals
   G. Rounding off decimals
   H. Dividing decimals

GENERAL MATH II

TERM I
I.   Arithmetic Review
   A. Whole numbers
   B. Fractions
   C. Decimals
II. Percents
   A. Read and write percents
   B. Percent to decimal
   C. Decimal to percent
   D. Percent to fraction
   E. Fraction to percent
   F. Three types of percent problems
   G. Finding percent of increase or decrease

TERM II
I.   Measurement
   A. Linear measuring devices
   B. Area
   C. Volume and weight
   D. Angle measurement
   E. Other measurements
II. Systems of Measurement
   A. United States Customary System of Measurement
   B. Metric system of measurement
   C. Other conversions

TERM III
I.   Geometric Figures
   A. Plane figures
   B. Polyhedrons
   C. Circle and angle measurement
   D. Solids with circular bases
II. Geometric Formulas
   A. Plane figures

TERM IV
I.   Geometric Formulas
   A. Solids
II. Geometric Constructions
   A. Lines and angles
   B. Triangles
   C. Triangles and circles

Exhibit 8-6 continued

GENERAL MATH III

TERM I
I. Review
   A. Whole numbers, fractions, decimals and percents
   B. Metric conversions
   C. Geometric formulas
   D. Geometric constructions

TERM II
I. Formulas from Industry
   A. Building trades
   B. Work and power
   C. Automobiles
   D. Miscellaneous formulas

TERM III
I. Exponents and Square Roots
   A. Exponents
   B. Solving square roots

II. Ratio and Proportion
   A. Ratios
   B. Solving proportions
   C. Similarity
III. Right Triangles
   A. The rule of Pythagoras
   B. Special right triangles
   C. Applications to area and volume problems

TERM IV
I. Trigonometry
   A. Trigonometric ratios
   B. Trigonometric tables
   C. Trigonometric formulas
II. Statistical Tables and Graphs
   A. Interpreting tables of data
   B. Pictographs
   C. Bar graphs
   D. Broken-line graphs
   E. Circle graphs
   F. Probability

GENERAL MATH IV

TERM I
I. Review of Mathematical Operations
   A. Whole numbers
   B. Fractions
   C. Decimals
   D. Percents
   E. Ratios and proportions
II. Solve for Cost Per Unit
III. Graphs
   A. Bar
   B. Line
   C. Circle
IV. Setting Up Random and Stratified Samples
   A. Average
   B. Percent of a number
V. Data
   A. Index numbers
   B. Interpolation
   C. Extrapolation

TERM II
I. Transportation
   A. Factors to consider when buying a car
   B. Charges that increase cost of a car
   C. Solving for sales and excise tax
   D. Three major types of car insurance

   E. Operation, repairs and upkeep of a car
   F. Renting a car
   G. Air transportation plans

TERM III
I. Taxes
   A. Federal taxes
   B. State taxes
   C. Other taxes
II. Banking
   A. Simple and compound interest
   B. Annual rate of interest for house, car and personal loans
   C. Checking accounts
   D. Credit cards and charge accounts

TERM IV
I. Insurance
   A. Life
   B. Medical
   C. Fire
II. Setting Up a Budget
   A. Housing costs
   F. Food costs
   C. Clothing costs
   D. Recreation costs
   E. Charge account costs

Source: Greater-Lawrence Regional Vocational-Technical School.

INSTRUCTIONAL AND CURRICULUM PLANNING

Total programming for the learning disabled in vocational education necessitates the consideration of both instruction and curriculum. Both instruction and curriculum have their specialized functions in meeting the needs of the learning disabled. The components of curriculum—particularly in application and meaning—are often determined by the specific trade area in which the individual is enrolled. Instructional alternatives may be more directly related to the environment, the conditions of learning, and the needs of the learner. These alternatives might be more appropriately developed by each instructor relative to the curriculum area and the individuals enrolled in the program. Instructional analyses of many types may be conducted by the instructor.

One step in the instructional analysis will be the completion of an analysis by teachers to identify the characteristics and qualities of their instructional procedures. This will seek to examine factors such as:

1. Grouping arrangement
2. Use of assessment information
3. Use of IEPs
4. Type of presentation
5. Manner in which concepts and skills are taught
6. Rate of instruction
7. Quantity of instruction
8. Manner of presentation
9. Concrete approach to instruction (hands-on demonstration)
10. Physical adaptations of workspace
11. Psychosocial adaptations
12. Matching of instructional time to student/attention span
13. Immediate intervention to praise or correct
14. Modification of materials
15. Assessment style
16. Appropriate individual goal-setting
17. Generalization training
18. Consideration of multiple goals for a given task
19. Increased frequency of instruction
20. Extended practice time to assure mastery
21. Flexibility of time schedule
22. Adapting objectives/skills to meet future demands
23. Alternative programs to include community involvement in on-the-job training
24. More application of basic skills

25. Transference of skills to a variety of jobs
26. More emphasis on process of learning, thinking skills, problem solving
27. More emphasis on social skills, self-concept
28. Other

Curriculum development in mathematics for vocational preparation must include both the general factor of mathematics skills and specific matter of application in trade or career areas. Within each of these, it must be recognized that a range of competencies exist. Exhibits 8-7 and 8-8 illustrate one approach. Using Electrical and Culinary Arts as examples, one can see the many areas of application and skill development that must be focused upon. The mathematics needed by the Cake Decorator might be quite different in its specifics from that needed by the First Cook or Restaurant Manager. The mathematics needed by the Master Electrician may be different in quality from that needed by the Electric Motor Repairman.

INSTRUCTIONAL PROCEDURES

Instructional procedures are the means by which we teach. When selecting an instructional procedure, there is the tacit recognition that curriculum decisions have been made and that the instructional activities are selected to deliver the content to the individual. Or, it is possible that the instructional procedures have been developed and they are such that they can be utilized with most content. One shortcoming of many instructional procedures is that they are not compatible with the content to which they are applied. Another shortcoming is that they require the teacher to make too many modifications in style.

The instructional analysis may highlight differences in the approaches used in the basic skills classroom and those found in the work center. Given the fact that the learning-disabled individual may have to make adaptations to both, it is important that each instructor be aware of the similarities and differences. Some of these are shown below:

BASIC SKILLS

Classroom	*Trade or Job Center*
1. Paper-pencil	1. Paper-pencil
2. Symbolic emphasis	2. "Hands-on"
3. Power emphasis	3. Speed emphasis

Classroom	*Trade or Job Center*
4. Tolerance for range of accuracy	4. Specific level of accuracy
5. Variation of performance standards (e.g., 75% = C)	5. Fixed standard (e.g., 100% accuracy or job is wrong)
6. Continuous programming topics and introduction to new topics	6. Repetition of topics and high degree of habituation
7. Teaches common content to all	7. Teaches specific content to few
8. Short period of time to instruct (e.g., 1 hour per day; different topic each month, year)	8. Long period to instruct (all day, multiple years)
9. Lecture-group	9. Demonstration-individual
10. Other	10. Other

The above list illustrates some of the conditions that influence instruction in the different settings and ultimately the manner in which the learning-disabled youngster is likely to approach the application stage. The setting may also influence the extent to which the youngster is likely to acquire basic skills and concepts and habituate them so that rapid responses are provided when problem situations are presented.

Special attention is defined in the regulations of Public Law 94-142 to include *specially designed instruction*. One approach to specially designed instruction for the learning disabled is interactive programming (Cawley et al., 1979).

The interactive unit constitutes the basis for the instructional design. The utilization of this technique presents an opportunity for the generalized implementation of a technique that was developed for use in two projects with the handicapped. The technique has a number of possibilities for use in the vocational education sector. The interactive unit was originally developed as a means of exchanging mathematics skills and concepts and for parceling out the effect of a disability in one area upon performance in another. Exhibit 8-9 illustrates the interactive unit. The sixteen combinations emerge from the interaction of four input and four output alternatives.

Nearly all concepts and most skills of mathematics can be presented using all sixteen combinations. Using the fractions as an example, Exhibit 8-10 illustrates each combination.

Exhibit 8-11 shows an instructional guide containing the multiplication of fractions. What we see in Exhibit 8-11 is the potential to present and/or measure mathematics concepts and skills in a number of ways. Furthermore, we see the potential to adapt input-output combinations to real

Exhibit 8-7 Components of Electrical Curriculum

ELECTRICAL
CURRICULUM HIGHLIGHTS

Mass. Electrical Code	National Electrical Code
AC Circuits	DC Circuits
Alternating Current Principles	Transformers
Basic Devices & Fittings	Overcurrent Devices
Wire Types and Sizes	Wire Size Selection
Wire Connections & Joints	Theory of Grounding
Wiring Methods	Service Entrances
Branch Circuits	Wiring System Planning/Installing
Heavy Appliance Wiring	Off-Peak & Special Rate Wiring
Oil Burner/Gas Burner Wiring	Apartment Building Wiring
Direct Current Motors (General)	Shunt Motors
Series Motors	Compound Motors
Source of E.M.F.	Magnetic Fields
DC Motor Calculations	Automatic Motor Control
DC & AC Generation	Single & 3 Phase Wiring Methods
Fluorescent Lighting	Technical Drawings
Troubleshooting	Job Estimating
Use of Test Equipment	Job Management (Foreman)

JOB OPPORTUNITIES

Journeyman Electrician
(Self-employed)

Master Electrician
(Self-employed)

Plant Electrician

Instructor

Maintenance Electrician
& Troubleshooter

Engineer

Marine Electrician

Electric Motor
Repairman

Electronics & Electrician

Source: Greater-Lawrence Regional Vocational-Technical School.

Exhibit 8-8 Components of Culinary Arts Curriculum

CULINARY ARTS

CURRICULUM HIGHLIGHTS

Sanitation	Food Safety
Equipment Safety	Equipment Usage
Meat Roasting	Sauteing
Deep Frying	Boiling
Braising	Vegetable Preparation
Meat Preparation	Basic Meats
Animal Structure	Meat Cuts
Sea Foods	Dining Room Procedures
Dining Room Layouts	Kitchen Layouts
Specialty Tools	Radar Cooking
Baking	Dessert
Wedding Parties	Specialty Foods
Purchasing	Storage of Foods
Kitchen Procedures	Traffic Flow
Hand Tools	Automatic Equipment
Portion Control	Cost Control
Beverage Control	Cake Decorating
Garnishing	Banquets

JOB OPPORTUNITIES

1st Cook/2nd Cook

Waiter/Waitress

Stockroom Steward

Baker

Baker's Helper

Caterer

Banquet Chef

Assistant Manager

Fry Cook

Cake Decorator

Source: Greater-Lawrence Regional Vocational-Technical School.

or contrived applications. In fact, one of the more valuable aspects of the interactive unit is its utilization in real and contrived applications.

Trade area teachers tend to use these alternatives because of the product nature of their program. Thus, the type of instruction the student receives should lead to greater understanding (concepts will be better understood)

Exhibit 8-9 The Interactive Unit

	Description
Manipulate	Manipulation of objects (piling, arranging and moving)
Display	(Instructor Interaction) Presentation of displays (pictures, arrangements of materials)
Say	Oral discussion
Write	Written materials (letters, numerals, words, signs of operation) and marking of these types of materials
Identify	(Learner Interaction) Selection from multiple choices of nonwritten materials (pictures, objects)

	INPUT	INSTRUCTOR		
OUTPUT	MANIPULATE	DISPLAY	SAY	WRITE
MANIPULATE				
IDENTIFY				
SAY				
WRITE				

and to more comprehensive interrelationships between skills and concepts and between skills and concepts and applications. There should be a reduced emphasis on rote computational activities (e.g., nearly all students can do ½ ÷ ½ = , but few can explain what is going on and why the answer is 1.) Given the fact that concept development will be enhanced, we have the opportunity for the meaningful use of calculators and minicomputers to which instruction can easily be adapted.

Contrived applications are those activities that take place in conjunction with the acquisition stage. They are primarily practice sessions (e.g., word problems) that utilize materials ordinarily found in textbooks or workbooks. Real applications are those activities in which the individual makes

Exhibit 8-10 An Interactive Unit

Input	Output	Component: Fractions, Concept: Fractions As Parts of Sets
		MANIPULATE/MANIPULATE M/M The instructor places 5 blocks on a table and encloses three of them inside a large rubber band. The instructor provides the learner with five blocks and a large rubber band and asks the learner to do the same thing.
		MANIPULATE/IDENTIFY M/I The instructor places 5 blocks on a table and encloses three of them inside a large rubber band. The instructor asks the learner to select, by pointing, from several representations on display the one that looks like that which the instructor made.
	"Three Fifths"	**MANIPULATE/SAY M/S** The instructor places 5 blocks on a table and encloses three of them inside a large rubber band. The instructor asks the learner to say the name of the fraction represented.
	$\frac{3}{5}$	**MANIPULATE/WRITE M/W** The instructor places 5 blocks on a table and encloses three of them inside a large rubber band. The instructor asks the learner to write the fraction represented.
		DISPLAY/MANIPULATE D/M ✻ The instructor displays several representations of fractions as parts of sets. The instructor provides the learner with blocks and a large rubber band. As the instructor points to each picture on display, the learner copies the representation.
		DISPLAY/IDENTIFY D/I ✻ The instructor displays several representations of fractions as parts of sets. The instructor gives the learner an activity sheet on which the same fractions are represented. As the instructor points to each representation on display, the learner marks its match on the activity sheet.

Input	Output	
	"Three Fifths" "Five Sixths" "Two Fourths"	**DISPLAY/SAY D/S** The instructor displays several representations of fractions as parts of sets. As the instructor points to each representation, the learner says the name of the fraction represented.
$\frac{3}{5}$ $\frac{5}{6}$ $\frac{2}{4}$		**DISPLAY/WRITE D/W ✻** The instructor displays several representations of fractions as parts of sets. As the instructor points to each representation, the learner writes the fraction represented.

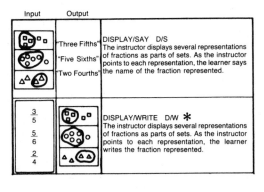

Exhibit 8-10 (continued)

	Input	Output
SAY/MANIPULATE S/M The instructor explains how part of a set can be expressed as a fraction of the entire set. The instructor says the name of a fraction. The learner, using blocks and a large rubber band, makes a representation of the fraction named.	"Three Fifths"	
SAY/IDENTIFY S/I The instructor explains how part of a set can be expressed as a fraction of the entire set. The instructor says the name of a fraction. The instructor gives the learner an activity sheet on which fractions are represented by way of pictures. As the instructor names a fraction, the learner marks the representation of that fraction.	"Three Fifths"	
SAY/SAY S/S The instructor explains how part of a set can be expressed as a fraction of the entire set. The instructor says the name of a fraction. The learner tells what the fraction means in terms of a set.	"Three Fifths"	"Three blocks out of five blocks"

	Input	Output
SAY/WRITE S/W The instructor explains how part of a set can be expressed as a fraction of the entire set. The instructor says the name of a fraction. The learner writes the fraction and draws a picture to represent the fraction.	$\frac{3}{5}$	"Three Fifths"
WRITE/MANIPULATE W/M ✱ The instructor shows the learner cards on which fractions are written. The learner, using blocks and a rubber band, makes a representation of each fraction.		$\frac{3}{5}$
WRITE/IDENTIY W/I ✱ The instructor shows the learner cards on which fractions are written. The instructor gives the learner an activity sheet on which fractions are represented. As the instructor shows a fraction, the learner marks the representation of the fraction.		$\frac{3}{5}$
WRITE/SAY W/S The instructor shows the learner cards on which fractions are written. The learner says the name of each fraction.	"Three Fifths"	$\frac{3}{5}$
WRITE/WRITE W/W ✱ The instructor shows the learner cards on which fractions are written. The learner writes the name of each fraction and draws a picture representing the fraction.	Three Fifths	$\frac{3}{5}$

Exhibit 8-11 Instructional Guide from Multi-Modal Math

MANIPULATE INPUT	Use a fraction piece representing one half. Cut that piece in half. Compare the one-half of one-half to one-fourth to show they are the same. Repeat for different fractions.

MANIPULATE OUTPUT	IDENTIFY OUTPUT	SAY OUTPUT	WRITE OUTPUT
Provide suitable materials. Direct the learner to do as you do.	Display representations of one-half, one-third, one-fourth, and one-sixth of wholes of the same size and shape. As you demonstrate each fraction of a part, ask the learner to point to the representation of the product.	Ask the learner to name the fraction represented by the piece you start with, and the fraction represented after you cut the piece. \\ //	Ask the learner to write the fraction represented by the piece you start with, and the fraction represented after you cut the piece. ¼

EVALUATION   After watching the instructor construct a representation of an expression such as ¼ × ½, ⅔ × ¾, the learner will (a) construct a representation of the same expression; (b) identify a representation of the same expression; (c) name the expression represented; (d) write the expression represented.

DISPLAY INPUT   Display representations like these:

½ × ½   ⅓ × ½   ¾ × ½

Exhibit 8-11 continued

MANIPULATE OUTPUT	IDENTIFY OUTPUT	SAY OUTPUT	WRITE OUTPUT
Provide suitable materials. Direct the learner to construct copies of the fractions represented by the shaded (colored) parts of the shapes on display 	Show representations like these: Ask the learner to match each representation to the correct representation on display.	Point to the entire part of the whole under consideration. Point to the colored (or shaded) part. Ask the learner to tell what fraction the smaller piece is of the larger (e.g., one-half of one-half; one-third of one-half, etc.).	Write expressions on the chalkboard: $\frac{1}{2} \times \frac{1}{2}$ $\frac{1}{3} \times \frac{1}{2}$ $\frac{3}{4} \times \frac{1}{2}$ As you point to each diagram on display, ask the learner to point to the expression represented by the diagram.

EVALUATION   After seeing a representation of an expression such as $\frac{1}{4} \times \frac{1}{2}$, $\frac{2}{3} \times \frac{3}{4}$, the learner will:
(a) construct a representation of the same expression; (b) identify a representation of the same expression; (c) name the expression represented; (d) write the expression represented.

SAY INPUT   Dictate expressions like these: "One-half of one-fourth; two-thirds of one half; one-half of one-third," and the like.

MANIPULATE OUTPUT	IDENTIFY OUTPUT	SAY OUTPUT	WRITE OUTPUT
Provide suitable materials. Direct the learner to show you by folding and/or cutting what each expression means. 	Display diagrams. Ask the learner to point to the diagram showing what a dictated expression means. 	Ask the learner to tell you how each dictated expression could be represented.	Ask the learner to write each dictated expression. Remind the learner that "of" can be used to indicate multiplication.

Exhibit 8-11 continued

EVALUATION   After hearing expressions such as "one-fourth of one-half; two-thirds of three-fourths," the learner will: (a) construct a representation of the same expression; (b) identify a representation of the same expression; *(c) tell how the expression could be represented; (d) write the expression.

WRITE INPUT   Direct the learner's attention to the appropriate activity sheet.

MANIPULATE OUTPUT	IDENTIFY OUTPUT	SAY OUTPUT	WRITE OUTPUT
Provide suitable materials. Ask the learner to show (by folding or cutting) what the expressions in part 1 mean.	Direct the learner to draw a path between each expression in part 1 and the representation of the product.	Direct the learner's attention to the models in part 2. Ask the learner to explain how to do the next two examples.	Direct the learner to compute the products in part 2, using the models as a guide.

EVALUATION   After seeing an expression such as ¼ × ½, ⅔ × ¾, the learner will: (a) construct a representation of the same expression, (b) identify a representation of the same expression; (c) explain how to compute the product; (d) compute the product.

direct application of the skills and concepts in job-related or social situations. The difference between the real and the contrived might be illustrated as follows:

Contrived: Problem in book. How many pieces of wood, each ½ inch long, can you get from a piece of wood that is 10 inches long?

Real: Problem in trade area activity. Tell me how many pieces of wood, each ½ inch long, you can get from a board which is 10 inches long?

In the first instance, likely to occur in the mathematics class, the expected response is 20. The response in carpentry class would be "about 18" because the individual would have to be aware that there is some loss in each cutting.

In the trade area, the problem is also likely to be given as:

> *Show* me how many pieces of wood, each ½ inch long, you can get from a board 10 inches long.

The manipulative act, that of cutting, is typical in the trade area. The symbolic act, that of computing in a paper-pencil task, is more typical of the basic skills classroom.

The combinations illustrated in the interactive unit lend themselves to the preparation of ten different types of workbook activities. Accordingly, a teacher could prepare up to ten different worksheet-based activities to cover the same content. This has many advantages in terms of small group instruction in contrast with a single presentation to the class as a group.

The interactive unit also provides a means through which teachers can cooperate to meet the needs of a given child. Assume a youngster is being served by a special education teacher, a regular math teacher, and a trade area teacher. Assume further that the appropriate mathematics for this youngster involves the division of a whole number by a fraction. Each teacher could use the same instructional guide; each could use selected interactive combinations; each could use different activity sheets. Yet, each would be focusing upon a direct need of the youngster within the context of his or her own instructional setting. The math teacher might decide to expand the conceptual structure for the child by introducing a new algorithm; the special education teacher might decide to increase rate of performance; the trade area specialist could emphasize a new or modified application.

SUMMARY

This chapter has focused on vocational education for the learning disabled. The thrust has been on the mathematics of the journeyperson-oriented program, rather than upon the socially oriented program of the work experience and survival skills programs. Vocational education for the learning disabled is an area where success can be realized and numerous skills and levels of proficiency attained. Although reading is integral to success in these programs, competency in mathematics is essential. For this reason, this chapter has stressed the development and implementation of comprehensive programs in mathematics as related to vocational education.

REFERENCES

Cawley, J.F. (1981). Commentary. *Topics in Learning and Learning Disabilities*, 1(3): 89-94.

Cawley, J.F., Fitzmaurice, A.M., Shaw, R.A., Kahn, H., & Bates, H. (1979). LD youth and mathematics: A review of characteristics. *Learning Disability Quarterly, 2,* 29-44.

Corman, L. (1980). Basic skill proficiencies of secondary school vocational education students. In *Vocational Education Study, Publication No. 4.* Washington, DC: National Institute of Education.

Jefferson County Public School. (1978). *Career exploration for handicapped junior high school students.* Jefferson County, CO.

McCabe, R.J. (1981). *A comparison of the accuracy achieved by students in shop-related vocational education classes through the use of metric and English linear measurement systems.* Unpublished doctoral dissertation, Auburn University, Auburn, AL.

McMillan, M.A. (1981). *A study of drafting abilities and mathematics abilities of high school students in a first-year course in industrial arts drafting.* Unpublished doctoral dissertation, East Texas State University, Commerce.

Osterman, P. (1980). *Getting started: The youth labor market.* Cambridge, MA: M.I.T. Press.

Phelps, L., & Lutz, R. (1977). *Career exploration and preparation for the special needs learner.* Boston: Allyn & Bacon.

Porter, M. (1980, March). Effect of vocational instruction on academic achievement. *Exceptional Children, 46,* 463-464.

Wilson, G. (1951). *Teaching the new arithmetic.* New York: McGraw-Hill.

Chapter 9

Applications of Mathematics in Other Subject Areas

Mahesh C. Sharma

Applied mathematical problem solving, especially the mathematics that apply to other content areas, is an important part of the mathematical education of any student. Applying mathematics to relevant problems is difficult for most children but more so for the student who is having difficulty in learning mathematics. They create a real dilemma for the high school mathematics educator. The dilemma is: what mathematics (what concepts, at what level) to teach these students and for what purpose; in other words what should be the nature of applications of this mathematics? The answer is not simple.

The pedagogical problems associated with this dilemma can be seen from the following cases. The first student had very high scores in everything but mathematics and mathematics-related subjects. The second student had demonstrated good performance in mathematics during classroom discussions and other projects and assignments but did extremely poorly on tests and examinations. The third student's level of performance was poor across the board in all subjects. The fourth student had high scores in the computational part of mathematics and did poorly in other areas.

All of these students were identified as learning disabled by school personnel. What is the reaction of these students when they see mathematics in other subject areas? What type of mathematics applications are best suited for the learning-disabled student in general? To understand this we have to understand what actually happens when we make an application of mathematics to other subject areas and what facets of this application are difficult for a learning-disabled student because of the constraints that his or her learning handicap puts on the learning and application of mathematics.

Mathematics in the secondary school is taught with several objectives in mind: perpetuation of a mathematical (cultural) tradition; development of intellectual (reasoning and logical) ability; preparation for higher mathematics; and presentation of a variety of topics involving applications of mathematics in everyday lives—in other words, preparing students for the real world. The underlying assumption here is that we are preparing our youngsters to meet the many different quantitative and qualitative situations they would encounter as adults in the world. Today society is highly technological. Computers generate and use vast amounts of information. This requires a facility in quantitative and qualitative mathematical skills. Quantification and representation of data is commonplace. As mathematics is becoming more and more a part of one's life, mathematics learning plays an important role in the development of a young person.

Other high school subject areas have similar objectives: to provide knowledge, to enable students to acquire and use information, and to enable them to gain proficiency in solving problems they will encounter in the future. It is in the last two areas that mathematics interacts with other subject areas. Mathematics helps in acquiring improved ways of identifying the variables to be studied in the context of given problems, collecting information about the variables, classifying the information, presenting and displaying the information, analyzing and systemizing information, and finally using the outcome of this experience in solving and resolving similar problems in other contexts. All subject areas use any or all of these mathematical problem-solving processes. But subjects such as the sciences, economics, psychology, home economics, and vocational trades require a substantial level of mathematical applications.

Almost all physical science problems and many of the problems in the social sciences lend themselves to representation through mathematical models. The range of mathematics concepts used in these modeling processes varies from simple arithmetic formulations to the most sophisticated expressions through calculus and other analytical tools. But the bulk of the mathematical applications, particularly at the secondary school level, remains at a very simple and manageable level. The mathematics of high school subjects is limited to a very few and simple yet important topics.

The major question that we want to focus on in this chapter is, Out of such a vast amount of mathematics, what topics are in the reach of a learning-disabled student for applications when he or she studies other subject areas? Or more accurately, What mathematical tools should he or she have acquired in order to study other subjects that involve mathematical concepts?

One vital consideration is that we are talking about the natural application of mathematics of significant value to other subject areas. Young people, for the most part, couldn't be interested in mathematics if its application did not have intrinsic and extrinsic value. For them mathematics should help in understanding other subject areas.

THE VALUE OF MATHEMATICS APPLICATIONS

Any problem that involves numerical data, spatial relationships, or requires careful logical analysis is a candidate for mathematical treatment. Where there is something to measure, something to be quantified, ranked, or compared, mathematics is being applied. By this criteria, there is hardly any aspect of life in which we do not measure, quantify, rank, or compare. Applications of mathematics are more pervasive than one realizes. There are several subject areas at the high school level where mathematical concepts or mathematical thinking is directly or indirectly used.

The following describes the process by which mathematics is applied to other disciplines: We begin with a situation in some other field, which we wish to understand or to act upon. We then examine it systematically, structurally, analytically. We try to represent it by a mathematical model. With a well-formulated problem in hand, we now work on it using whatever mathematical reasoning is appropriate. We find a solution, if possible, to this mathematical problem. We then go back to the original situation and interpret the solution that we have found to explain the physical phenomenon.

Mathematical applications have a variety of purposes. They range from better understanding of the original situation to action taken as a result of the analysis.

Most mathematics educators believe teaching of application is an important instructional activity. The belief is usually predicated on one of three supporting arguments. The first involves the researchable hypothesis that teaching students to apply mathematics enables them to become more analytical in making decisions in life. The second argument focuses on the idea that applying mathematics is of paramount importance in learning mathematics. Finally, mathematics is the language of science, in order to understand and use sciences, students have to know mathematics.

The application of mathematics to other content areas is one of the largest and most urgent tasks in mathematics curriculum development.

Application of mathematics to other subject areas provides students opportunities for such mathematical activities as generalization, abstraction, theory building, and concept formation. Mathematics teaching at the secondary level seems incomplete and inconceivable without applications. There is, however, another more important role of applications in the high school curriculum and that is to motivate learning of the subject matter not only for those who have a special interest in mathematics and a special aptitude for it, but also for those students who have difficulty in mathematics.

Methods and Approaches

Along with the high motivation factor and the significance of the material used, a change in methods of teaching mathematics is also in order if we want students to apply mathematics. Everyone talks about new methods, new techniques, and new materials to aid the learning of mathematics, but one may well question how much actually gets implemented in the classroom. It is one thing to study the best available clues to the learning/ teaching of mathematics, but it is quite another thing altogether to build classroom experiences making use of this knowledge.

In developing new teaching techniques or using new techniques and materials the following important variables should be kept in mind:

1. The cognitive and intellectual levels of the students
2. The mathematical learning styles of the students
3. The constraints that the learning handicaps put on the learning capacity and style of the students
4. The career objectives of the students

No one particular type of material or approach is appropriate for all students, all topics, and all grades. The teacher has to look for the match: the match between the student's cognitive level, style, and handicap and the concepts being taught; the level of difficulty and the manner in which the concept is being taught. It is not easy and it is not automatic, and we can be sure of one thing: there is no panacea.

If we are to work for the mathematical instruction of students with learning handicaps in mathematics, then it seems we are not only obligated to construct methods of instructions that reflect what is important in mathematics for these students but that our methods must be based on sound pedagogical principles in terms of what we know about these students' capabilities, potentials, and needs. We must determine how they conceptualize, use, and retrieve information.

Everything we know about children and young adults and the way they develop and the constraints that any learning handicap puts on their learning styles and capacity would seem to indicate that the tasks that are laid before them must have meaning and importance now in the present rather than the future if the students are to become interested in them. For example, involving a 16-year-old planning to buy a car in a study of automobile insurance and financing may well attract a good deal of interest. Michael T. was identified as a learning-disabled student in elementary school and he has been having problems in mathematics throughout his school career. He has always been behind in mathematics by a grade or two. When he was 14 years old his mother opened a bank account for him. He became interested in the comparison of cars—prices, performance, and value. The same student who could not do simple arithmetic earlier now can explain the difference between different types of compound interests, rates of depreciation and appreciation, and best buys in cars by analyzing several variables at the same time. His favorite newspaper is the *Wall Street Journal*.

What about the teacher in all this? For teaching meaningful applications of mathematics the teacher (whether a mathematics teacher or other subject matter teacher) must have:

1. a good knowledge of mathematics
2. a knowledge of subject matter other than mathematics
3. the ability to represent problems through mathematical modeling
4. an understanding of how the interaction between mathematics and other subject matter areas takes place
5. a background in the history of the development of mathematical ideas.

The development of mathematical concepts takes place through two major approaches: one is when physical phenomena are explained through a mathematical model. That model is studied as a mathematical problem. It is generalized and abstracted. This process of study, generalization and abstraction, gives rise to new concepts and ideas and therefore a new body of mathematical knowledge. The other approach is when a particular concept in mathematics is explained through a physical or sociological phenomenon. In this process there is not always a neat and direct fit and therefore more mathematics is created through this intermediate refining process. The areas of mathematics that have come into existence as a result of the first activity are algebra, geometry, calculus, trigonometry, systems of equations, etc. The second situation has given us complex analysis, differential equations, Boolean algebras, number theory, etc. (Of course, there is the third approach, when mathematicians create mathematics without any particular application in mind. Many of them "do" mathematics for mathematics sake.)

Types of Applications

Mathematics applications can be classified into two types. The first type of application is to develop and explain concepts in other disciplines. This process involves developing mathematical models representing the problem or phenomenon arising from and existing in other fields. This particular approach is seen in the fields of biology (applications of geometry and probability), physics (algebra, geometry, and trigonometry), chemistry (algebra and trigonometry), and business or economics (arithmetic and algebra). The second type of application is to explain mathematics concepts by physical, chemical, biological, or sociological phenomena.

Two types of books have mathematics applications. One type includes books such as biology texts (for applications of geometry and probability), physics texts (algebra, geometry, and trigonometry), chemistry texts (algebra and geometry), business or economics texts (arithmetic and algebra). A second type of book is the one written for students of other subjects— *The Mathematics of Biology, The Mathematics of Home Economics,* etc. Such books are for scientists, managers, draftsmen, electricians, nurses, technicians, machinists, carpenters, biologists, police officers, consumers, etc.

Some newer branches of mathematics are so allied with applications that it is difficult to pick up a text without finding applications in it. Recently there have appeared a large number of pamphlets for use with hand calculators; these have applications. Statistics books usually deal with real problems. Probability texts have always contained material on games of chance; conversely, books about card games or gambling often have much to say about probability.

Applications of mathematics in other content areas are quite diverse, from applications of one branch of mathematics to another such as simple arithmetic to calculus.

Other than the applications of higher mathematics to professional fields, the mathematics used at the high school level can be divided into three major categories: arithmetic, algebra, and geometry. In many of the high school content areas these three have an important part to play. Geometry, which deals with form and shape, or "spatial relationships," continually employs arithmetic and algebra. Trigonometry is a special kind of mathematics that employs all three. Almost every practical problem employs some algebra and geometry and a substantial amount of arithmetic.

The mathematical needs of high school students include mathematical knowledge for daily living and mathematical insight necessary for understanding other subject areas. Of course, the amount of mathematics needed for future professional needs of these students varies so enormously that hundreds of books are written on the subject of applications of higher mathematics. Their contents vary from simple arithmetic for real estate agents to calculus and complex analysis for electronic engineers.

Obstacles and Incentives

The major problem that students face in learning meaningful mathematical applications stems from these factors:

1. The teaching of mathematics and the teaching of content areas have become estranged; the training of teachers is too limited to their specific subject areas.
2. Mathematics teachers do not have enough time and expertise to include lectures on other subjects in their courses in order to show real applications of mathematics.
3. Teachers of other subject areas have a fear and very little knowledge of mathematics.
4. The bulk of mathematics that does apply to other fields is too advanced for the ordinary student.
5. By high school many students have developed a real "phobia" about anything mathematical and most teachers have very little expertise in helping students to remove their anxiety about mathematics.

Mathematics training provides two direct and at least one indirect advantage in life. Direct advantages have to do with the knowledge and problem-solving skills one gains, the indirect advantage is that a person who has studied mathematics should be able to live more intelligently than one who has not. And, up to a point at least, the more mathematics studied, the more intelligent one's life may be said to be.

MATHEMATICAL CONTENT FOR THE HIGH SCHOOL STUDENT

Advanced Arithmetic

- *Operations with very large and very small numbers*
- *Integers (signed numbers)*
  Adding, subtracting, multiplying, and dividing signed numbers; forming equations involving signed numbers; solving simple equations

involving signed numbers; reading Fahrenheit and Celsius thermometers and converting from one system to another; reading profit and loss statements.
Used in physics, chemistry, business, and vocational courses.

- *Fractions, decimals, and percents*

Adding, substracting, multiplying, and dividing fractions and decimal numbers; converting fractions into decimals and decimals into fractions. Writing small and large numbers in the scientific notation form. Contructing equations and solving equations involving fractions and decimal numbers. Interconversion of fractions, decimals, and percents. Applications of decimals and percents to problems such as profit and loss; sales, commissions, depreciation, and appreciation; averages; wage calculations, tax computations; solution and mixture problems.
Used in physics, chemistry, business, and vocational courses.

- *Ratio and proportion*

Identifying ratios; forming ratio and proportions; setting up ratio and proportion equations; solving equations involving ratio and proportion.

Used in physics, chemistry, vocational areas, business courses, home economics, economics, biology, art, and photography.

Algebra

- Writing algebraic expressions involving variables and performing fundamental operations using algebraic operations.
- Setting linear equations and inequalities in one variable. Solving linear equations in one variable.
- Uses of variables in formulas. Solving for one variable.
- Rates, ratios, and proportions involving variables.
- Setting up relations: correspondences, mappings, functions.
- Setting nonlinear equations, quadratic equations.
- Laws relating to exponents; radical expressions.
- Maxima-minima problems; linear programming.
- Rates and slopes.
- Coordinate systems; representing functions and graphs using coordinate systems.

Geometry

- Identifying common geometrical shapes and calculating areas, circumferences, volumes, and surface areas of common, practical geometrical shapes.
- Understanding the relationships between points, lines, planes, and angles. Application of parallel lines, angle relationships to practical situations.
- Right triangle and the Pythagorean theorem.
- Ideas of similarity and congruence in geometry.
- Ideas of scales, proportion, symmetry, transformations, and perspective in geometry.
- Introductory coordinate geometry and non-Euclidean geometry concepts.

Trigonometry and Logarithms

- Basic trigonometric relations and reading tables.
- Logarithms and exponents.

Probability and Statistics

- Deriving permutation and combination relationships.
- Understanding probabilities and expectations.
- Classification, presentation, and interpretation of data: graphs, bar graphs, histograms, charts and tables; mean, mode, median, frequency distribution of data.

Number Theory

- Important elementary number theory relationships.
- Development of number concepts (rational, irrational, and complex number system).
- Binary system

Computer Literacy

- Preparing flow charts.
- Task analysis and sequencing of tasks.
- Writing programs using simple algorithms.
- Understanding computer capabilities and limitations.

MATHEMATICAL APPLICATIONS

Mathematics of Biology: Number and Forms in Nature

A professional biologist uses a great deal of mathematics, generally in the category of higher mathematics: graphs and algebra, rates of growth and decay, prediction, extrapolation and interpolation, variability, correlation studies, geometry of body form, etc. To a high school student the interaction of mathematics and biology comes in the form of understanding the functioning of the body and its physiology. With today's consciousness of nutrition and good health, it is important to understand measurement and ratio (ratio of input to output).

The major mathematical concepts used in biology are probability and statistics and permutation and combination from simple algebra. It is assumed that students can perform operations with rational numbers (fractions and signed numbers).

Examples of Mathematics Applications in Biology

- Biologists have estimated that on the average ten pounds of useful food is needed to produce one pound of body tissue in a living animal. This varies from animal to animal and additional food is needed to maintain body tissue and to provide energy for functioning. Extrapolating this information for human beings, let us assume that it takes twelve pounds of food consumption for the production of one pound of body tissue. We can determine the approximate amount of food necessary for a baby to reach a weight of 100 pounds. Let us also assume that it takes ten pounds of grain to produce one pound of animal meat. How much grain is needed to produce the meat necessary for the daily consumption in America if the daily intake of meat by an American is half a pound? (The population of the United States is 230 million people.)

- It is reported that the weight and length of an animal are nearly linearly related. If a 45 cm long animal weighs 5 kg, what is the weight of the animal when it is 127 cm long?
- Biologists have found that the number of chirps crickets of a certain species make per minute is related to the temperature. The relationship is very close to linear. At 68° F those crickets chirp about 124 times a minute. At 80° they chirp 183 times a minute. Find the linear equation relating Fahrenheit temperature F and the number of chirps C. If you count chirps for only ten seconds, how can you quickly estimate the temperature?

In biology and other related sciences precision instruments are an important means of obtaining accurate data quickly. Microscopes and automatic analyzers, for example, are necessary to examine bacteria culture, blood cholesterol level, and tissue samples. In recent years, the computer has provided an efficient tool for storage of vast quantities of scientific information. In some cases, the computer has been programmed to give preliminary results, but a student needs to understand the mathematics behind the results.

Mathematics of Physics

Very little meaningful physics can be understood or used without mathematics; mathematics is the language of physics. Physics even at the secondary level uses mathematics that is quite sophisticated—ratio and proportion in the lever principle, trigonometry and geometry in optics and its uses, matrix algebra and calculus in simple relativity theory and quantum mechanics. A learning-disabled student with difficulty in mathematics also faces major difficulties in understanding physics and its applications. Even at the secondary level a good understanding of physics involves among others the following mathematical concepts:

- signed number operations
- ratio and proportion
- forming linear equations and their solutions
- exponents
- simultaneous linear equations
- quadratic equations
- functions and graphs
- geometry and trigonometry

Examples of Mathematics Applications in Physics

- Gear A has 120 teeth; gear B has 60 teeth. If gear A revolves a times per minute, how many times per minute does gear B revolve? Call a positive when the turn is counterclockwise. Call a negative when the turn is clockwise. Is the answer to the first part of the question different if we consider the direction?

- Applying the principles of relativity, we find that as an object travels at velocity v, its original mass m_o will become m, where $m = \dfrac{m_o}{\sqrt{1 - \dfrac{v^2}{c^2}}}$ and c = speed of light $\approx 3 \times 10^5$ km/sec.

  (a) At half the speed of light, by what factor is an object's original mass multiplied?

  (b) If this formula is used for a velocity very close to the speed of light, what happens to the mass?

- According to Newton's law of gravitation, the magnitude of the force between two objects is proportional to the product of their masses and inversely proportional to the square of the distance between their centers. That is,

$$g = G \cdot \frac{m_1 \cdot m_2}{d^2}$$

where d is the distance between them. At what point on the line joining the centers of the earth and the moon do the gravitational forces on an object due to the moon and earth have the same magnitude?

  mass of earth $= 5.98 \times 10^{24}$ kg
  mass of moon $= 7.35 \times 10^{22}$ kg
  mean distance from center of the earth to center of the moon $= 4.60 \times 10^8$ m.

- An electric motor is designed to run on any voltage in a range from 200 to 210 volts, plus or minus 5 percent. What is the actual range of voltages within which the motor will run as designed?

Mathematics of Chemistry

Though we rely on products of chemical research every day we seldom realize how many hours chemists worked to develop such things as plastics, synthetic fibers, and antibiotics.

Chemists investigate the properties and composition of matter and try to put this knowledge to practical use. They design and conduct laboratory experiments and describe their results in reports that may be published in scientific journals.

Modern chemistry needs a substantial grounding in mathematics but chemistry concepts at the high school level can be understood with a good understanding of arithmetic and introductory algebra. The two most important concepts from arithmetic used in chemistry are operations of signed numbers and ratio and proportion. The major concept from algebra is forming linear equations and solving them.

Geometric models and mathematical equations help chemists understand the structure and behavior of atoms and molecules and reactions between chemicals and elements. For example, geometrical models are useful in illustrating the lines of symmetry that may exist in a molecular structure. The mathematical equation $N_1V_1 = N_2V_2$ describes the reaction between two chemicals. Here N_1, N_2 represent the chemical strengths of the chemicals and V_1, V_2 represent the volumes of the chemicals used. By this equation we can calculate one of the variables if the values of the other three variables are known. For example, if we know the value of V_1, V_2 and N_2 then $N_1 = N_2 \dfrac{V_2}{V_1}$. This equation is obtained by using the knowledge of ratio and proportion.

Examples of Mathematics in Chemistry

- There are three temperature scales in common use in chemistry. Celsius (or centigrade), Fahrenheit, and Kelvin. Conversions from Celsius temperatures to those measured on the Fahrenheit or Kelvin scale can be carried out by means of the formulas

  $$F = (9/5)C + 32, \ K = C + 273$$

  A chemistry textbook describes an experiment in which a reaction takes place at a temperature of 400° Kelvin. What are the corresponding Celsius and Fahrenheit temperatures?

$$400 = C + 273$$
$$127° = C$$
$$F = (9/5)(127) + 32$$
$$= 228.6 + 32$$
$$= 260.6°$$

- French scientist Jacques Charles in 1787 discovered, by applying linear extrapolation, that gases expand when heated and contract when cooled. Charles used this linear relationship to find volume and temperature if one of them is known. Suppose a particular gas had a volume of 500 cc at 27°C and a volume of 605 cc at 90° C. Using these data a linear equation can be obtained. Similarly, using this equation the temperatures can also be obtained for different volumes.

- A malfunction in the sewage system of a town causes a toxic chemical to be introduced into a lake, which is the town's source of water. Thus it is necessary to stop using the water. If the level of toxicity is 10 times the safe level, and the lake has a natural flushing action of about 50 percent in 10 days, what estimate should the county Board of Health give to residents concerning the time lag until the water will be usable?

Mathematics for General Science

Mathematics belongs to every inquiry, biological as well as physical. Even the rules of logic, by which it is rigidly bound, could not be deduced without its aid. Every theory in the physical and biological sciences gets its expression through mathematics.

The concept of mathematics is the concept of science in general. It is only through mathematics that we can thoroughly understand what science is.

With an acquaintance with trigonometry and the elements of algebra, one may take up and understand popular scientific and technological information.

Geology

Geology is part of the general field of environmental science. Many high schools offer courses in this field. The study of geology involves studying the structure, composition, and history of the earth's crust and analysis of mineral structures by X-ray techniques and complex instruments that permit close study of rock formation.

In geology, as in all sciences, a working knowledge of mathematics is an essential tool. Identification of shapes and solid structures, geometrical transformations, coordinate and solid geometry, pattern recognition and its extension are some of the topics considered.

Examples of Mathematics in Geology

- In 1970 the known coal reserves in the world were estimated at 5×10^{12} tons. The rate of consumption was about 2.2×10^9 tons a year.

  (a) At this rate, how long would those reserves last?
  (b) How long would they last if the rate of consumption increased 5 percent a year?
  (c) How long would they last if the rate of consumption remains at a level 10 percent below the current level?
  (d) What if the actual coal reserves were four times as great as the known ones?

- Crystals are classified by their symmetries into 32 classes, which in turn are grouped into six systems: cubic or isometric, hexagonal, tetragonal, orthorhombic, monoclinic, triclinic. Find out what a crystal of each system would look like and describe the types of symmetries.

Mathematics of Business

Students in general think that business courses at the secondary level require little mathematics, but contrary to this belief the business courses require a good proficiency in basic arithmetic and algebra. The concepts involved are

- ratio and proportion
- signed numbers and their operations
- exponents
- percentages and averages (simple and compounded interest formulas)
- simple equations

Mathematics at a higher level, including the secondary level, is a means of supplementing language. It provides a thought form and expression that helps a businessperson to be exact, concise, and logical. A great deal of the essential facts of the financial sciences and countless social and political problems are easily accessible to those who have a sound training in mathematical analysis and logic. Today, to make a fitting use of knowledge in any field of endeavor, it is as necessary to be able to compute, to think in averages and maxima and minima, as to be able to read comprehensively and to write well.

Examples of Mathematics in Business

- On the average, 1½ percent of the items produced by a company are found to be defective before shipping. So, on the average, how many items should be manufactured in order to ship 5,000 nondefective items?

$$X = \text{number of items manufactured}$$
$$X - .015X = 5000$$
$$.985X = 5000$$

About 5078 items

- An estate valued at $10,000 is to be divided among a wife, a son, and a daughter. Each is to receive $1,000 and then the rest is to be divided so that the wife receives twice as much as the daughter and the daughter twice as much as the son. How much does each receive?

$$X = \text{additional inheritance of son}$$
$$3000 + 4X + X + 2X = 10,000$$
$$7X = 7000$$
$$X = 1000$$

wife: $5,000; son: $2,000; daughter $3,000

- Two companies, A and B, offer a student a sales position. Both jobs are essentially the same, but A pays a straight 20% commission and B pays $150 per week plus 15% commission. The best salespeople with either company rarely have sales greater than $5,000 per week. For what amounts of sales will company A pay more money?

$$.20X > 150 + .15X$$
$$.20X - .15X > 150$$
$$.05X > 150$$
$$5X > 15,000$$
$$X > 3000$$

For $X = 4,000$, company A will pay more money.

- Linear depreciation is one of several methods approved by the Internal Revenue Service for depreciating business property. If the original cost of the property is C dollars and it is depreciated linearly over N years, its value V at the end of N years is given by

$$V = C \left(1 - \frac{n}{N}\right)$$

A machine having an original cost of $20,000 is depreciated linearly over 20 years. When will its value be $15,000?

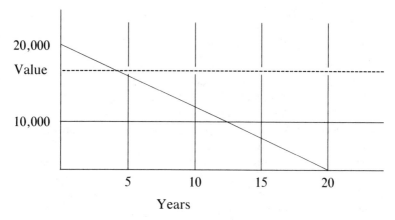

$$15,000 = 20,000 \left(1 - \frac{n}{20}\right)$$

$$\tfrac{3}{4} = 1 - \frac{n}{20}$$

$$\frac{n}{20} = \tfrac{1}{4}$$

$$n = 5 \text{ years}$$

- An apartment building then worth $3,000,000 was built in 1950. What is its value (for tax purposes) in 1989 if it is being depreciated linearly over 50 years?

- In 1960 the BBB Cab Co. purchased $80,000 worth of new cabs. What is the value of these cabs in 1989, if they are being depreciated linearly over a period of 30 years?

- A simple example of algebra arises in the study of compound interest. There the interest is added to the principal at regular intervals of time and thereafter earns interest. The interval of time between successive calculations of interest is called conversion period. If the conversion period is one year, we say that the interest is compounded annually and if we borrow (or invest) P dollars compounded annually at the interest rate i, then the amount we owe (or have coming) at the end of n years is given by

$$A = P(1 + i)^n$$

If $10,000 is invested at 10% (compounded annually), then the value of this investment after 5 years is given by:

$$A = 10,000 (1 + 0.10)^5$$
$$= 10,000 (1.10)^5$$

Mathematics in Vocational Subjects

For all the higher arts of vocational activities some acquaintance with mathematics is indispensable. To be a carpenter one has to master skills that involve constant reference to quantitative ratios and proportions and calculations with special fractions. In the construction industry calculations abound. The surveyor upon the results of whose survey the land is purchased; the architect in designing a mansion to be built on it; the builder in preparing his estimates; his foreman in laying out the foundations; the mason in cutting the stones; and the various artisans who put up the fittings—are all guided by quantitative rules and geometrical truths.

Every vocational field relies heavily on arithmetical calculations and geometrical explorations. The extent of the mathematics used is ordinary eighth-grade mathematics. The topics include

- estimation
- basic operations of addition, subtraction, multiplication, and division of whole numbers, fractions, decimals, and signed numbers.
- calculating areas, volumes, weights, surface areas, capacities of geometrical shapes and solids.
- calculating ratios, percentages, averages, and proportions
- solving mixture problems
- isolating variables and relating variables to understand the mutual effects of variables and their individual contributions to problems or solutions.
- reading of all kinds of meters, bills, and reports relating to specifications.

The mathematics of vocational subjects takes into account the practicability of a solution along with finding optimal solutions using mathematical methods. The mathematics of the vocational arts has certain characteristics:

- Mathematics of the vocational arts uses more estimation (close or relevant) compared to actual calculations. One uses different levels of accuracies in estimating answers.
- Even the ordinary calculations of the vocational subjects have many more variables to contend with. For example: Given a 10″-long piece of wood, show how many pieces of 2″-wide pieces can be cut from this piece. (Answer: 5 pieces).

  The answer given above is a mathematical answer. The answer in the "shop" will not be 5 or the five pieces will not have 2″ as their width, as there is wastage when the pieces are cut. Therefore mathematics in the "shop" has to take these factors into account. Mathematics in the shop has to be practical.

Examples of Mathematics in Construction

We come in contact with the products of the construction industry in almost every aspect of our daily lives, from the house we live in, to the roads we travel upon. The building trade encompasses a wide range of occupations: surveyors, carpenters, electricians, plumbers, bricklayers, and masons, to name a few.

Mathematics is important in the construction process from the planning stage to the finishing touches. Successful planning of any construction project involves applying mathematical principles to problems of structure and design. Precision in carrying out the architect's plans is needed to guarantee the quality of the finished structure.

A careful look at a building structure under construction will reveal applications of geometric principles, particularly those involving parallel and perpendicular lines and planes.

- For a certain construction job five pieces of floor joints are needed. The required lengths of the pieces are as follows: 11 feet, 8 feet, 4 feet, and 3 feet. What is the total length to be purchased, allowing 1 foot for waste?

- Suppose a 4,000-foot-long railroad rail is solidly anchored at both ends (with no expansion joints) and expands in length by 2 feet on a very hot day, buckling up as shown:

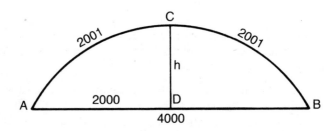

Let us assume that the height is h feet. Now consider the following diagram (a right-angled triangle). Using the Pythagorean theorem, we get

$$(2001) = h^2 + (2000)$$
$$4001 = h^2$$
$$63 \cong h$$

If no expansion joints are allowed, the buckling effect will be approximately 63' in height.

- You can estimate the height of a tree (XY) by placing a mirror (R) on the ground and moving backward in line with the tree to the point B where you observe in the mirror the image of the top of the tree.

    (a) If a person's eyes are 5'5'' from the ground and he finds BR = 5 ft. and RX = 20 ft., estimate the height of the tree.

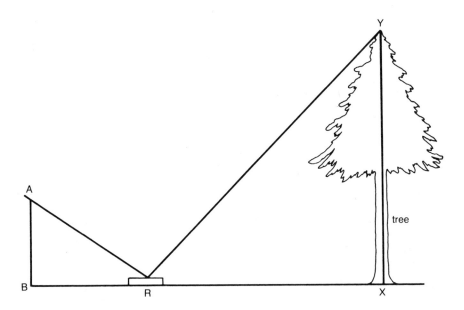

IMPORTANT MATHEMATICS SKILLS FOR A HIGH SCHOOL STUDENT

Although we earlier identified the mathematics that a high school student needs, we find that along with the basic arithmetic skills, a few key mathematics skills are used more often than others. In this section we shall discuss these key concepts.

The Number Line and Its Applications

To help understand numbers and their uses, many models have been used. One of the most successful of these ways to picture numbers is the use of the number line. The number line is used in many forms in our everyday life. A ruler is a fine example, of course. The common application of a number line appears in a thermometer, comparison of profits and loss in a financial statement, and many other measurement devices. Graphing in two- or three-dimensional coordinate systems is an extension of number line application, where two or three number lines are used as axes.

Applications of Number Line

• *Signed Numbers: How To Manipulate Plus and Minus Signs*

The plus and minus signs in arithmetic are operations of addition and subtraction respectively, but in algebra − is regarded as the reverse of +. Any number with a + before it is a gain, increase, asset, or lies on the right of zero on the number line, while any number with a − sign before it is a loss, decrease, debt, or lies on the left of zero on the number line. If + indicates a measurement along the scale in one direction, then − indicates measurement along the scale in the opposite direction. If +17 means a temperature of 17 above zero, then −17 means a temperature of 17 below zero. If +500 means a deposit to an account (credit), then −50 means a withdrawal from the account (debit). If 1,500 means 1,500 ft. above sea level, then −1,500 means 1,500 ft. below sea level. If +568 means A.D. 568, then −568 means 568 B.C. If +10 means 10 paces forward, then −10 means 10 paces backward.

These numbers with a sign attached are called *directed* or *signed* numbers.

• *Operations of Signed Numbers*

Consider the following examples:

(a) $+6 + 2 = ?$	(e) $+6 \cdot +2 = ?$	(i) $+6 \div +2 = ?$
(b) $+6 - 2 = ?$	(f) $+6 \cdot -2 = ?$	(j) $+6 \div -2 = ?$
(c) $-6 + 2 = ?$	(g) $-6 \cdot +2 = ?$	(k) $-6 \div +2 = ?$
(d) $-6 - 2 = ?$	(h) $-6 \cdot -2 = ?$	(l) $-6 \div -2 = ?$

In examples (a) and (d) both numbers have the same signs indicating the same activity. In such a situation we apply the following rule:

Rule 1. For the same signs we add the numbers and use the common sign.

Thus $+6 + 2 = +8$, $-6 - 2 = -8$

In examples (b) and (c) the two numbers have opposite signs indicating opposite activity. In such situations we apply the following rule:

Rule 2. In the case of opposite signs we subtract the numbers and use the sign of the larger number.

Thus $+6 - 2 = +4$, $-6 + 2 = -4$

In multiplication and division we have the following rules.

Rule 3.	$+ \cdot + = +$	$- \cdot - = +$
	$+ \cdot - = -$	$- \cdot + = -$

Rule 4.	$+ \div + = +$	$- \div - = +$
	$+ \div - = -$	$- \div + = -$

Thus

$$+6 \cdot +2 = +12 \qquad +6 \div +2 = +3$$
$$+6 \cdot -2 = -12 \qquad +6 \div -2 = -3$$
$$-6 \cdot +2 = -12 \qquad -6 \div +2 = -3$$
$$-6 \cdot -2 = +12 \qquad -6 \div -2 = +3$$

Scientific Notation

We can write 3000 as 3×10^3 and 298 million as 298×10^6 or as 2.98×10^8. These are compact ways of writing the number. Also, it is easy to compare several large numbers written in this form. For example, we can tell at a glance that 4.2×10^{12} is bigger than 8.4×10^7 without counting decimal places in 4200000000000 and 84000000. This notation often simplifies calculations with large numbers. It is a common practice in scientific and engineering work to represent numbers in this way, namely in the form

(a number between 1 and 10) $\times$ (a power of 10).

The number is then said to be written in *scientific notation*. A number is said to be expressed in scientific notation if it is written as the product of a decimal numeral between 1 and 10 and the proper power of 10. If the number is a power of 10, the first factor is 1 and need not be written.

Sometimes *"scientific notation"* is referred to as *"power of ten"* notation. Scientific notation is commonly used with very large and small numbers such as population and budget information and mathematics in chemistry, physics, biology, and earth sciences.

Example

Since the earth does not travel in a circular path, the distance from the earth to the sun varies with the time of the year. The average distance has been calculated to be about 9.3×10^7 miles. The smallest distance from the earth to the sun would be about 1½ percent less than the average; the largest distance would be about 1½ percent more than the average.

(a) The smallest distance will be
   $9.3 \times 10^7 - (1\frac{1}{2}\%)$ of 9.3×10^7

(b) The largest distance will be

$$9.3 \times 10^7 + (1\frac{1}{2}\%) \text{ of } 9.3 \times 10^7$$
$$1\frac{1}{2}\% = 1.5\% = .015 = 1.5 \times 10^{-2}$$
$$(9.3 \times 10^7) \times (1.5 \times 10^{-2}) = (9.3 \times 1.5) \, 10^5$$
$$= 13.95 \times 10^5$$
$$= 1.395 \times 10^4$$
$$= 1.4 \times 10^4 \text{ (approximately)}$$
$$\text{smallest distance} = (9.3 \times 10^7) - (1.4 \times 10^4)$$
$$\text{largest distance} = (9.3 \times 10^7) + (1.4 \times 10^4)$$

Decimals and Percents

The two most commonly used mathematics concepts in any subject (other than mathematics) are the decimal representation of quantity and the percent operation. With the use of calculators, the use of decimal numbers has become even more important and the understanding of the percent operation is the key to successful transactions in many areas.

Percent is a particular form of fraction in which the denominator is always one hundred. Percent means per hundred (cent); 5% means 5 percent or 5 per hundred or $\frac{5}{100}$. The important thing to understand is that 100% (one hundred percent $= 100$ per $100 = \frac{100}{100} = 1$) is 1 and that we may therefore multiply by 100% without changing the value. In order to express any fraction or decimal as a percentage we multiply it by 100%, as in the following examples:

$$\frac{1}{4} = \frac{1}{4} \times 100\% = 25\%$$
$$\frac{1}{2} = \frac{1}{2} \times 100\% = 50\%$$
$$\frac{1}{5} = \frac{1}{5} \times 100\% = 20\%$$
$$\frac{9}{10} = \frac{9}{10} \times 100\% = 90\%$$
$$\frac{1}{3} = \frac{1}{3} \times 100\% = 33\frac{1}{3}\% \times 33.3\%$$
$$.25 = .25 \times 100\% = 25\%$$

When we multiply a decimal by 10 the decimal moves to the right by one place; when we multiply by 100, the decimal moves to the right by two places; etc.

Fraction	$\frac{1}{10}$	$\frac{1}{5}$	$\frac{1}{4}$	$\frac{1}{8}$	$\frac{3}{4}$	$\frac{9}{10}$	$\frac{1}{3}$	$\frac{2}{3}$
Decimal	0.1	0.2	.25	0.125	0.75	0.9	0.333	$.666 = .\overline{6}$
Percent	10	20	25	12.5	75	90	33.3	66.6

Conversion

- From fraction to decimal:
  divide the numerator by the denominator.
- From decimal to percent:
  move the decimal point two places to the right.
- From percent to decimal:
  move the decimal point two places to the left.
- From fraction to percent:
  multiply the fraction by 100% and simplify.
- From decimal to fraction:
  express the decimal as a fraction and reduce it.

Use of Decimals and Percents

Interest is usually expressed as a rate percent per annum. If the rate is, for example, 6 percent per annum, this means that if you lent $100 for a year, you will receive $106 back, the additional $6 00 being the interest. If you had left the money on loan for two years, on this basis, you would have been entitled to $12 interest.

This assumes that the interest is not asked for until the end of two years. If, in the case of the $100 for two years at 6 percent per annum, the interest had been paid by the year there would have been $106 owing at any time during the second year. As 6 percent of $106 is $6.36, this means that at the end of two years you would have been entitled to $112.36, not $112. This is called *compound interest,* the additional $.36 is interest on the first year's interest, which is put in and regarded as part of the loan. Every adult deals with money and interest and therefore it is important to understand the difference between different rates and types of interest to make the best use of one's money. The idea of interest comes up in loans, credit card buying, time payments, and mortgages.

Thus, in order to understand interest and its implications one has to acquire the following skills:

- basic operations of addition, subtraction, multiplication, and division
- percentages
- estimation

- basic operations of addition, subtraction, multiplication, and division of whole and decimal numbers
- comparison
- extrapolation

Writing Number Sentences

All of us use sentences every day. We use sentences in talking. When we read, we read sentences. In mathematics we need to deal with many kinds of sentences. We use sentences to explain physical phenomena and then translate physical phenomena into mathematical sentences. We use sentences to explain mathematics and to discuss mathematics. Whenever there is any application of mathematics in any other subject area it results in some type of mathematical sentence. A number sentence using the symbol "=" indicates equality. The sentence, $X + 4 = 9$, makes the statement that "$X + 4$" and "9" are different names for the same number. We call such a sentence an *equation*. The mathematical sentence "$X - 5 \geq 7$" is called an *inequality*. This sentence indicates that the number represented by "$X - 5$" is *greater than or equal to* the number represented by "7." Other examples of inequalities are "$X + 4 < 17$" or "$3X \neq 18$."

Use of Number Sentences and Equations

- The AA Car Rental Company charges a daily rate of $25 and 25¢ per mile after the first 100 miles. BB Car Rental Company charges a daily rate of $20 and 20¢ per mile. If you used the car for 600 miles in two days which one is the better buy? If you traveled 100 miles in a day, which would be the better buy then? In these two situations the decisions are different. The same type of decision making is faced by almost everyone quite regularly. The mathematics involved in this type of problem is:

Charges = daily rate × no. of days + (no. of miles − free miles) × mileage rate

In calculating AA Car Rental Company charges we have
Charges = $25 × 2 + (600 − 100) × $.25
= $50 + $125
= $175

In calculating BB Car Rental Company charges we have

Charges = $20 × 2 + (600 − 0) × $.20
= $40 + $120
= $160

It involves simple arithmetic, but the main thing is setting up the equation. For 100 miles the calculations are:

AA Company   BB Company
    $25 $20 + $.20(100) = $20 + $20 = $40

- A formula used in finding simple interest is written as I = prt (where I is the interest in dollars, p is the principal (or amount borrowed), r is the rate (percent) of interest per year, t is the time in years). This is an example of an equation at the junior or high school level.

The information Bob has 20 coins in nickels and dimes, the total value of which is less than $10, can be represented by one equality and one inequality.

$$x + y = 20$$
$$x = \text{no. of nickels}$$
$$y = \text{no. of dimes}$$
$$.05x + .10y < 10$$

Equations and inequalities are found in almost all areas of physical and social sciences.

- The rate for first-class mail in the United States is 20 cents for the first ounce or fraction thereof, 17 cents for each subsequent ounce or fraction. That is, a letter weighing not more than one ounce costs 20 cents, a letter weighing more than one ounce but not more than two ounces costs 37 cents, and so forth. The following table represents the above information.

w (weight) in oz.	c (cost)
$0 < W$ and $W \le 1$	20¢
$1 < W \le 2$	37¢
$2 < W \le 3$	57¢
. . . .	. . . .

If a letter weighs W ounces, the equation for cost will be

$$W = 20 + (W − 1)17$$

Similar examples are seen in other content areas.

Estimation

In life, in day-to-day living, and other subject areas we use estimation more often than actual calculations. An important aspect of quantitative work is estimation. For example, when one says that the answer to 12 × 18 is close to 200, one is estimating. Estimating the size of an answer is important because this sort of approximation may be good enough for many of the problems one faces or many times the estimation is a good check on the exact answer whether produced by man or machine.

Estimation procedures become even more important now that pocket calculators and minicomputers are beginning to be commonplace items.

The most common and popular meaning of estimation is in finding approximate answers to numerical problems, where the approximation is used to generate a "rough" answer by translating the given problem into the numbers involved in the original problem. "Rounding off" of numbers is a key skill. For example:

> 67 → 70 (67 is rounded off to 70)
> 19 → 20
> 727 → 730
>
> round off to nearest 100s
> 671 → 700
> 195 → 200
> 7345 → 7300
>
> round off to nearest 1000s
> 671 → 1000
> 7951 → 8000
> 9834 → 10,000
>
> round off to the nearest whole number
> 6½ or 6.5 → 7.0
> 9¼ or 9.25 → 9.0
> 681.78 → 682.0

Rule: If the number in the digit immediately to the right of the place being rounded off is more than or equal to five, then the number in the intended place is increased by one more; otherwise it remains the same.

Learning to estimate—learning the scales and dimensions by which we make quantitative judgments about the environment and appropriate action in that environment—is an important component of mathematics learning. Estimation is indispensable to measurement, as one must estimate to choose appropriate units of measurement and to determine whether results are reasonable.

Example of Estimation

- John wants to carpet his family room. The room is 11½′ long and 9¾′ wide. How much carpet should he buy? Since in carpeting the room there will be some cutting and wastage involved, he approximates the numbers (12 feet long and 10 feet wide) by "rounding off" and finds the answer by multiplying the new numbers.

Ratio and Proportion

When we want to compare two things quantitatively we talk about the *ratio*. When we want to study the relative change in two variables we talk about proportion. The comparison of two ratios is a *proportion*.

Ratio is another name for division. Thus the ratio 2 to 4 is the same as 2 divided by 4. Since division can always be expressed also as a fraction we often see the ratio of two numbers written as a fraction. The ratio of 2 to 4 can be written in the following three ways, all of which have equal value: 2:4; 2/4; and 2 ÷ 4.

A ratio is expressed as 2:4 and is read as "2 is to 4" or "the ratio of 2 to 4."

A proportion shows that two ratios are equal, as 1:2 = 2:4 (or 1:2: : 2:4). It may read either

1 is to 2 as 2 is to 4

or

the ratio of 1 to 2 equals the ratio of 2 to 4

Important Principles of Proportion

Working with proportion is simple if we learn to apply these three important principles:

1. The product of the extreme terms (extremes) is equal to the product of the middle terms (means).
2. The product of the extremes divided by either mean gives the other mean.
3. The product of the means divided by either extreme gives to the other extreme.

Examples

- According to an advertisement, with respect to energy use, railroads are twice as efficient as automobiles and four times as efficient as airplanes. If the statement is valid, what are the relative efficiencies of the three modes of transportation?

- Type paper A costs 40¢ per hundred sheets, type paper B costs 45¢ per hundred sheets. By ratio this can be expressed as

    paper A : paper B : : 40¢ : 45¢

In the fractional form it can be written as

$$\frac{\text{cost of paper A}}{\text{cost of paper B}} = \frac{40¢}{45¢} = \frac{8}{9}$$

The ratio of the cost of two paper is 8 : 9.

- In the proportion 36 : 18 :: 12 : X. Find the value of the missing term, X.

    According to rule 3, the missing extreme, $X = \dfrac{18 \times 12}{36} = 6$. In the proportion 9 : X :: 6 : 24 (see rule 2) the missing term, $X = \dfrac{9 \times 24}{6} = 36$.

Geometry: Lines, Shapes, and Angles

Drawing pictures and diagrams helps us solve many problems. Engineers draw pictures of each component of a new piece of machinery or equipment to help them study the problems involved. Architects, designers, and decorators make drawings of floor plans and pictures of how completed buildings, interiors, and objects will look before the actual work is started. Theatrical directors sketch the stage and the location of objects, actors, and scenes to help decide how a certain scene should be staged. Carpenters make drawings of the objects they are building. Electricians make diagrams to show how a machine should be wired. Many of the problems that high school students encounter in other subject areas will be much easier to solve if they develop the habit of drawing pictures to help them see the relationships in their problems. The two most important concepts that are useful in applications are

1. ratio and proportion (for scale drawings)
2. right triangle and the Pythagorean theorem

The type of drawings and diagrams mentioned above use a scaled version of the original (or actual object). This requires an understanding of ratio and proportions.

Every craftsman makes use of the right angle. The Greek mathematician-philosopher Pythagoras noticed that a 3-4-5 triangle (a triangle where the sides are in the ratio 3, 4, and 5) has a right angle in it and found that the sum of squares of two sides is equal to the square of the third side, that is $9 + 16 = 25$. From more observations Pythagoras was able to prove that in *any* right triangle, *the area of the square on the hypotenuse (longest side) is equal to the sum of the areas of the squares on the other two sides.* This is the *Pythagorean Theorem.* Simply stated $c^2 = a^2 + b^2$, where c is the hypotenuse of the right triangle whose other sides are a and b, or $(hypotenuse)^2 = (base)^2 + (altitude)^2$. In other words, if we know two sides of a right triangle, we can calculate the third one.

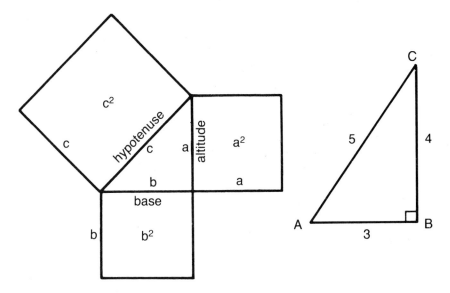

For example: In triangle ABC, B is 90°, AC is the hypotenuse, BC is the base, and AB is the altitude. Then, by Pythagoras' Theorem, we have $(AC)^2 = (BC)^2 + (AB)^2$. Let us assume that $AB = 3$, $BC = 4$, then $(AC)^2 = 3^2 + 4^2 = 9 + 16 = 25$. $AC = 5$ units, as we see from the diagram above.

Another use of triangles is in scale drawings, enlargements, contractions, and map making. When two triangles have the same shape, corresponding angles are equal, and one triangle is a larger version of the other, such triangles are said to be similar. The principle of similarity is not restricted to triangles. If, for example, we examine a specimen under the microscope the image seen is similar in every way to the original object. Every time an architect or engineer makes a scale drawing, or a photographer makes an enlargement, or we use field glasses or a telescope, this principle is realized. For example, the triangles ABC and XYZ are similar. AB↔XY, BC↔XZ, AC↔YZ

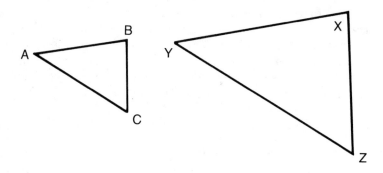

Then $\dfrac{AB}{XY} = \dfrac{BC}{XZ} = \dfrac{AC}{YZ} = \dfrac{1}{2}$.

If we know the dimensions of one triangle and the scale of transformation, the dimensions of the other triangles can be calculated.

Areas, Surfaces, and Volumes

Plane (flat) surfaces are so common about us that we solve for areas without thinking of geometry at all.

Area of a Square of a Rectangle

The area of a rectangle is equal to the product of its length multiplied by its width (A = 1w). If two sides of a rectangle are 10″ and the other sides are 5″, the area is 50 square inches.

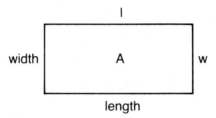

Area of a Parallelogram

The area of a parallelogram is the product of its base multiplied by its altitude. If AC is the altitude and BD is the base, the area of the parallelogram is 4 × 10, or 40 square inches.

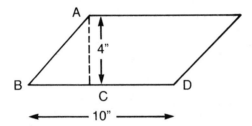

The altitude is the perpendicular distance between two parallel sides.

Area of a Triangle

The area of a triangle is equal to the product of one-half the base multiplied by the altitude. The altitude of a triangle is always the perpendicular distance from a *vertex* (any of the points where the sides of a triangle intersect is a vertex) to the opposite side, called the base.

This means that in either of the figures illustrated the area is 1/2 (AD × BC). If BC is 5 inches long and AD is 6 inches long, the area is 15 square inches [½ (5 × 6) = 15]. The area of an equilateral triangle (three equal sides) is given by ¼ (side)^2 · $\sqrt{3}$. The area of a triangle in general is given by Area = $\sqrt{S × (S - a) × (S - b) × (S - c)}$. Where S = ½ (Sum of the sides) = ½ (a + b + c), a, b, c, three sides.

Area of a Polygon

A surface that is enclosed by three or more straight lines is called a polygon. We may call triangles, squares, hexagons, pentagons, etc., polygons. The area of a polygon is given by the number of regular triangles formed from the polygon times area of one regular triangle in the polygon.

The regular hexagon is divided into six regular triangles as indicated in the diagram. Therefore, the area of the hexagon ABCDEF is 6 times the area of any regular triangle (say △ABO).

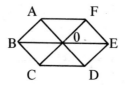

Area of a Circle

The area is found by multiplying the square of the radius by 3.14 or 22/7. This may be written in the form of Area $= \pi r^2$ where r represents the radius of the circle.

Area of the Surface of a Cylinder

To find the lateral area of a cylindrical surface, find the distance around the circle (circumference) and multiply this distance by the height. If the diameter of a cylindrical tank is 20 inches and the height 5 feet, the lateral surface area of the cylinder may be found by the formula

$$\begin{aligned} \text{Area} &= 3.1416 \times \text{diameter} \times \text{height} \\ &= 3.1416 \times 20 \times 60 \\ &= 3769.92 \text{ sq. inches} \end{aligned}$$

Volume of a Cube

The volume of a solid with a rectangular cross-section may be found by multiplying the area of the base by the height or the product of its length, width, and height. The volume of a cube may be found by the same method as for any other solid with a rectangular cross-section. However, as the edges of a cube are all equal, the product of its length, width, and height is the same as the cube of one of its edges. Therefore we say: Volume of a cube $=$ its edge cubed $= (\text{edge})^3$.

Volume of a Cylinder

A cylinder is similar to a solid with a rectangular cross-section. The total surface of a cylinder, not including the base, is a rectangle. The total lateral surface of a cylinder is equal to the area of the base times height; and since the base is a circle, the volume may be expressed as

$$\text{Volume} = 3.1416 \times r^2 \times \text{altitude}$$
$$r = \text{radius of the base}$$
$$\text{altitude} = \text{height}$$

Tables and Graphs

There are many instances of calculations that are often repeated where it is a great saving of time to have a set of answers worked out, carefully checked and neatly tabulated for future use. Banks, supermarket checkout counters, sales clerks, physicians, and many others have ready-made charts, graphs, and tables. Newspapers, promotional materials, annual reports from corporations and organizations, and many other individuals and groups present information through graphs (bars, histograms, pie charts, tables) and other visual materials. Understanding these visual aids to information requires mathematical expertise ranging from simple numerical tabulations to percentages and ratio and proportions.

Probability and Statistics

Almost every game, however high a degree of skill it demands of the players, has its own elements of chance. The part that chance plays in the final result varies enormously. It is these elements of chance, this infinite variety of circumstances that may arise by accident, that forms part of the appeal of many games; were it not so, it would be useless for players of unequal skills to compete with each other since the result would be a foregone conclusion.

While it is possible in some games to calculate the chances of certain situations arising, or of a particular player being successful, in others no amount of calculation can estimate the effects of chance. Calculating odds for the winning of a particular team, for getting a particular card or groups of cards in a bridge or a poker game, for getting a particular number in the game of roulette, etc., involves some understanding of permutations and combinations. But the calculation of chance factors and their occurrences is not limited to games only. When we talk of 50 percent chance of rain and 20 percent probability of one's selection for a task we are talking of calculating chance or the probability of that happening.

When we read in the press that according to the latest MNP poll 46 percent of the people favor discipline in schools or that 60 percent of those who voted in the last presidential election favored marijuana decriminalization, what does that mean? There is a great deal of information in these statements and a lot of mathematical thought lies behind these simple statements, which most people are ready to accept without question.

SUMMARY

As we have seen mathematics applications in other subjects are quite common, and more and more mathematics will appear as society continues to become more technological. Mathematics educators need to acquire competence in relating mathematics concepts to other   subjects and at the same time learn to deal with the anxiety of those who have difficulty in learning mathematics.

REFERENCE

Joint Committee of the Mathematics Association of America and the National Council of Teachers of Mathematics. (1980). *A sourcebook of applications of school mathematics*. Reston, VA: National Council of Teachers of Mathematics.

Chapter 10

Adapting the College Preparatory Program for the Learning Disabled

Robert A. Shaw

Initial information that foreshadowed this chapter appeared in Chapter 6. The major conclusions were that (1) a learning disability is independent of intelligence, (2) learners must develop compensating skills, and (3) if learners are to enter a college preparatory program, they must have had some success in learning the fundamentals of arithmetic. (Perhaps they developed compensating skills early in the elementary school program.)

As the mathematics program becomes more structured at the secondary level, students are expected to perform at a higher level with respect to achievement and all students are expected to perform in a similar manner. However, such an expectation is in direct conflict with the needs of individuals with learning disabilities as they each require alternatives to compensate for any disability. Indeed, perhaps the major obstacle to obtaining acceptable and challenging mathematics programs for the learning disabled is the changing belief systems of rigid content-oriented specialists.

Alternative methods and strategies must be a refinement of what already is happening in a classroom if there is to be a chance of success. Instructors must acquire an awareness of specific learning disabilities, participate in formal and informal assessment/evaluation procedures, and learn of the different content strategies and methods. An instructor must assume the responsibility of trying to obtain the optimal match among content, strategies, methods, and the abilities of the learners.

Some initial guidelines were also presented in Chapter 6 in regard to structure, method of presentation, and sample alternatives. Based on this introduction and the guidelines of Chapter 6, a college preparation program in mathematics will be outlined and discussed in the remaining sections of this chapter.

CURRICULUM CONCERNS

The first curriculum concern in secondary school mathematics is organization. The various tracks of a program need to be well defined in a sequential manner, with alternative routes along the tracks. A learner should be able to move from one track to another as the need arises.

Exhibit 10-1 contains a sample mathematics course sequence for a large secondary school system. The usual sequence is straight across each row. Individual students may move to a "higher" or to a "lower" level whenever appropriate. Levels are defined as H, honors; A, advanced; S, standard; B, basic; R, remedial. Small school systems may have only the standard sequence as their highest level because of size of staff and the enrollment required to conduct a class.

Each course within the program should be well documented in terms of prerequisites, both as to previous courses with acceptable grades and acceptable scores on any prognostic tests; and in terms of requisites, what a learner must achieve in order to continue successfully into other courses or into another track in the mathematics curriculum.

COLLEGE PREPARATORY PROGRAM

While there are many variations of course offerings in a college preparatory program in mathematics, for the purposes of this chapter, we will explore the standard sequence as outlined in Table 10-1.

The two courses of algebra and geometry constitute a minimum offering in mathematics and some colleges and universities admit students with only this minimal background in mathematics; however, we will explore the total sequence in this chapter.

Table 10-1 A College Preparatory Program

Grade	Mathematics Course
8	General Mathematics (Pre-Algebra)
9	Algebra I
10	Geometry
11	Algebra II
12	Pre-Calculus

Exhibit 10-1 Sample Mathematics Course Sequence for a Large Secondary School System

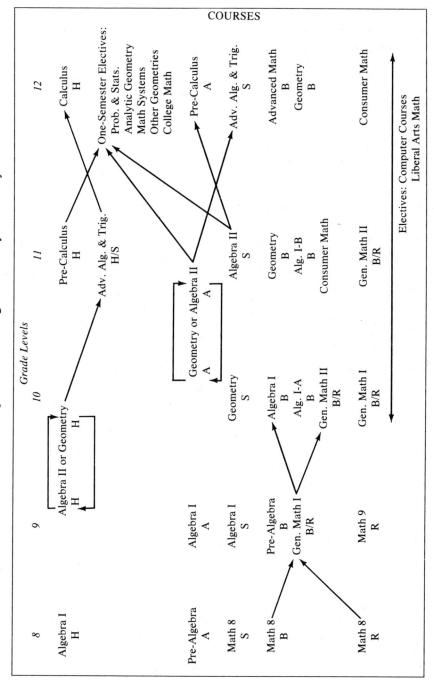

While we should not have to mention the content knowledge of secondary teachers of mathematics, this has become a critical issue today with many good teachers now leaving the profession for higher-paying positions and better working conditions. If an individual is placed to teach a secondary mathematics course for which he or she is not completely prepared, then very likely as this individual is struggling to stay ahead of his or her students, little attention will be given to providing learning alternatives. Or, if an older content specialist is hired after he or she has retired from another job, the belief systems of this individual may be rather rigid and lack of knowledge concerning young adults may compound the situation. Individuals who are responsible for planning mathematics programs for learning-disabled students must become aware of current teaching situations in mathematics, become active in the hiring procedures, and inform others of possible consequences of various administrative decisions. This issue is critical in meeting the guidelines to be presented below.

As the student is prepared to enter a college preparatory program, the program should be prepared for the student. At the end of the general mathematics sequence students should be given a prognostic test for algebra to obtain some indication of the probability of success in the first year algebra course. A student should have the option of taking this prognostic test in the usual paper-pencil format or orally. Every effort needs to be made to obtain a fair representation of a learner's ability. Previous performance levels and compensating skills should be identified and made available to teachers of secondary school mathematics. Awareness on the part of instructors is the first step toward redesigning classroom procedures.

Many program changes that will be suggested in this chapter are "common sense" changes in regard to the development of a sound mathematics program. Perhaps many departments of mathematics already have sound programs in place and need only to widen the scope.

CURRICULUM ESSENTIALS

For each course within the curriculum sequence objectives must be listed in terms of desired learner attitudes, concepts, and skills. Each student must know precisely what is expected. While this seems like an obvious request, in practice, it is not a common occurrence. In some cases we appear to be afraid to list objectives and students become aware of them only when they are tested. (Are objectives considered when tests are constructed?) This is especially true if instructors offer no more material than is contained in the textbook.

One step removed from no list is a listing of content topics. What are learners expected to know about these topics—definitions, relationships, what . . . ? From this simple listing of topics we often expect students to solve problems involving concepts and skills derived from basic knowledge. Such a situation lacks structure and creates a huge gap between facts and problem solving and places the learning-disabled individual at a disadvantage. The objectives must be complete, precise, and well ordered. For example, a student in an algebra class must know what procedures for factoring are acceptable to the instructor. Must all calculations be presented? Will a calculator be permitted? If learners know what is expected, they have the opportunity to organize, to plan, and to seek help when it is needed.

Arguments against a detailed listing of objectives center on the notion that such a listing serves to produce a program that is not flexible. One answer to this is that a listing of objectives is a proposed plan of action and it will need changes as the course develops. (Of course, students must be made aware of these changes). The objectives should be in written form and distributed to both students and their parents. In addition, all instructors should orally review the objectives for each unit of work and allow students to tape this review (and all presentations of content) if they wish. Assessment and evaluation procedures should be completed in terms of written and stated objectives.

Content overviews that contain major topics to be studied, sections from text materials, major assignments, and any supplementary materials should be available in both oral and written form for each major unit or chapter of work in each course of study. The objectives may be a part of the overview that is to be presented on the first day of a new unit of work. As instructors present the overview they need to make students aware of how this new unit of work relates to previous materials; therefore, the first lesson of a new unit is an overview lesson.

TYPES OF LESSONS

Other types of lessons are developmental, reinforcement, and review; however, before we can discuss these types of organizational lessons it is necessary to consider the typical classroom procedure in a secondary school mathematics classroom. A typical class period is often divided into three time segments with the first segment being devoted to going over homework or answering questions. During the second time period new material is presented and assignments are made. Time remaining is used to get started on assignments with the help of the instructor. This patterned procedure becomes unacceptable if it is inflexible and the instructor does nothing more than restate text material. Time must be variable across a unit of work instead of within a given class period. More time-on-task seems to lead to higher levels of achievement; therefore, the maximum amount of time should be spent on instruction and interaction among learners and the instructor. Careful attention must be given to how learning-disabled individuals acquire and demonstrate competencies in a class, a course of study, or the total mathematics curriculum.

Developmental Lessons

Several developmental lessons were presented in Chapter 6. The major instruction objective of this type of lesson is to provide background information to learners as they use previously acquired knowledge to make new information meaningful. Since learning-disabled individuals may have difficulty in receiving information, storing this information rapidly, or retrieving the information, we need several alternatives in our delivery systems. Some individuals may need a combination of input modalities, for example, written material to review while listening to an oral presentation. However, many will need to isolate an input modality in order to store information; for example, an individual may tape a lesson and listen to the tape in a darkened room to achieve maximum input attention. For this type of learner the instructor should demonstrate, discuss, and summarize classroom presentations of content. The presentations should contain only one new mathematical concept per lesson.

As new content is developed, instructors need to explore different presentation strategies in an attempt to reach as many learners as possible. Students need to be allowed to tape classroom presentations. Outlines and study guides should be provided. Perhaps, strategic workmates should be identified and the individuals should be encouraged to do classwork together. A list of tutors should be kept for parents or interested individuals who inquire about the availability of tutors. The guidance function of a secondary school is very important since learning-disabled individuals must develop self-confidence as they face a rigorous schedule and workload. Some estimates of workload indicate that the learning-disabled individual will have to work three times as hard as any other student to achieve the same successful results.

Reinforcement

A reinforcement lesson may become an application lesson and provide an excellent opportunity for an instructor to determine how each individual student functions. Such a lesson also requires us to rethink our philosophies or belief systems in regard to assignments and testing. Somehow homework has become something that teachers feel required to give, but careful thought is usually not devoted to assignments. For example, we may say, "Do all of the 'even-numbered' exercises on such-and-such a page." Often we do this whether or not the appropriate material has been completely taught and learned. What happens in this case is that homework becomes a self-teaching exercise.

Homework should be given for reinforcement purposes and with the understanding that all learners will have a high degree of success with the assignment. Homework should *not* be given on material that has not been taught or on material where there is some doubt as to the possible success of the learners. More attention should be given to the processes used by the learners; therefore, teachers must check the homework in some manner and *not* just indicate whether students have attempted the work or not. Again, some learners may need to respond orally instead of in written form.

Review

Testing should follow similar patterns (as with homework). Together, evaluation of homework and testing should serve as monitoring procedures to enable us to check the progress and plan alternatives for learning-disabled individuals. Oral responses should be considered. Review lessons may be used to determine if learners are ready for an examination and to plan alternative or differentiated tests for various learners. If we want learners to be successful a flexible program is essential.

METHODS AND ALTERNATIVES

How learning-disabled individuals are taught and how they respond to such teaching are questions that must be considered if we are to influence their learning. Since we are branching from a normal classroom situation, let's suggest some procedures in addition to those discussed in the beginning of this chapter.

One alternative for the study of a unit of work is performance contracting in which there is an agreement between the teacher and student regarding assignments and responsibilities. There are two general types of perform-ance contracts: grade contracts and time contracts. In a grade contract a learner agrees to do a certain amount of work and attempts to score at a certain test level for a particular grade. With a time contract the learner agrees to complete a certain amount of work in a given time period. Initial contracts should be short, not involve more than seven days of the usual class work, and all elements of the contract should be clear to all individ-uals involved.

Independent study for credit is an example of contract learning. In this situation, teaching and learning are self-directed; therefore, the individual must be highly motivated to be successful. Other self-instructional units involve programmed materials, audiotapes, filmstrips and worksheets, computer-assisted instruction, or some appropriate combination of strat-egies, materials, and methods.

Methods are concerned with how materials are presented *and* how the material is learned. Experimentation is a necessity. Always consider the interactives. What do learners do—what is their output behavior—in response to what the instructor does?

In terms of general methods we can hypothesize that

1. Background information should be presented to learners in a direct, dynamic telling mode with clues as to how to organize and use the new information.
2. Mathematical rules and principles should be developed carefully with a good deal of interaction between the input behaviors of the instruc-tor and output behaviors of the learners.
3. Guided discovery and laboratory approaches should be used to develop generalizations and problem-solving skills.

A PLAN OF ACTION

The beginning sections of this chapter serve as an overview of the scope of problems to be considered in developing a college preparatory program for learning-disabled individuals. In this section we will develop a plan of action that follows the program outline of Table 10-1. Under this plan we will assume that a mathematical sequence has been defined, minimum and maximum sequences of topics have been determined for each course, and the instructor is able to select objectives to match the content with the abilities of the learners. The plan is for that group of learners who, from all indications, have a chance to be successful if provisions are made to compensate for any disabilities. Preassessment data indicate that the learners have a favorable attitude and possess the general mathematical concepts and skills that are prerequisite for the pre-algebra course.

The general plan for each course that unites with the other courses for the overall plan of action has the following characteristics. With the pretesting data on participating students on hand the instructor selects and organizes the content of the course, collects materials, and develops a long-range plan (or schedule) for the year. An overview for each major unit or chapter is developed by identifying major topics and objectives for these topics that match the abilities of the learners. Perhaps the objectives should be organized in a criterion-referenced manner so that monitoring of the progress of the learners can occur. Support services should be identified and made known to the learners, for example, the teacher's schedule and available tutors. The flowchart in Figure 10-1 will serve to model each course.

An important element of this flowchart procedure is monitoring progress. Every effort needs to be made to assist the learners involved. To reinforce the concepts there should be some overlap in the examinations and near the end of a course, students should be given a prognostic test of the next course in the sequence. Discussions with students should be realistic in terms of their abilities, successes and failures, and requirements for future work.

ALGEBRA I: THE COURSE SEQUENCE

Algebra may be defined as the symbolic language of real numbers; understanding algebra is knowing the relationships among the language elements and where to use these relationships to solve problems; and doing algebra is manipulating the symbols to produce other relationships and solutions to examples, exercises, and problems. Any disability in reading or writing can cause the abstract reasoning ability of learners to be underdeveloped.

Research on information processing is relevant to understanding the needs of learning-disabled students. Wittrock (1979) investigated how learners process information that is presented during instruction. An active role was advocated to enable learners to make the connection between information presented and past experiences. Students will spontaneously generate relevent relationships or learn to construct relevant relationships. However, if material is not explained clearly, they are unlikely to generate relevant relationships (p. 10). This situation presents a real challenge for a teacher of algebra to make verbal presentations so clear that learners will be able to develop a mental image of the rules and relationships of

Figure 10-1 Model for Course Organization

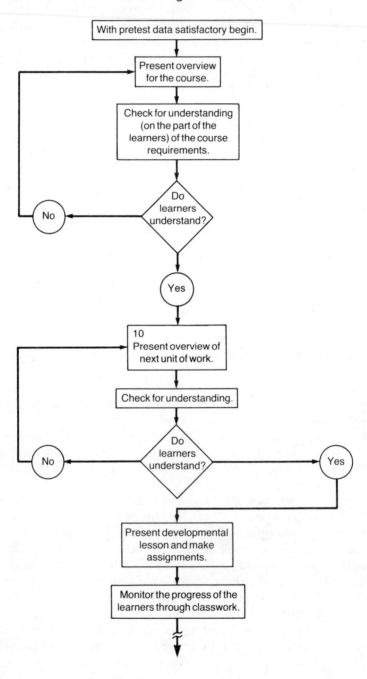

Figure 10-1 continued

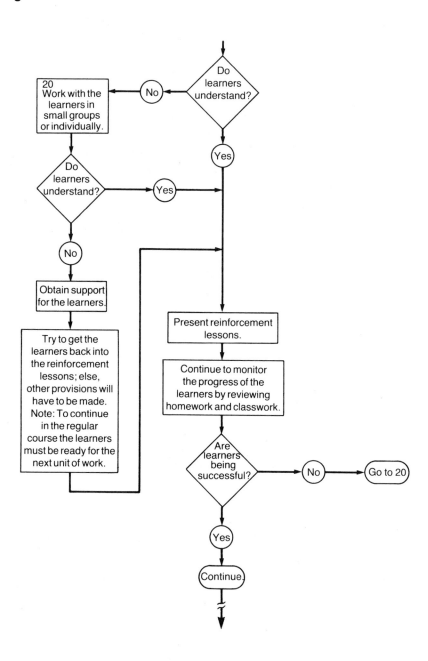

Figure 10-1 continued

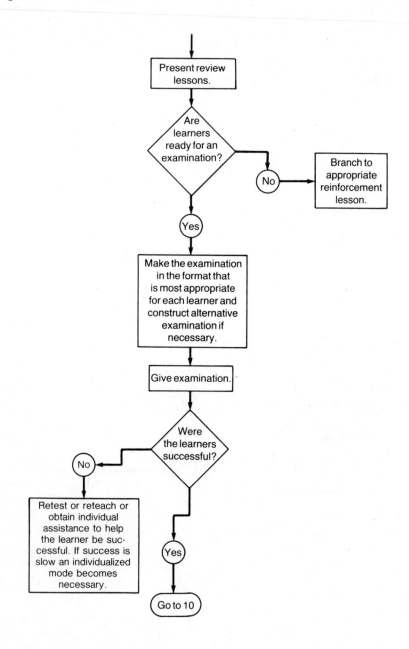

algebra, along with a speaking vocabulary. Ultimately, they must understand the rules and be able to apply them.

To illustrate these ideas we will simulate the presentation of a difficult concept from algebra—the product of two negative numbers is a positive number. No written symbols will be used. Listeners would be encouraged to make any notes or diagrams to assist in the understanding of the concept. A learning-disabled individual should be allowed to tape the presentation.

Today we are going to continue our discussion of products of real numbers. Actually, we will be considering only certain real numbers, the integers. Some of the previous lessons have been on examples of positive and negative integers, their sums and differences. We discovered that multiplying positive integers is like multiplying whole numbers. For example, positive eight times positive two gave positive sixteen as eight times two is sixteen. We concluded that the product of two positive numbers is a positive number. We also used the property of zero for multiplication noting that any real number times zero or zero times any real number is equal to zero. Think of some examples to illustrate this zero property for multiplication.

Yesterday we used the zero property to develop the rule that the product of a positive number and a negative number is a negative number. Let's review this concept. Think of some positive integer between zero and ten. Let this number be your first factor and let the second factor be zero. You now have some single-digit, positive integer times zero. The answer or product is zero. Now, change the zero factor (your second factor) to a single-digit positive integer plus its additive inverse (opposite)—a single-digit negative integer. You now have a single-digit positive integer times an indicated sum (a single-digit positive integer plus its negative) which is equal to zero.

We used the distributive property to develop our rule. We distributed our first factor across the indicated sum and produced a sum of two products—a positive integer times a positive integer plus *a positive integer times a negative integer. Think of your numbers in this format. From past experiences, we know that the positive integer times the positive integer was a positive integer. In order for the sum of the two products to equal zero, the second product—the positive integer times the negative integer— had to be negative. After several examples we concluded that this was indeed true and we used the commutative property to show that a negative integer times a positive integer was also a negative integer.*

We want to extend the concepts of your previous lesson. Think of some negative integer between zero and negative ten. [Pause] Again, this will be your first factor of an indicated product. [Pause] The second factor will be zero. [Pause] You now have a negative integer times zero which equals zero. [Pause] Now, change the zero factor (your second factor) to a single-digit positive integer plus its additive inverse (or opposite)—a single-digit negative integer. [Pause] You now have a negative integer times an indicated sum (a positive integer plus its opposite negative integer) which is equal to zero. [Pause] Use the distributive property again. [Pause] Distribute the negative integer (the first factor) across the indicated sum to produce a sum of two products. [Pause] The sum is a negative integer times a positive integer plus a negative integer times a negative integer. Think of your numbers in this format. [Pause] We learned in the last lesson that a negative integer times a positive integer is a (negative) integer. [Pause] The first part of our sum is negative. The next part of our sum is a negative integer times a negative integer. For our sum to be zero (we already have a negative number), the negative integer times the negative integer must be a (positive) integer. [Pause] A negative number times a negative number is a positive number.

This description represents one time through the procedure. The instructor should repeat this procedure, perhaps with specific values, until students make the connections with past experiences. Our presentation illustrates the verbal detail that is necessary and that will pay dividends later in the development of *word* exercises and problems. For example, think of two consecutive positive integers with a sum of 35. The thought process is similar to the learning of rules as the student attempts to think of something that will satisfy a given condition.

Students need training and practice to think of numbers that will satisfy two conditions at the same time. For example, think of two integers that have a *sum* of six and a *product* of nine. This type of mental processing is essential in factoring such expressions as $x^2 + 6x + 9$.

GEOMETRY

The plane geometry course of the secondary school serves to formalize the intuitive and informal geometry of the middle/junior high school. It broadens the scope of the secondary mathematics program. While we have discussed geometry as a content strand in Chapter 6, it is considered here to continue the framework that was established with algebra—working with those individuals who have disabilities in reading and writing the symbolic language of mathematics.

Diagrams and pictures may be used to aid the learning-disabled individual by providing that individual with an alternative input modality. A diagram of parallel lines is an abstract concept, but with a picture of the rails of a railroad track, the parallel concept may be enhanced. Angle measure can be determined by using cardboard models of various sized angles. Models that the learners construct will also be useful (see Chapter 6 for simple models such as angle bisectors). The concept of congruence may be introduced by using tracing paper on which to copy the angles and other figures and moving the copy over other diagrams to make comparisons.

A central concept area of geometry has to do with theorems and their proof. We will demonstrate the modifications of content presentation that can be made to serve the needs of the learning disabled as we develop an analytical proof of the Pythagorean Theorem. In a right triangle, the square of the length of the hypotenuse (longest side or side opposite the right angle) is equal to the sum of the squares of the lengths of the legs of the triangle. This is a statement of the Pythagorean Theorem. By contructing a right triangle (for example, with sides equal to three, four, and five centimeters, respectively) and a square from each side of the triangle (three squares—one with side length of three centimeters, one with side length of four centimeters, and one with side length of five centimeters), the learner has the necessary elements to develop a proof for the theorem. Patterns should be made of all three square regions. The two small square regions should be cut and placed on the large square region. With some experimenting the learner should discover that all pieces of the two small square regions will fit exactly on the large square region with no overlap or gaps (see Figure 10-2). Each symbol now has a model. This type of development can also be used for area and volume formulas and to enhance the type of thinking necessary for problem solving.

ALGEBRA II

Algebra II is an extension of first year algebra. It makes use of some geometric concepts, it is used to expand verbal problem development, and it serves as an introduction to relations and functions. To continue into this area of study learners must be able to manipulate and understand real numbers in symbolic form because they will be expected to combine a series of operations into a complex procedure to obtain the solution to an exercise or problem. Compensating skills for any disabilities must be refined in order to be successful in Algebra II within a reasonable amount of time.

Figure 10-2 Pythagorean Relations

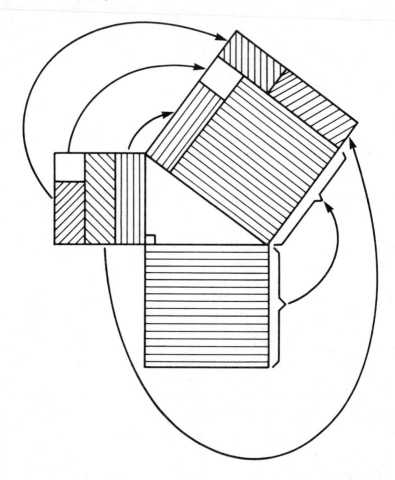

One of the first major topics is solving equations. Concepts and skills that lead to equations include algebraic expressions. Most textbooks in Algebra II include many oral exercises involving simplifying algebraic expressions. The instructor should make use of these exercises to assess the readiness of learners to begin solving equations. Since the oral exercises contain skill and concept building activities, they are essential for organizing steps to solve an equation. Certain rules become evident; for example, collect like terms and perform the necessary operations to isolate the unknown on one side of the equation.

Since development of equations and inequalities involves verbal discussion, some learning-disabled individuals may show a growth in understanding. By the very nature of the topic, multiple input modalities are necessary. Graphing provides another input possibility as linear relations and functions are introduced. It is at this point that we want to suggest some organizational changes so that learners may relate their new experiences to past algebraic experiences and organize the new concepts and skills into a meaningful pattern. With pattern organization we have problem solving.

We begin by graphing the relation *and* function, y = x, on the coordinate graph using the domain of real numbers. The learners discover that the graph is a straight line at a 45° angle to both the x and y axis and in the first and third quadrants. They should be asked to speculate on how the

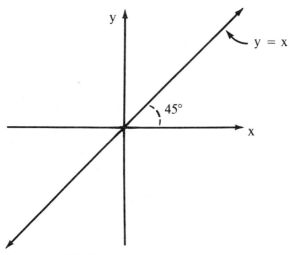

graph of the function will change if you increase the numerical coefficient of x from one (1), e.g., y = 2x. With some experimentation, mentally or graphically, students should discover that the line is steeper and closer to the y-axis—the slope is increased. What happens if the numerical coefficient of x becomes zero? . . . becomes negative? Students will note that slope changes but the graph always goes through the origin (point (0, 0)). What do we do to the equation to move the graph away from the origin? Perhaps learners will suggest adding some constant term to the right side of the equation. We continue the development until the general form of the linear equation is produced, y = mx + b, where *x* is the independent variable, *y* is the dependent variable, *m* is the slope, and *b* is the y-intercept. If the learners have a good understanding, they will be able to explain x = ny + a.

Figure 10-3 Parabola from a Locus Definition

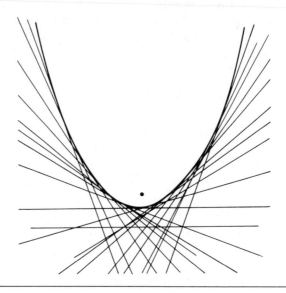

A similar procedure should be followed with quadratic relations and functions where a simple form of the equation is presented and expanded into standard form. Preliminary to the development of any standard equation is an introduction to the special quadratic relations of the conic sections—parabola, hyperbola, ellipse, and circle. Using wax paper and a locus definition each of the conic shapes (and graphs) may be constructed prior to a formal introduction. We will discuss one such construction.

On a clear piece of wax paper draw a line segment along one edge of the paper. In the middle of the paper and one-half to one inch above the line segment locate a point. Now fold the paper so that a portion of the line segment goes through the point. Make a crease. Unfold the paper and fold the paper so that another point of the line segment touches the point. Make another crease. Continue to follow this procedure and you will produce a set of intersecting lines. The points of intersection will form a parabola because each point of the parabola will be the same distance from the line segment and the point above the line segment (see Figure 10-3). The symbolic development of the parabola begins with the equation, $y = x^2$, and is extended to $y - k = \frac{1}{p}(x - h)^2$. It is important that students build a structure and relate experiences to past experiences. The development of quadratic equations should be systematic and similar to the development of linear equations.

PRE-CALCULUS

Pre-calculus or elementary functions is an extension of Algebra II and may include a section on analytic geometry. Complex numbers are included, but the major effort is the study of relations and functions. Exponential and logarithmic functions are graphed, defined, and related in inverse relationships. Circular functions and trigonometry are developed in detail. Applications and problem solving are significant elements of this course.

For the purposes of this chapter we will explore the unit circle. Using the definition from geometry that a circle is a set of points in a plane at a given distance from a point in the plane called the center, a unit circle is a circle with the given distance equal to one unit. If (x,y) represents any point on the circle, then the equation for the unit circle with its center at the origin in the x,y plane is $x^2 + y^2 = 1$. There is symmetry about the x-axis and about the y-axis. The circumference of our unit circle is 2π units. The learner must understand that it is meaningful to speak of distance along a circle. With this understanding every real number can be paired with a point on the unit circle. This concept is one strategy for producing the functions of trigonometry. For example, for each real number r (where r is the distance from P (1,0) counter-clockwise around the circle to a selected point) one and only one point P (x,y) on the unit circle exists. By assigning to each real number r the first coordinate x of P, we can define a function of domain in the set of real numbers and with a range of all first coordinates of points on the circle. This function is called the cosine function (cos) over the real numbers. Other functions can be described in a similar manner.

SUMMARY

In this chapter we have introduced a college preparatory program, described curriculum elements and types of lessons, overviewed methods and strategies, developed a plan of action, and given selected examples from higher mathematics. Continuing to build on past experiences by providing alternative learning conditions is the key to structuring mathematics at the secondary level for individuals with learning disabilities.

REFERENCE

Wittrock, M.C. (1979). The cognitive movement in instruction. *Educational Researcher, 8,* 5–11.

Chapter 11

Organizing the Secondary Mathematics Program for Learning-Disabled Students

Raymond E. Webster

Effectively organizing the secondary mathematics program for LD students is a very difficult task because of the numbers of people involved. Politically based issues such as territoriality, self-perceived mission for a department, biases toward individualized or group instruction, declining enrollments, and a score of existing and new interpersonal conflicts can become major obstacles to coordination and implementation.

One of the first concerns is that of territorial domain. Each department has its own unique mission and procedures for attaining it. Implicit to each is the philosophy of the department administrators. The mission for many secondary mathematics departments is to teach students how to use mathematics either in further academic study or daily living. The procedures to fulfill this mission usually relate to the expected performance levels for a group of students. If a student is unable to keep pace, placement in a lower-level class with a different curriculum is sought. This general model has worked rather effectively for many years in education and is one supported by many mathematics teachers.

The mission and procedures for special education are similar yet different in substantial ways. The mission of special education is more general in that it exists to serve students across all subject areas. It strives to achieve this by emphasizing the learning styles and needs of the individual as distinct from the rest of the class. Often, special education supports individualized instruction within a regular class setting. In some districts special educators identify themselves as child advocates. What is implied is that other staff are antagonists toward students.

An adversarial or at least a potential conflict situation is often created when trying to coordinate a mathematics program for LD students. Mathematics teachers may feel they are being told what and how to teach by staff with little or no experience in group teaching, much less mathematics. Many staff may feel that their professional integrity is being questioned.

All staff may feel overly burdened and that they are doing the work of special education. The mathematics department administration may view coordination as a lowering of influence, administrative esteem, or outright demotion.

Such issues must be addressed openly and honestly early in the process of making organizational plans. Mathematics teachers possess extensive knowledge about their subject area. They know many ways to make complex concepts more understandable for classes of students at grade level or higher. The special educators have expertise with teaching methodologies and student learning styles. Each of these knowledge bases complements the other. Neither department should be organized in an overt or implied dominant position. The focus of coordination between departments is to capitalize on the expertise within each so that teaching becomes more effective for all students and especially those with learning disabilities.

A second point for consideration and resolution is the way in which the mathematics and special education departments operate. Mathematics departments usually are centralized. The curriculum for any given year has been approved by the board of education. The school and department administrations supervise its implementation so that all students receive the same content from year to year. The teacher has flexibility in how to teach the content but is not authorized to make curricular changes independently.

Special education programming is governed by the child study team. This group of professionals and parents decides what will be taught and how it will be presented. The more special education oriented the class placement for the student the easier to implement team decisions. If a student is placed in a regular mathematics class and receiving special education services, the curriculum scope and sequence are already determined by board action. Here is where the complementary relationship between mathematics and special education becomes vital. Special education can assist in developing in-class techniques, alternative groupings, and other kinds of teaching or environmental modifications so that LD students can learn at rates about consistent with that of the class. To do this most effectively the special educator needs to observe and work in the mathematics class to understand how teaching occurs. Merely presenting the results of psychoeducational evaluations and teaching recommendations at a child study team meeting will never accomplish the kind of organization needed for LD students.

ORIENTING THE MATHEMATICS PROGRAM

The general philosophy of the mathematics program for LD students should reflect a dual commitment to instruction in basic skills as well as those related skills important to life and work. To do this the mathematics curriculum must be organized around four basic principles that offer direction to its scope.

Curriculum Scope

The first principle is that many LD students are capable of learning at rates and levels consistent with those for students of average or higher learning ability. The curriculum scope should not be diluted or limited only to the most basic mathematics facts merely because a student has been identified as learning disabled. These kinds of decisions cannot be made on the basis of teachers' expectations about the performance levels or progress of LD students in general in mathematics. Decisions about what content to include should be made only after the special education child study team *and* the mathematics teacher have carefully evaluated and determined the specific learning characteristics and hypothesized learning progress rates for each LD student in the class. Even then, the curriculum cannot be adapted in the same way for all students. More precise information on success in mathematics can be collected after the teacher has had time to observe the student actually perform in class. Different LD students will achieve at different levels and rates. Few generalizations can be made for groups of LD students. Curriculum modification will need to be done on an individual basis.

Program Coordination

The second principle around which the secondary level mathematics program should be organized is that mathematics must be coordinated with other subject areas the LD student is studying. Coordination increases the student's opportunities to apply and practice concepts in a useful way, develop understanding about the uses of mathematics as a tool, and reduces the burden on teachers to develop appropriate programs of study for LD students.

Coordination between teachers offers more variety to each content area and increases the number of meaningful and challenging activities that can be used in each class. Greater program variety allows teachers to meet the individual learning needs and ability levels of both LD and average students in the same class. Coordination increases the teacher's flexibility to use new techniques in class. Some content areas where integration can be done easily include economics, the physical sciences, social studies, industrial arts, vocational-technical trades, and physical education.

Subject matter integration is an idea that is easier talked about than done. The issue of orchestrating people to work toward a common goal arises. First, staff in other subject areas must be willing to participate in the project. This means that the relevance of mathematics to these areas must be stressed. How will integrating mathematics more fully in another subject enhance that subject? How much extra work will be required of the teacher in the related area? Does coordination mean that the related subjects teacher is getting another supervisor and more demands without more technical and material support?

The situation becomes even more complicated when related subjects coordination for LD students is raised. Teachers are being asked to integrate another subject into their program for students who have defined learning problems. These two factors together are enough to frighten the most willing and competent teacher.

Several curriculum items must be attended to in order to help staff focus their teaching. Related subjects staff will need a lesson plan listing goals, objectives, teaching procedures, methods and materials, and content of the unit. This information helps the mathematics teacher identify appropriate skills for inclusion. The mathematics teacher can help select relevant mathematics tasks, do a task analysis, and describe effective teaching procedures. Once the overlapping content areas have been defined the relevant skills can be taught in both classes. Although this process may sound onerous, once it is done it can be used for several years with minor adaptations.

When coordination involves LD students the special education teacher becomes a third source of skill reinforcement. Special education staff can give input matching student learning characteristics with teaching methods in all classes. In the resource room lessons can use the content from the regular classes presented with teaching styles more sensitive to individual needs.

Who should implement and monitor the coordination process? Several options exist, depending on the specific characteristics of the school setting. Either the mathematics teacher or a related subjects teacher could oversee the process. One could be designated as mainly responsible for paperwork and related details, while both would evaluate and monitor the program. Neither teacher should become a "supervisor" for the other. Another option is to assign an administrator or supervisor to monitor the program and ensure that a peer relationship is maintained between teachers. In fact, this option is preferable when more than two staff are involved.

Motivation

Maintaining student commitment to learning is the third principle characterizing the secondary mathematics program. One of the best ways to maintain motivation is by presenting students with activities that are challenging and likely to result in successful and meaningful learning experiences. During the initial stages of learning some failure is expected. But frequent failure or giving students assignments that are consistently beyond their ability unless they devote large amounts of time to studying can cause personal frustration, a negative self-concept, or behavior problems. Secondary mathematics should provide a variety of tasks for students where they use facts and concepts meaningfully. These tasks should be controlled by the teacher so the student experiences success at least 80 percent of the time. The remaining 20 percent of the tasks might require the student to spend time in one-to-one tutoring or individual studying until 100 percent mastery of all concepts taught is attained. The more skills not learned by the student the more difficult teaching becomes later in the year. Because of the cumulative nature of mathematics it is recommended that a criterion level for mastery of at least 90 percent and preferably 95 percent to 100 percent be set.

Problem Solving

Finally, a primary focus of the mathematics program should be on developing problem-solving skills. In fact, problem solving must be considered as one of the basic skills in mathematics. Rather than spend large amounts of time on repetitive drills to learn number facts, teachers should instruct students in the use of computational aids such as hand calculators to do basic arithmetic operations. Teaching should stress comprehension of the meaning and use of these basic computations. Minimal class time should be devoted to rote learning tasks. The goal of comprehension activities would be to teach the LD student how to reason logically in problem solving.

Preparation for a Productive Life

This discussion has stressed four general principles that should form the basis of the secondary mathematics program for LD students. These principles apply to all students across all levels of ability and skill development. Teaching creativity, curriculum coordination, practical application, and development of problem-solving skill in a success-oriented environment are essential to preparing students to assume roles as autonomous and productive members of society.

CONTENTS OF THE MATHEMATICS CURRICULUM

Secondary level LD students face a unique dilemma. All secondary schools have a defined curriculum plan in mathematics. This plan is based on the school board's decisions with input from professional staff about what to include in each course. The specific contents for each course are based on the expectation that students have mastered the majority of mathematics facts and concepts from earlier grades. The secondary program uses these concepts to present even more complex ideas and problems.

The truth is many LD students have gaps in their knowledge of mathematics. Some may be able to solve geometry problems and understand what they are doing, while have difficulty with long division. Others can perform basic whole number operations and be overwhelmed by fractions. There are many reasons why these gaps exist. Some relate to the learning characteristics of the LD student; others to the quality of the student's past learning experiences.

Whatever the reasons for these gaps it is important to identify each student's strengths and relate them to content most needed by the student. It is very difficult to define those areas most needed, given the diversity of ability levels in the group and the multifaceted nature of society. Some LD students may attend college while others will have trouble working at a part-time job. Even at the college level the range of job possibilities upon completion extends from driving a taxi cab to working in a biology laboratory.

The situation becomes more complicated when one considers the variety of secondary mathematics curricula available. At least three tracks are offered: college preparatory, business, and general. Some schools also offer a vocational training track. To which track are LD students assigned? No easy answers are available. At least two general factors must be examined: the characteristics of the student and the nature of the track for which he or she is being considered.

Student Characteristics

Perhaps the single most important student characteristic is previous school performance in mathematics and in general. Has the student stayed close to grade level in spite of the LD? At what grade level is the student now functioning? Does performance in mathematics suggest large gaps in basic facts? If so, can these gaps be filled in so the student can perform in the desired track? Other characteristics include estimated intellectual ability, levels of motivation and aspiration, and record of attendance. Finally, is the learning disability so extensive and severe that it precludes success in certain kinds of topics requiring some degree of abstraction?

Tracks

The second factor to be examined is the nature of the track. How receptive and sensitive are teachers and students to a student who may ask questions or not grasp facts as rapidly as they do? What is the impact of these responses, if negative, on the LD student? What is the implied expected level of achievement for students in the track? What is the stated level of attainment as set by board action? Does the teacher have any *real* flexibility in not meeting established curriculum timelines or will there be negative reactions from supervisors? What kinds of content are covered during the year? Is the content too abstract or complex given the student's learning styles? Even if the answers to all these questions point to placement in a higher level track the last item to examine concerns that of *diminishing returns*. Will the student need to put in more and more study time and learn less? Even if the student is highly motivated and capable, it may be physically impossible to study enough to stay even close to the pace of the class.

The critical point in determining the mathematics track most appropriate for the LD student is to find a *match* between the student's characteristics with those of the placement. In this way many program, administrative, and personal problems can be circumvented.

Basic Competencies

There are at least four areas of mathematics in which all LD students must be competent. These are (1) basic computations for whole numbers and fractions, (2) using mathematics practically, (3) problem solving, and (4) understanding concepts.

Computation

LD students must be skilled in the four basic number operations and their meanings. They must know when and how to use these processes appropriately in school and other life situations. It is not so important that they be skilled in the rote aspects of number operations as long as they understand what each operation means and when to use it. Using computational devices can save the student and teacher time and effort and allow more teaching time to deal with the substantive uses of mathematics in solving problems. Students should also understand the meaning of fractions and have some skill with computations and decimal conversions using a calculator.

There are many diagnostic tests available to assess number meanings and calculations (see Chapter 2). To mention two, the *Buswell-John Diagnostic Arithmetic Test* (Buswell & John, 1926) which can be given either individually or to a group and is designed to assess whole number computations in the four basic number operations and *The Mastery Test for Basic Essentials of Mathematics-Revised* (Steck-Vaughn Company, 1975), another useful test for individuals or groups, which includes decimals, fractions, and word problems. Effective teaching identifies what mathematical skills the LD student has and uses them to focus future programming.

Using Mathematics Practically

Mathematics is a tool that lets people solve problems logically and consistently. Instruction must be clear in showing the practical uses of mathematics in various situations. Mathematics is relevant to a person's job and daily life. Its daily uses range from simple addition when purchasing fruit to more complicated budgeting using percentages and projected expenses. Students must know how to apply mathematics in these situations. Too often, teaching produces students who can perform specific tasks in a specified context. For example, a student may be able to multiply two two-digit numbers with 100 percent accuracy in class but not be able to find the surface area of a wall being prepared for painting. The student has learned a skill, but does not understand its meaning and use. If students cannot use mathematics in these kinds of situations they should not be viewed as skilled even if they can do the computation in class.

Problem Solving

Using mathematics to solve real problems is one facet of teaching students to become effective problem solvers. Another is the ability to analyze issues logically and develop reasonable solution options. Analytic reasoning skill involves knowing when to use a given operation and understanding why it is used. It also means the ability to interpret and reduce a problem to its critical elements. The mathematics program should address these skills in the context of daily life skills. It might be more appropriate to spend class time with students explaining how and why they would use a certain mathematical operation to solve a word problem and less time on arriving at the correct answer.

Class assignments and tests could be given in the format shown in Exhibit 11-1. With this format a greater emphasis is placed on the process

Exhibit 11-1 A Problem-Solving Format Emphasizing Processes to
Solution

PROBLEM: You are building a ranch house and are now constructing the roof. The size
of the roof is 38'-0" with a 16" overhang on each side. The rise is 6" per foot
of run. You will be using 2" by 6" rafters that are spaced 16" on center.

1. Why do you space rafters 16" on center?
2. What are the advantages of using 24" on center spacing?
3. What are the disadvantages of 24" spacing?
4. What is the formula to figure rafter length?
5. Why is a formula used to figure rafter length?
6. Is this formula similar to anything you learned in geometry class? If so, to what is
it similar?
7. Why do you add the overhang to the length of the run?
8. What is the rafter length for the roof you are building? Show each calculation
clearly step by step.
9. Sketch how the roof on your house will look. Specify the dimensions for the rise,
run, line length, and rafter length.
10. If rafter boards cost 67 cents per linear foot what is the cost for one 10' rafter?
11. How did you calculate the cost for this rafter?
12. How much will it cost you as the contractor for rafters for this house? Show each
step clearly.
13. If the total selling price for this house is $67,900 how much of the cost is for the
rafters? Do not include labor costs in your computations.

---

than the answer itself. The student must be able to distinguish between
important and nonessential details in the problem and apply them to each
question asked. This requires more reasoning than merely giving the student the formula to compute the base of a triangle without showing the
practical uses of the formula. Such a lesson can be included in either the
mathematics or special education classes and is useful for both LD and
average students. If the format is utilized by the mathematics teacher the
special education teacher can give additional drill during resource time.

Concepts

The final focus in the secondary curriculum is on developing an understanding of some mathematics concepts. It is not important that students
understand all or even most mathematics concepts. They must know the
meaning of numerals, number operations, and specific concepts related to
life. Specific concepts should be related to the individual experiences and
goals of the student. Understanding the meaning of numerals means more
than being able to represent the value of "6" using six blocks or verbally

identifying 2,973 correctly. The student must understand the meaning of sets, place values, decimals at least as related to money, and fractions.

The IEP

Now that the main areas of mathematics have been outlined it would seem easy to orient the curriculum to stress each, varying only the levels. But the LD student's educational program is defined using the Individualized Educational Program (IEP). The IEP is similar to a map that outlines areas for teaching. The IEP in mathematics should be cumulative from year to year and reflect a four-year program. The mathematics teacher has a major role in determining the extent and complexity of topics taught and in establishing a content sequence. Input can cover techniques and experiments to make mathematics more real and to integrate mathematics into other subjects. Most IEPs are developed in a segregated way with mathematics goals only for mathematics class, science goals only for science class, and so on. The special education teacher can help the mathematics teacher to adapt methods and materials so the IEP can be extended across several subjects. This makes the IEP more fully describe the student's educational plan and program.

MEETING THE EDUCATIONAL NEEDS OF THE LD STUDENT

Offering a mathematics program to meet the educational needs of LD students is a complex task. This programming requires a variety of class options to be most effective and appropriate. It is not possible to offer one or two resource room classes and expect that the needs of most or even many LD students will be met. Merely modifying the regular mathematics program by reducing the number of topics taught or lowering standards for acceptable performance will not produce a better educational program. Appropriate programming occurs only when there are different kinds of classes available to teach mathematics. Each class will differ according to the degree of disability of the students, the technical expertise of staff in special education and mathematics, and the specific topics taught during the school year. The overall mathematics program must recognize the diverse academic and emotional needs of students and be responsive to differences in performance existing among LD students even at the same grade in school.

The organization of the secondary school typically leads teachers to make assumptions about student learning and achievement. Grade levels and curricula provide a sequence to the educational system. This sequence implies that a tenth grader has successfully mastered most of the important information given in ninth grade. If the student did not, then he or she would be repeating ninth grade.

In general, this assumption is not true for LD students. Yet many teachers present material according to predetermined timeliness set by the curriculum. The school administration typically reinforces teaching all the information in the curriculum. Even in many regular education classes students have not mastered basic skills from the preceding grade.

Teaching a skill does not ensure that students have learned the skill even if the student passes the course with a grade of "C" or better. Some students may have learned the skill initially and forgotton how and when to use it. Others may have learned the skill in a rote manner to pass a test but not understand how to use it beyond the test situation. Some may have never learned the skill at all and still passed the course.

Each situation poses different problems for the mathematics teacher. In the first case the student can learn and understand. The problem seems to be in the frequency of using the skill. A brief review may be all that is needed to go on to new material. The latter two cases involve students with varying degrees of learning problems. Ideally, the mathematics program would be organized so each could be taught capitalizing on learning abilities rather than highlighting inabilities.

The remainder of this section discusses several classroom organizational models to teach mathematics. They are (1) regular class models, (2) special education support models, and (3) alternative setting models. The section concludes with a discussion of some strategies to coordinate mathematics with other subject areas.

Regular Class Models

There are several ways the mathematics teacher can organize the class to meet the needs of most mildly LD and some moderately LD students.

Teaching Methods

One way begins by examining the teaching methods used in class. Is information presented using mostly a lecture approach with few opportunities to use skills? Giving students immediate feedback while monitoring how they use skills has several benefits. It prevents students from developing incorrect ways of getting answers to in-class assignments, even if the answers are correct. Students must learn how to solve problems correctly and understand the processes used to get the answer. During class assignments the teacher might ask students to explain the solution process

either individually or to the group. This not only helps the teacher determine if the student has learned the skill but it also gives other students a
review of the lesson. Care should be taken in using this approach with LD
students in front of the class, particularly if the student has difficulty with
verbal expression. Individual explanations let the teacher give feedback
immediately. The student can continue with the assignment using the right
procedure.

Some other relatively easy modifications include reducing the amount
of information taught during class and using several different ways to teach
it, handing out diagrams that are color-coded to highlight key points put
on the chalkboard, and telling students which points during class are most
important and should be learned.

Small Groups

If the student's progress fails to improve after using these adjustments
on a consistent basis the next option is to determine the appropriateness
of dividing the class into smaller groups according to their understanding
of the material. Students can be grouped in one of two ways: homoge-
neously according to level of performance in the unit or heterogeneously
with more advanced students serving as tutors for slower ones. Both
groupings require the teacher to have small group activities ready for most
classes to follow up the initial teaching. Each class might be concluded
with students summarizing what was taught and how it can be used either
in a class project, real-life situation, or both.

Tutoring

A third option for organizing the class is one-to-one tutoring from an
upper-class student or an adult. Tutoring sessions may be given only for
topics with which the student is having difficulty. Sessions could take
place outside class either during study periods or after school. Direction
from the mathematics teacher is critical for the student to benefit from the
tutor.

Regular class models are designed mainly for mildly LD students who
can function in mathematics in spite of their learning disability. Some skills
may give this student trouble. With the appropriate teaching flexibility and
adjustments, the student's learning rate can be about equal to that for the
rest of the class. Special education may be consulted for specific questions
about teaching. The mathematics curriculum is not modified in any substantive way.

Increasing the variety of methods used to present concepts paired with
the necessary material modification, practical application, and creative

class organization can enhance learning and achievement. Some other classroom options include using computer-assisted instruction, providing independent class assignments often, and setting up a mathematics laboratory in a corner of the room where there are handouts, worksheets, and experiments for students to work on and get step-by-step directions to solve each task.

Special Education Support Models

Many moderately LD students can succeed in regular mathematics classes when given support services from special education. These services could range from spending one hour a week in a resource room for help in organizing work assignments to being in a full-time self-contained class and integrated into mathematics on a selective basis. The main characteristic distinguishing these students from those discussed above is their inability to function successfully without consistent and specialized help from special education.

Resource Room

The most frequent special education support given to LD students is the resource room. Two basic options are usually offered. Either the student spends part of the day receiving help in mathematics while attending regular mathematics classes daily or the student receives the entire mathematics program from special education. With the first option the efforts of both teachers must complement each other. Sometimes the special educator is seen by the mathematics teacher as an unauthorized supervisor rather than a consultant on teaching strategies. The potential for staff conflicts increases if teachers become possessive about their own program of study. In the second option staff conflicts are less likely to arise over student programming but mathematics is taught by special education. The issue becomes the special education teacher's knowledge of mathematics beyond basic concepts. Because the special educator has probably not had the depth of training in this subject there is a limit imposed on the range of topics to be taught. The teacher's knowledge about methods and materials is also restricted. There may be many LD students in a self-contained class who can learn advanced concepts and skills when given proper programming but these concepts may not be taught because of the special educator's lack of training in the area. Other options are available to make maximum use of the small group setting and services offered by special education.

Lab/Workshop Areas

Special education may be able to set up a mathematics laboratory or workshop area in the regular mathematics class. The topics in the area would correspond with those being taught in mathematics. During the first part of class the mathematics teacher would teach using many of the strategies discussed earlier. The second half of class would involve small group projects or independent study tasks. At this point any student having problems with the lesson could work in the laboratory with the special education teacher. A maximum of five students should be allowed at any one time. The special educator would clarify concepts from the lesson and then return students to the rest of the class where they would either work alone or in small groups under the direction of the mathematics teacher. Slower students could spend their entire second half of class in the laboratory area. A major advantage here is that both the mathematics and special education teachers work closely with the same students on the same topics. Ideas can be exchanged on how to modify teaching for both LD and average students. The problem of curriculum coordination no longer exists and the opportunity for staff communication is increased. Because the laboratory is open to all students the LD students are not singled out because of their disability.

Scheduling

Special education staff can also provide these services outside mathematics class for students having problems with specific topics. Most LD students will not have problems with all content areas. There will be certain areas that do give individual students trouble. The LD student could leave for part of each mathematics class to receive more help in the resource room. The remaining students in mathematics class might be involved with a class assignment or receive more in-depth information about the topic during this time. A high level of planning and coordination is needed for presenting information according to a timeline and scheduling of classes.

The student might also leave mathematics class early and complete the class in a resource room. The student also could attend the resource room first and then mathematics class or leave for part of the mathematics class and return to complete the period. The first option is the easiest in terms of scheduling, but may not be best for students socially. The second lets the special education teacher help the student get prepared for class and review important information to be used in class. The third allows the special educator to be sure that the student understands and can apply the lesson. The last two options require more coordination between teachers but offer more opportunity to monitor student performance.

Multigrade Classes

A third option is for the mathematics department to identify one staff person who enjoys working with LD students and set up a separate class. The group could have LD students from several different classes. Because of its size the teacher could be flexible in adapting teaching strategies and materials to meet student needs. The special educator would be a consultant to help with these modifications. At times, the special educator might conduct evaluations to assess student learning behaviors. This approach can be a practical and cost-effective way to meet the educational needs in mathematics of LD students in the least restrictive environment. The class should have no more than ten students at any time and preferably fewer if the students have severe learning problems. The mathematics teacher will need additional planning time daily to prepare lessons. This teacher should also have a rather generous budget to buy texts and supplies. Finally, this teacher will need to be involved with inservice training to increase skills about the learning disabled.

Co-Teaching

A final option is to offer mathematics courses that are co-taught by special education and mathematics. Co-teaching could be done for the entire course or only specific topics. This approach has many of the advantages discussed in the model first presented in this section. The major distinction is that the special educator assumes a much more active role in daily teaching activities. With the first model the special educator listens to the lesson during the first half of class and co-teaches only during the second half.

Any of these models can be effective and efficient ways to provide mathematics programming for LD students who need more than just the regular class. The last two models are appropriate for moderately learning-disabled students needing a smaller class setting, less peer pressure, and more frequent adaptation of teaching methods. There is still a third group of LD students that must receive instruction. They are the severely learning disabled.

Alternative Setting Models

Severely learning-disabled students have learning styles that are so inefficient that placement in a highly specialized academic setting is necessary. They may have good measured intellectual ability but experience difficulty organizing these abilities during learning. They may be easily distractible, have low frustration-tolerance levels, or show behavioral/

emotional problems. The number of teaching presentations needed before this student learns and retains something may be four times or more as much as mildly and moderately learning-disabled students. Placing these students in one of the regular or special class support models is inappropriate. Even if the teacher can meet this student's educational needs, achievement is so slow that the gap between the student and peers increases even when support services are given. Two basic program options exist. The first is the self-contained class; the second is the alternative school.

The Self-Contained Class

In a self-contained class most of the student's academic program is given in the same one or two rooms by one to three special educators. Typically, students spend nearly all day in one room with the same teacher. Mathematics is taught by a special educator who usually stresses basic "survival skills." The mathematics curriculum may more resemble that at the primary-elementary levels than a secondary plan.

There are many advantages for programming. Because of the special education training of the teacher and the small class size there is ample opportunity to individualize teaching. Instruction need not be geared to a large group or even a small group. The intensive nature of the placement makes mathematics programming easier. In a class of seven students it is possible for the teacher to have seven different mathematics programs going simultaneously.

The disadvantage of such a class is in the highly specialized nature of the setting. Mathematics may be taught in a traditional way stressing basic number operations. In part, this may be due to the skill level of the student. But it might also be because of the special educator's unfamiliarity with teaching mathematics conceptually. Students may not be shown how to apply mathematics to life and work beyond basic survival skills. Even if mathematics is practically oriented students may use it only on paper-and-pencil tasks. The special educator is trained to use educational tests and specialized teaching strategies to enhance student learning. This teacher is not a content specialist as is the mathematics teacher. One can expect major differences in the priorities each places. This problem can be reduced somewhat by assigning a mathematics teacher to consult on a regular basis with the special educator about the curriculum.

The Alternative School

The alternative school offers a viable educational option for many severely learning-disabled students. It overcomes many of the disadvantages of the self-contained class while retaining individualization. The major differences between the two lie in physical location, staffing, and philosophy. Placement in an alternative school presumes that students can be educated most appropriately in a setting that is different from the typical school setting. To emphasize this difference the actual physical location of the school must be separate from the high school. Sometimes the school is located in an unused school building but it may be in a former store or factory.

In many ways the alternative school is a magnified version of the self-contained class with a wider range of courses and teaching specialists. Mathematics may be taught by a mathematics teacher who has had additional training in special education. Special education teachers and consultants at the school facilitate staff communication for student programming.

The alternative school usually has fewer students than the high school. A typical alternative school may have one administrator, ten teachers, and a counselor for 75 to 85 students, depending on their academic needs. The small environment lets mathematics be integrated readily into other subjects. An example of this kind of subject coordination is shown in Exhibit 11-2. These materials are from a unit on painting developed by Webster (1981) for use with severely learning-disabled students in an alternative vocational high school. The vocational teacher prepared information sheets for students and staff outlining the content for the unit. The English and mathematics teachers received copies to help them focus their lessons. A mathematics unit on weights and measurements was started, while an English lesson using vocabulary from this unit taught spelling, dictionary work, reading, and writing. The content from English and mathematics was used in the vocational class. Similarly, mathematics was used in both English and vocational classes. Measuring student learning became easier because only one test was given to students. The test included skills and concepts from all three subjects. Learning increased because students were being saturated with the same or similar content in three different classes. Each class highlighted the practical uses of the lesson using many different teaching strategies and activities.

Such curriculum coordination can be extended throughout the student's entire day and program. As students become more skilled in using basic mathematics more advanced concepts can be presented. Exhibit 11-3 presents some of the teaching objectives that accompanied this unit.

The disadvantages of the alternative school lie in the social area. Students risk being identified by peers and the community as odd or different. Establishing an alternative school requires careful planning to anticipate such issues before they become problems.

Exhibit 11-2 An Example of Curriculum Coordination Relating Mathematics to Other Content Areas

Painting
Information Sheet—Liquid Measurement
Paint and Solvent Containers

Caution/Danger: Whenever you use paint, solvents, acid, or other chemicals make sure that you read the label and understand what you are using. If you have trouble reading or understanding the directions and cautions on the label, ask for help before you proceed. Many labels tell you about danger by using big red letters or the skull and crossbones.

Pint
- One pint equals 16 fluid ounces.
- Two pints equal one quart.
- You can buy most paints, stains, and varnishes in one pint containers.

Quart
- One quart equals 32 fluid ounces.
- Four quarts equal one gallon.
- You can buy most paints, stains, and varnishes in one quart containers.

Gallon
- One gallon equals 128 fluid ounces.
- Most paints, stains, and varnishes come in one gallon cans that are round.
- Most paint thinners and turpentine come in one gallon cans that are rectangular.

Five-Gallon Bucket
- If you paint large areas you can buy five-gallon buckets of paints.

Information Sheet—Surface Preparation Supplies

Caution/Danger: Whenever you use paint, solvents, acid, or other chemicals make sure that you read the directions and cautions on the label and understand what you are using. If you have the trouble reading or understanding the directions and cautions on the label, ask for help before you proceed. Many labels tell about danger, or caution you, by using big red letters or the skull and crossbones.

Tri-Sodium Phosphate (T.S.P.): Very strong powdered cleaner that is mixed with water. T.S.P. will dissolve grease and oil on surfaces to be painted.

Muriatic Acid: Used to prepare concrete for painting.

CAUTION: Muriatic acid is dangerous in many ways.
- If it touches your skin, it will burn you.
- If you breathe in the fumes, it will hurt your lungs and get into your bloodstream.
- If it is swallowed, it will burn you inside and poison you.

Use muriatic acid only:
- Under the teacher's direct supervision.
- While wearing rubber gloves and eye protection.
- Only with proper ventilation of the work area.

Exhibit 11-2 continued

White Pigmented Shellac: Used to seal water stains in ceilings and walls and to prime and seal new wood when thinned with alcohol.

Plaster of Paris: White powder mixed with water and used to patch cracks and holes in plaster walls and ceilings.

Wallboard Compound: Comes premixed and used to patch holes and cracks in sheetrock walls and ceilings.

Caulking Compound: Comes in tubes and used to fill cracks, holes, or seams in outside areas.

Exhibit 11-3 A Sample of Student Objectives in Mathematics for a Unit on Painting

---

Given a geometric figure student will identify and measure width.

Given a geometric figure student will identify and measure length.

Given a list of measuring instruments and units of measure student will match them with an appropriate definition.

Given 2 columns of liquid measurements student will match Column I with Column II.

Given an addition problem involving liquid measurements student will express answer in simplest way.

Given a subtraction problem involving liquid measurements student will express answer in simplest way.

Given a multiplication problem involving liquid measurements student will express product in simplest way.

Given a division problem involving liquid measurements student will express quotient in simplest way.

Given a liquid measure student will convert to an indicated equivalent measure.

Given an angle and protractor student will measure the given angle correct to within 2 degrees and classify as acute, obtuse, or right.

Given applications of area, perimeter, and volume and these kinds of measurements: linear, square, and cubic student will select the type of unit that would be used in solving the problem.

Given a list of geometric terms student will draw a picture and label each.

Given a group of line segments student will measure to nearest $\frac{1}{2}$, $\frac{1}{4}$, and $\frac{1}{8}$ inch.

In developing this type of school it must be decided whether the school will serve only students from one district or be a cooperative effort among several districts. A system-wide school is probably best, placed administratively at some level outside the regular and special education systems. Students already have been unable to achieve in either of these systems. The alternative school is a third system option. This option should not be a replica of the two systems in which the student has already failed.

Of course, the school must follow all board policies and procedures. The requirements for graduation should be the same as for any other student. The major distinction lies in the teaching strategies used to enhance learning and the emphasis placed on solving real problems. The school principal should be someone capable of being creative and resourceful. This person is required to maintain a successful balance of educational leadership, supervision of teaching, and administrative detail responsibilities. One description of an alternative high school for severely learning-disabled/emotionally disturbed students may be found in Webster (1981).

A cooperative alternative school involves many more issues to be resolved including school policies and procedures, daily operational format, graduation requirements, discipline and curriculum, to name but a few. Will the school have a board or council made of representatives from each sending district? How will membership or voting power be determined? What will be the role and limits of this council? What will be the duties for the principal? Will tuitions be charged and how are the rates set? Although cooperative schools are a financially beneficial delivery system, they present many problems and offer a high potential for continuing problems. A great deal of time may be spent in meetings dealing with group process and communication styles.

COORDINATING MATHEMATICS WITH OTHER SUBJECT AREAS

As we discussed in Chapter 9, mathematics is an important tool in many areas. In some subjects inability to use mathematics is a major obstacle to success. Mathematics deficits also interfere with performance in many vocational areas. Most trades mandate knowledge about applying number operations and concepts from geometry, algebra, and trigonometry to solve problems. Even semiskilled jobs such as cashiering or maintenance require competence in mathematics.

Coordinating mathematics with other subjects can be an effective way to make a school program more interesting for both students and staff. With proper planning and cooperation coordination can be done without imposing on any one person.

Coordinated teaching shows students the practical uses of mathematics outside class and how apparently dissimilar subjects are related. Student motivation can be raised as these relationships are clarified and used to reinforce each other. Student achievement levels can increase because of practice from using concepts in several classes. Staff can prepare complementary in-class assignments or homework involving reasoning and problem solving.

The painting unit presented earlier offers many opportunities for innovative teaching over the entire school day. The contents for English, mathematics, and vocational classes have already been outlined. The vocational class might also have actual in-class tasks or outside work experiences with students painting surfaces solid colors and adding various geometric patterns. Students could calculate area, the amount of paint needed, plan the design using a scale-model drawing, do a cost analysis, and actually paint the surface. Lessons using these skills for reading, science, health, and any social skills training are also possible.

More severely learning-disabled students, reading four years or more below expected grade level, might work on basic sight words such as "gallon," "quart," "acid," or "caulking." More advanced activities would include a language experience approach. Word and phrase meanings using both verbal and quantitative definitions are also appropriate. Students needing work in reading comprehension might be given verbal word problems using reading and mathematics. During reading the mathematics in the problems is minimized because the emphasis is on comprehension and/or word decoding. Higher functioning students could be given written materials describing the uses of surface preparation supplies and their effects on different surfaces.

In science the student might be introduced to the chemical structure and interactions for each of these materials as well as an analysis of geometric representations of their atomic structures. In health the effects of each material on different body areas could be explored. An introduction to basic human anatomy and body chemistry is necessary. Finally, criterion-referenced rating scales can be made to rate academic performance and behavior. These scales can be used in every class or only one class. Two examples of such scales are presented in Exhibits 11-4 and 11-5. Exhibit 11-4 is an example of a content-based scale, while Exhibit 11-5 deals with interpersonal behavior.

It is not necessary that all the specific operations taught during mathematics also be taught in every other class. What is necessary is that teaching in other classes complement and reinforce what is presented in mathematics. The mathematics teacher should do the same for related subjects. Practically speaking, coordinating mathematics requires at least one full academic year. Once it is established the total school program becomes more meaningful for everyone.

Formal and Informal Relationships

Many formal and informal relationships must be established to make coordination successful. The formal relationships involve clarifying the

Exhibit 11-4 A Rating Scale Used To Assess Student Performance in a
Content Area (Vocational Skills)

	yes	no	shows improvement	needs improvement	comments
1. Student demonstrates knowledge of the different types of paint, stains, and varnishes (verbally).					
2. Student can match (verbally) proper brushes, roller covers, and accessory equipment to the following painting tasks:					
a) flat finish latex on smooth surfaces					
b) semigloss latex on smooth surfaces					
c) semigloss latex on rough surfaces					
d) enamel (oil, alkyd, & urethane) on smooth surfaces (wood and metal)					
e) enamel on concrete floors					
f) primer (oil) on new wood and bare metal					
g) stain (oil) on new wood.					
3. Student demonstrates knowledge of procedures and solvents used for cleaning of painting tools. Ref #2.					
4. Student demonstrates acceptable manipulative skill levels with brushes in the following tasks (criterion includes neatness, smooth finish, no runs, drips, or brushmarks):					
a) cutting in walls, ceilings, & hardware					
b) painting small surface areas and doors					
c) painting sash and trim					
d) applying varnish or shellac.					
5. Student demonstrates acceptable manipulative skill levels with rollers in the following tasks (criterion includes neatness, no runs, drips, or tracking):					

Exhibit 11-4 continued

a) rolling sheetrock & plaster walls						
b) rolling ceilings (smooth & texture)						
c) rolling concrete walls						
d) rolling concrete floors						
6. Student demonstrates ability to accomplish acceptable surface preparation on listed materials: a) new wood						
b) previously painted wood						
c) cement and concrete						
d) metal						
e) sheetrock and plaster						

administrative arrangements for program implementation such as budget, materials, schedules, and curriculum. In districts with declining enrollments the security of both mathematics and special education must be ensured. Any innovation that even hints at possible staff reassignments or layoffs will be met with resistance.

Informal relationships refer to the quality of interactions between staff in the two departments. How do members of one department view those in the other? Does a basic degree of professional and personal respect exist? How has special education been seen in general throughout the district? Staff in both departments must be shown that their efforts will actually make teaching easier and more creative.

Beyond these adult-centered and logistical issues there lies the attitudes and expectations of staff about the LD student. Concern about their ability to function in mathematics, doubt about having the skill to teach them, and reluctance to deviate from the curriculum because of overt or subtle administrative pressures are but a few of the items that might arise. Special educators may be protective of their students and make unrealistic requests on other staff about standards for behavior, attendance, or grades. If allowed to magnify, these issues can destroy the entire program.

Staff Development

One way in which these concerns can be addressed is through a staff development and inservice training program that operates on a daily basis. Obviously, speakers cannot be brought in daily. But they can be brought in monthly. A system can be set up where the speaker's ideas are used and evaluated. Most of the speakers should be practical and have specific

Exhibit 11-5 A Rating Scale Used To Assess Student Social Skills in a Content Area

	never	rarely	usually	shows improvement	needs improvement	comments
Student observes safety practices involving co-workers, work areas, and tools and equipment.						
Student works effectively with peers in team work situations.						
Student follows oral instructions promptly and discharges tasks without repeated instruction.						
Student asks questions when he or she does not understand procedures.						
Student stays on task for 45 min. without constant supervision.						
Student utilizes break periods constructively and returns from breaks on time.						
Student demonstrates leadership ability when assigned as job foreman.						
Student demonstrates ability to match proper tools with assigned tasks.						
Student wears clothing appropriate to assigned tasks.						

Exhibit 11-5 continued

Student maintains tools and supplies in a responsible, constructive manner.						
Student participates in clean-up operations upon job completion without constant supervision.						
Student demonstrates neatness, organization, and pride in his or her work.						
Student demonstrates enhanced self-image due to newly acquired skills.						
Student demonstrates physical strength and stamina necessary to accomplish assigned tasks.						

suggestions about curriculum, teaching, student management, or whatever else staff see as needed. Issues speakers should be kept to a minimum especially during the first year or two of operation.

In addition to the technical aspects of the school, there are human factors that must be addressed. It is not suggested that work be a place for ongoing personal group or individual therapy, but a mechanism to discuss work problems that occur and affect the program should be available. If morale and commitment are not maintained there is little point in continuing the effort.

Staff meetings discussing school information should be held weekly. They should be brief and lively with a structured agenda. On occasion, these meetings may focus on problem solving a group issue such as staff communication styles.

Effective staff development requires enough release time from class duties on a regular basis so that mathematics teachers can observe special educators teaching and vice versa. Observation helps staff understand what is occurring in other classes. Once staff from each department are familiar with other teaching styles, arrangements can be made for team teaching. Both teachers will need time after observations to explain and analyze what was seen. Class observations need not be limited to just one school. They can be done at neighboring schools when the purpose is inservice training rather than coordination. As the coordinated effort continues successfully, the frequency of class observations can be reduced. Observations should be required of all staff at least once every three months after the first year of experience. Throughout staff training supervisory staff can be involved to as great a degree as they wish.

ASSESSING STUDENT PERFORMANCE

Awarding a high school diploma indicates the successful completion of a prescribed course of academic study. Completion implies that the recipient has achieved at least a minimal level of competency in basic academic areas. Often, though, a high school diploma signifies only that the student was able to attend school for four years. The diploma has little reference to standards of performance attained or to the course of study pursued. In some school districts students in special education are not required to meet even minimal requirements for graduation aside from possibly the attendance criterion. Even there board policy may be waived because the student has been identified as handicapped.

Special education is not designed to give students an easier route to a high school diploma. Special education was developed to give students another option within the educational system. This option uses alternative teaching techniques adapted to individual needs to present the required curriculum. It was not designed as a watered-down version of the regular education system or a program with lower standards for achievement.

There are two basic ways to evaluate the LD student's competency in mathematics. The first is to evaluate learning progress according to the goals given in the IEP. If the student attains 70 percent of these goals during a quarter he or she either passes for the quarter or the performance is converted into some letter-grade equivalent. Although this seems appropriate it can be very misleading to the student, parents, possible employers, and other educators. For example, an eleventh grade LD student may be working on basic operations using fractions as outlined in the IEP. The student attains 80 percent of these goals during the first half-year and receives a grade of B + at midyear. The course name is "Mathematics 3—General." To someone not familiar with the curriculum certain presumptions will be made about where and how this student is performing in mathematics. It appears as though he is doing above-average work in eleventh grade mathematics. In fact, the student is really working on fifth and sixth grade mathematics, some five and six years below his current grade placement. A second limitation is the difficulty caused in preparing course outlines because of the wide differences that could exist among IEP goals from one student to the next.

Another way to rate performance is by modifying the tests used in the regular mathematics class so the student is not penalized for his or her learning disability. Modify does not mean make the test easier. Rather, it means that adaptations may be made in how the test is given (orally instead of written), how the student responds to items (demonstrations rather than written solutions), or how the test is organized physically (using large letters, color-coding, and blocked off areas to stress the separate pieces of information presented). A list of information necessary for the student to know to pass the test could be given to the special educator about two weeks prior to the test to help focus studying. The student might also be given the test several times until a passing grade is achieved. The rationale here is criterion-to-mastery of the material, not the typical "test-grade-teach something new" format used by many teachers. The goal is to get the student to learn regardless of how many times it takes to reach a satisfactory criterion level.

Courses could be organized according to the competencies learned. When a student has mastered the criteria at one level, he or she is then free to go to the next until all mathematics requirements for graduation are met. Some students may need only six months to complete a level, while others may need much longer. It is important that students are taught until attaining some prescribed level of consistent performance.

This approach also addresses the appropriateness of minimal competency testing (MCT) for the learning disabled. Students must be prepared to deal with the demands of society after leaving high school. Once they leave school people no longer will modify treatment of them because they are learning disabled. They are members of the social mainstream and must be able to function appropriately if they are to be happy and productive. If they do not have the mathematics skills demanded by society, employers typically are not going to adjust their work standards to meet their needs. Participating in MCT and being given instruction needed to help them pass the test are experiences all but the most severely learning-disabled students should have.

INTRODUCING NEW PROGRAMS

The rapid technological advances of the past decade have changed the applications of mathematics in our lives. The inexpensive cost and simple operation of hand calculators have nearly eliminated doing basic whole number operations using paper and pencil. Basic skills in mathematics have been made easier. But the rise of a high technology industry and the increased use of computers at work and at home have created a need for different kinds of mathematical skills. These developments have significant implications for programming at all levels. Programs will need a core of information that is supplemented with more contemporary skills valued by industry and society. New programs teaching these skills will be phased into the mathematics program regularly. The relationship between program and technological advances may be represented as follows:

Technological Changes/Improvements
↓
Changes in Mathematics Curriculum
↓
Graduation of Students with Relevant Skills
↓
Technological Changes/Improvements

The mathematics program must be flexible to accommodate new programs while retaining constancy in presenting a core of basic skills needed by everyone. The program cannot exist independently from the society for which it is preparing students. There must be a reciprocal relationship between the two that keeps the program student-centered, future-oriented, and realistic.

The decision to include new skills in the program should be based on a systematic and objective analysis of current and anticipated trends in society. Skills that have some durability, rather than reflecting passing fads, should be included. This avoids confusion and adjustment to frequent reorganization. Perhaps the most effective way to make these decisions is to analyze data collected from several representative sources. For example, the rise of computers is well known. There are many kinds of computer systems, languages, and skills available. The decision to include computer training in the mathematics program is easy. But deciding which model to use, which languages to teach, and which specific programming skills are needed comes from a clear delineation of the goals for the program and a sampling of the needs of industry in a 25- to 50-mile radius from the school.

Meeting with representatives from several different size companies covering several technological areas will give an adequate sampling of data on which to base decisions.

Other issues relevant to implementing new programs include the amount of money available in the department budget beyond essential equipment and supplies, the amount of time needed to organize the program, and the level at which the program content will be oriented. It will be necessary to do a task analysis of the mathematics skills needed to succeed and rank order them.

Beginning new programming is a complex and time-consuming activity when done correctly. It is the only way the mathematics program can remain up to date to prepare students for productive roles in society.

SUMMARY

In this chapter we have examined the major components of philosophical, organizational, curricular, instructional, and interpersonal issues relevant to mathematics programming for the secondary level learning-disabled student. Setting up a viable coordinated mathematics/special education program is a complicated process that requires anticipation and resolution of potential problematic areas before they develop into real problems. Once personnel have to react to a series of unexpected problems or concerns, the real focus of the programming can easily be lost. The resistance of the staff to adjust to the demands made by coordinated programming can be great. The benefits to students, staff, and society are even greater if this effort can be implemented successfully.

REFERENCES

Basic essentials of mathematics test—Level II. (1975). Steck-Vaughn Publishing.

Buswell, G., & John, L. (1926). Diagnostic studies in arithmetic. *Supplementary Educational Monographs*, No. 30.

Webster, R. (1981). Vocational-technical training for emotionally disturbed adolescents. *Teaching Exceptional Children, 14(2),* 75–79.

Index

A

Achievement tests, 33-34, 39-40
  group criterion-referenced, 38-39
  group norm-referenced, 37-38
  individual criterion-referenced,
    35-37
  individual norm-referenced, 34-35
Addition
  decimals, 146
  fractions, 128, 133-138
  whole numbers, 92-97
Advanced arithmetic, 214-242
Advancement scores, 37
Algebra, 242, 279, 283, 285-289
Algorithmic variations, 20-23
Alternative schools, 305-310
Alternative setting models, 305-310
Angles, 167-171, 188-191
Area, 191-196, 266-268
Arizona State University Child Service
  Demonstration Center, 68
Assessment
  achievement tests, 33-40
  diagnostic tests, 40-44, 298
  informal, 44-48
  measurement scales, 32-33, 311
  performance, 76-77, 79, 311,
    316-317
  proficiency tests, 48-56
  prognostic tests, 274, 279
  purposes, 31-32
  strategies, 30-31
  vocational proficiency tests, 210-213
  whole number skills, 113-114

B

Basic skills, 84-86, 205, 207-210,
  297-300
Biology applications, 244-245
Business applications, 249-252
Buswell-John test, 43-44, 298

C

Calculators, 71, 91-92, 109, 111-113
California Achievement Tests, 38
Career education, 201. *See also*
  Vocational preparation

CBA. *See* Curriculum-based assessment

Centimeter, 182-183

Chemistry applications, 247-248

Child Service Demonstration Center,
   Arizona State University, 68

Circles, 177
   area, 194-196, 268
   circumference and diameter, 187-188
   unit, 289

Circumference, 187

Classroom organization
   alternative setting models, 305-310
   regular class models, 301-303
   special education support models,
      303-305

Classroom procedures, 64-66, 275-276

Clinical interviews, 46-47

Clinical Mathematics Interview (CMI),
   46-47

Closure, 115-119

CMI. *See* Clinical Mathematics
   Interview

College preparatory programs
   algebra I, 279, 283-284
   algebra II, 285-289
   course offerings, 272
   curriculum, 272
   curriculum objectives, 274-275
   geometry, 284-285
   lesson types, 275-277
   plan of action, 278-279
   pre-calculus, 289
   teacher qualifications, 274
   teaching method alternatives,
      277-278

Compensatory education, 25, 29, 30

Comprehensive secondary school
   programs, 204-205

Computation competency, 297-298

Computer-assisted instruction, 72, 113

Computer literacy, 244

Concept and Skills Assessment, 37, 47

Congruence, 172-175

Content
   high school mathematics, 241-244
   modification, 66-69

overviews, 275

Co-teaching, 305

Counting numbers, 116

Criterion-Referenced Curriculum
   (CRC), 36

Criterion-referenced tests
   achievement, 35-40
   curriculum-based assessment, 76-77
   description, 33
   diagnostic, 43-44
   group, 38-39
   individual, 35-37
   performance, 311

Curriculum, 218-220, 222, 272, 274,
   293

Curriculum-based assessment (CBA),
   76-77

Cutoff scores, 37, 43

Cylinders, 268, 269

D

Decimals
   activities, 143-145
   applications, 259-260
   concepts, 142
   job-related use, 209
   operations with, 145, 258-259
   reading and writing, 145

Decimeter, 181-182

Dependent sheltered employment
   setting, 202

Developmental lessons, 25, 276

Developmental variations, 13-19

*Diagnosis: An Instructional Aid in
   Mathematics, Level B*, 36

Diagnostic Chart for Fundamental
   Processes in Arithmetic, 43-44

Diagnostic Inventory of Basic Skills,
   36, 37

Diagnostic Mathematics Inventory
   (DMI), 39

Diagnostic tests, 40-44, 298

Diameter, 187

Division
   decimals, 146

fractions, 139-141
whole numbers, 106-109
DMI. *See* Diagnostic Mathematics
Inventory
Domain-referenced tests. *See*
Criterion-referenced tests

E

Employment settings, 202-203
Error analysis, 45-47
Estimation, 262-263
Euclidean geometry, 151. *See also*
Measurement

F

Feet, 186
Fractions
activities, 122-132
addition and subtraction, 128,
133-138
concepts, 119
division, 139-141
multiplication, 138-139

G

General science applications, 248
Geology applications, 248-249
Geometry
angles, 167-171
applications, 264-266
circles, 177
college preparatory course, 284-285
concept modeling, 161-162
course content, 243
goals, 151
guidelines, 154
introductory lesson model, 155-161
measurement lesson model, 162-166
modification approach, 155, 284-285
prerequisite skills, 153-154
proof, 166

rectangles, 176
similar polygons, 177
structure of, 151-153
triangle congruence, 171-176
See also Measurement
Grade contract, 278
Graphing, 269, 287

H

Homework, 277

I

Inches, 186
Independent study, 278
Individual Criterion-Referenced Tests,
39
Individualized Educational Program
(IEP), 300
Individualized instruction
advantages of, 61-63, 79-80
classroom procedures and, 64-66
content modification, 66-69
definition, 63-64
delivery system modification, 72-74
pace modification, 69
performance assessment, 76-77
procedures, 75-79
sequence modification, 69-70
task demand modification, 70-71
teaching method modification, 74-75
Informal assessment, 44-48
Informal geometry, 155
Institute in Learning Disabilities,
University of Kansas, 68
Integers, 116-117
Interactive units, 223, 225-232
Iowa Tests of Achievement and
Proficiency, 56
Irrational numbers, 118

K

Key Math Diagnostic Arithmetic Test,
41-42

L

Laboratories, 304
Learning disabled
    algorithmic variations, 20-23
    characteristics of, 5-13, 23-24
    classification problems, 62-63
    course content problems, 83-84
    developmental variations, 13-20
    program design for, 24-25
Length, 180-181
    centimeters, 182-183
    circumference, 187-188
    decimeters, 181-182
    diameter, 187-188
    inches, feet, and yards, 186
    metric ruler activity, 183-184
    perimeter, 186-187
Lines, 161-162, 180-188
Logarithms, 243
Lowest common denominator, 133,
    135-137

M

MASI. *See* Multilevel Academic Skill
    Inventory
Mass, 198-199
*Mastery Test for Basic Essentials of
    Mathematics-Revised*, 298
Math Concept Inventory, 36
Mathematics applications
    benefits of, 241
    biology, 244-245
    business, 249-252
    chemistry, 247-248
    general science, 248
    geology, 248-249
    learning disabled needs, 235-237
    physics, 245-246
    prerequisite skills, 241-244
    problems, 86, 241
    role of, 237-238
    skill needs, 255-270
    teaching methods and approaches,
        238-239
    types, 240-241
    vocational subjects, 252-254
Mathematics Instructional Tests, 38-39
MCT. *See* Minimal competency tests
Measurement
    angles, 188-191
    area, 191-196
    function, 179-180
    length, 180-188
    line segments, 162-166, 180-188
    mass, 198-199
    number system and, 117-118
    prerequisite skills, 180
    scientific, 198-200
    vocational preparation and, 207-208
    volume, 196-198
Measurement scales, 32-33, 311
Metric measurement, 181-184
Metropolitan Achievement Tests, 38
Microcomputers, 72, 113, 244
Minimal competency tests, (MCT), 317
Minimum Essentials Test, 56
Modified employment setting, 202
Multigrade classes, 305
Multilevel Academic Skill Inventory
    (MASI), 39
Multi-Model Mathematics, 36, 37, 46
Multiplication
    decimals, 146
    fractions, 138-139
    whole numbers, 102-106

N

New program integration, 318-319
Normal competitive employment
    setting, 202
Norm-referenced tests
    achievement, 34-35, 37-38
    description, 32-33
    diagnostic, 41-43
    group, 37-38, 43
    individual, 34-35
Number line, 255-257
Number sentences, 260-261
Number theory, 243

O

One-to-One Instruction, 73-74
Out-of-level testing, 38, 43

P

Parallel Alternate Curriculum (PAC),
    68
Parrallelograms, 193, 267
Peabody Individual Achievement Test
    (PIAT), 34, 35
Peer tutoring, 72-73
Percentages, 147-149, 258-260
Performance contracting, 277
Performance tests, 76-77, 79, 311,
    316-317
Perimeter, 186-187
Physics applications, 245-246
PIAT. *See* Peabody Individual
    Achievement Test
Place value, 91-92
Planes, 161
Points, 161, 162
Polygons, 177, 193-194, 268
Power-of-ten notation, 257-258
Pre-calculus, 289
Prevocational education, 203-204
Probability, 243, 269
Problem solving, 295, 298-299
Productive sheltered employment
    setting, 202
Proficiency tests
    commercial, 56
    description, 48-50
    development of, 52-56
    objectives sample, 50-52
Prognostic tests, 274, 279
Programmed instruction, 73
Program organization
    alternative setting models, 305-310
    basic competencies, 297-300
    curriculum scope, 293
    design factors in, 24-25
    new program introduction, 318-319

performance assessment, 316-317
principles of, 292-205
problems of, 300-301
problem solving skills, 295
regular class models, 301-303
special education support models,
    303-305
student motivation, 294
subject matter coordination, 291-294,
    310-316
track assignments, 296-297
Project MATH, 36
Proof, 166
Proportion, 263-264
Protractors, 190-191
Pythagorean Theorem, 265, 285

R

Ratio, 263
Rational numbers
    decimals, 142-146, 209,
        258-260
    description of, 117-118
    fractions, 119, 122-142
    objectives, 119-122
    percent, 147-149, 258-260
Real number system, 115-119
Rectangles, 176, 192-193, 266-268
Regular class models, 301-303
Reinforcement lessons, 277
Remedial education, 25, 29-31
Resource room, 303, 304
Review lessons, 277

S

SAMI. *See* Sequential Assessment in
    Mathematics Inventory
Scales, 32-33, 311
Scientific measurement, 198-200
Scientific notation, 257-258
SDMT. *See* Stanford Diagnostic
    Mathematics Test

Self-contained class, 306
Sequential Assessment in Mathematics
    Inventory (SAMI), 44
Signed numbers, 256-257
Similar polygons, 177
Small group instruction, 73, 302, 304
Special education support models,
    303-305
Staff development, 313, 315-316
Standardized tests, 76. *See also*
    Assessment
Stanford Achievement Tests, 38, 56
Stanford Diagnostic Mathematics Test
    (SMDT), 42
Statistics, 243, 269-270
Subject area coordination, 310-311
    alternative school setting, 307
    problem of, 293-294
    staff development, 313, 315-316
    types of relationships, 311, 313
Subtraction
    decimals, 146
    fractions, 133, 135-138
    whole numbers, 97-102
Surfaces, 266-268
Survival skills, 84
System Fore, 36

T

Tables, 269
Teacher-made tests, 47-48, 76-77
Teaching methods
    application oriented, 238-239
    college preparatory program,
        277-278
    modification, 74-75
    regular class model, 301-303
    vocational education, 222-223,
        225-232
Time contract, 278
Track assignments, 296-297
Triangles, 171-176, 193, 265-267
Trigonometry, 243
Tutoring, 302-303

U

Unit circles, 289
University of Kansas Institute in
    Learning Disabilities, 68

V

Vocational preparation, 57
    basic skills, 205, 207-210
    curriculum, 218-220
    description, 29-30, 201
    employment settings, 202
    instructional and curriculum
        planning, 221-222
    instructional procedures,
        222-232
    mathematics applications,
        252-254
    mathematics programs, 203-205
    trade area needs, 210-218
    whole number skills, 84-85
Vocational proficiency tests, 210
Vocational-technical schools, 204,
    206-207
Volume, 196-198, 268-269

W

Weight, 198-199
Whole numbers, 116
    addition, 92-97
    assessment, 113-114
    basic skill needs, 84-86
    calculator use, 109, 111-113
    division, 106-109
    instructional objectives, 86
    microcomputer use, 113
    multiplication, 102-106
    place value, 91-92
    reading, writing, and identification,
        88-91
    subtraction, 97-102

Wide Range Achievement Test (WRAT), 34-35
Woodcock-Johnson Psychoeducational Battery, 34
Workshops, 304

WRAT. *See* Wide Range Achievement Test

Y

Yards, 186

About the Editor

John F. Cawley is Chairperson, Department of Special Education, University of New Orleans. He is especially concerned with curriculum and instruction for the handicapped.

About the Contributors

Colleen Blankenship is Associate Professor, Department of Special Education, University of Illinois. Her primary interests are data-based instruction and mathematics for the handicapped.

Anne Marie Fitzmaurice Hayes is a mathematics educator with extensive research in curriculum development for the handicapped. She is presently Assistant Professor at the University of Hartford, where she teaches courses in mathematics and special education.

Henry Goodstein is an Adjunct Professor of Education as well as a Research Associate in the Corporate Learning Center at Vanderbilt University. Currently he is the Manager for Human Resource Planning at Northern Telecom, Inc., of Nashville, Tennessee. His special interests are assessment and curriculum and instruction in mathematics for the handicapped.

Mahesh C. Sharma is Director of the Center for Teaching/Learning of Mathematics, Framingham, Massachusetts. Dr. Sharma also directs the Mathematics Institute at Cambridge College, Cambridge, Massachusetts. He has written extensively in the area of learning disabilities and mathematics and is noted for his client-centered efforts.

Robert A. Shaw is Professor of Mathematics Education, University of Connecticut. He has worked extensively in the area of mathematics and the handicapped and has been active in the curriculum development process.

Raymond E. Webster is Assistant Professor, Department of Psychology, at East Carolina University. Prior to this position, he served as a teacher, psychologist, and administrator for 13 years. He has published extensively in the areas of information processing, mathematics, and the handicapped.